"I have wanted a book like this for r  sensed
something was missing. Steven Smit ervice
to pastors and churches everywhere i)ect of
preaching, even expository preachin, pture,
this professor of preaching shows us . a text
should shape the substance and structure of the sermon. Why we did not see this all along I
do not know. With the publication of this book, we no longer have an excuse!"

Daniel L. Akin, *president,*
Southeastern Baptist Theological Seminary

"Great biblical preachers are rare, and great books on preaching are rarer still. In *Recapturing the Voice of God*, one of this generation's greatest expositors, Steven Smith, helps the
preacher know how to let the text shape the sermon outline and the sermon itself. Helpfully,
Dr. Smith works through different literary genres, thus bringing the reader a most helpful
template of how to truly let the text speak. I highly recommend this book for all who preach
and for all who love the art and science of homiletics."

Jason K. Allen, *president,*
Midwestern Baptist Theological Seminary and College

"If you want to preach in a way that is fully faithful to the full expression of Scripture,
Steven Smith can help."

Kenton C. Anderson, *president,*
Northwest Baptist Seminary;
professor of Homiletics at ACTS Seminaries of Trinity Western University

"*Recapturing the Voice of God* is really about how God presents the message of Scripture
and preaching accordingly. Paying attention to genre matters. So read and learn to be sensitive to how God presents his message as you preach."

Darrell Bock, *senior research professor of New Testament Studies,*
Dallas Theological Seminary

"In light of the mountains of new scholarship on the significance of biblical genre, Smith
provides a much-needed and very helpful resource for preachers who want the special
structure, as well as the specific content, of each biblical text to inform the message communicated to God's people."

Bryan Chapell, *senior pastor,*
Grace Presbyterian Church

"Steven Smith provides a refreshing and much-needed reminder that our sermons are the
most biblical when they not only reflect the message of the text but also mirror the form
of the text. In *Recapturing the Voice of God,* you will find wise and reliable guidance for
crafting sermons that are truly faithful to Scripture."

J. Scott Duvall, *professor of New Testament,*
Ouachita Baptist University

"It's no surprise that much of today's church is being fed with spiritual junk food from pulpits across the land. For some, the Bible is just a means to a sermon or, worse, a mere footnote in it. However, when the people of God return to the Word of God, reformation is inevitable. In this book, Dr. Smith has compiled all of the tools a preacher needs to hone his skills in expository preaching. In simple, practical terms, the reader is given a roadmap for preaching through every genre of Scripture. Drink richly from the pages of this book before you stand behind the sacred desk to deliver God's Word. Your people will be glad you did."

Robby Gallaty, *senior pastor,*
Brainerd Baptist Church

"Steven Smith carefully leads preachers through the territory of preaching various biblical genres. He helps preachers appreciate the contours of these landscapes so that they can develop sermons that respect the shape of the genre itself. This text-driven homiletic is explored in these helpful pages—and preachers will benefit from reading each chapter and applying Smith's words to their preaching."

Scott M. Gibson, *professor of Preaching,*
Gordon-Conwell Theological Seminary

"The Word of God, proclaimed by men of God, remains the lifeblood for the gospel. In *Recapturing the Voice of God,* Steven Smith effectively articulates the need for the sermon's shape to mirror the Scripture's shape, theologically considering genre in text-driven preaching. Steven Smith's experience as a pastor and professor, combined with his prowess as a pulpiteer, creates a reference work for the study and classroom alike. I highly recommend this book for all who desire to reach the world as they preach the Word!"

Robert Jeffress, *senior pastor,*
First Baptist Church, Dallas, TX

"This is a book that would have saved me from many sub-par and misguided sermons, had I read it in seminary and/or the early days of pastoral ministry. Chapter one alone, in my estimation, is worth the cost of the book. Further, I will most likely come back to the genre-specific chapters (nine in all) each time I begin a new book/series, as I seek to re-orient myself to the unique features and aims of that genre of Scripture. I'm so thankful for Dr. Steven Smith's work to help us all grow in 'recapturing the voice of God.'"

Ryan Kelly, *pastor for preaching,*
Desert Springs Church, Albuquerque, NM

"Books on preaching are legion. But this one stands out. It discusses preaching the way it should be done, one genre at a time, based on the premise that genre determines the shape of the text and the shape of the text (including its genre) should determine the shape of the sermon. If you long to recapture the voice of God in the Word of God, this book is for you!"

Andreas J. Köstenberger,
senior research professor of New Testament and Biblical Theology,
Southeastern Baptist Theological Seminary

"One of the great overarching concerns of the preacher in faithfully proclaiming God's Word must be the genre of the text. Finding the central thrust of a passage of Scripture is a matter of capturing the thunder of the very voice of God. Steven Smith's *Recapturing the Voice of God* is an excellent tool for students, pastors, and all who seek to discover the larger picture of what God is saying to us through his Word. Use this book often as you recapture the true intent of the biblical text in the confident knowledge that it will not return to you void."

Steven J. Lawson, *president,*
OnePassion Ministries

"When talking with students about preaching with genre sensitivity, I have lacked resources to offer them. Now I have one! Steven Smith helps us understand the need to re-present not just the meaning of the biblical text but also the spirit and the shape of the text in our expositional sermons. If (aspiring) pastors will implement what Steven is saying, I can't help but believe that local churches will be enriched, blessed, and built up as they hear the voice of God from the Word of God. I wholeheartedly recommend it."

Tony Merida, *pastor for preaching and vision,*
Imago Dei Church; associate professor of Preaching,
Southeastern Baptist Theological Seminary

"Expository preaching is the heart of Christian worship and central to the pastoral task. The Word of God constrains and compels every aspect of preaching. Steven Smith understands this. *Recapturing the Voice God* helpfully reminds us that the text must drive every aspect of truly expository preaching. In this book, preachers will be encouraged and equipped for the all-important task of rightly dividing the Word of Truth."

R. Albert Mohler Jr., *president,*
The Southern Baptist Theological Seminary

"*Recapturing the Voice of God* is a needed resource for sermon prep and discipling the next generation of faithful preachers."

Anthony Moore,
Fort Worth campus pastor, The Village Church

"It's rare to find a book that seamlessly weds a scholar's mind with a preacher's heart, but in *Recapturing the Voice of God*, Steven Smith provides a unique and overdue resource that will both inform and inspire preachers to more faithfully communicate God's Word!"

R. Scott Pace,
Reverend A. E. and Dora Johnson Hughes Chair of Christian Ministry,
Oklahoma Baptist University

"If you are searching for a fresh approach to preaching, Dr. Steven Smith's *Recapturing the Voice of God* will condition your own heart to think God's thoughts after him and will spur your congregation to abandon the pace of the walking horse and rise to become derby racers. In a style unique to Smith, the text of Scripture leaps to life from the pages of the Bible and electrifies the heart. You have waited for this book for years. Now feast on it."

Paige Patterson, *president,*
Southwestern Baptist Theological Seminary

"Steven Smith's treatment of the biblical genres and the directive they provide for sermon development and delivery is critical for us to hear God's voice and help our listeners to do the same. God's voice is our only hope of transformation into Christ's image."

Jim Shaddix,
W. A. Criswell Chair of Expository Preaching,
Southeastern Baptist Theological Seminary

STEVEN W. SMITH

RECAPTURING THE VOICE OF

GOD

SHAPING SERMONS
LIKE SCRIPTURE

B&H
ACADEMIC

NASHVILLE, TENNESSEE

Dewey Decimal Classification: 251
Subject Heading: PREACHING\SERMONS\BIBLE

Printed in the United States of America
1 2 3 4 5 6 7 8 9 10 • 20 19 18 17 16 15
VP

CONTENTS

Acknowledgments

This work owes a great deal to many people. I'm very thankful for them all and to others who, regrettably, I am unintentionally excluding.

First, I am thankful to Paige Patterson for fostering an environment where writing and research are valued. Thank you to Danny Akin for encouraging me to submit this work. I'm grateful for the opportunity to write provided by B&H's Jim Baird, and for the patient counsel and help of Chris Cowan and Chris Thompson. I'm grateful for the careful editing of Allen Davidson, who read each chapter and created the subject index. In chapter 2 I was dependent on the research of Denny Autry in his dissertation on Jean Claude and, therefore, Charles Simeon. I am especially grateful for the über-gifted Dave Wright for creating the graphics throughout the book. The full-color ones he created, not used in the book, are even better. Once in print the master graphic looks very similar to that in Köstenberger and Patterson's *Invitation to Biblical Interpretation*. While this was unintentional, it reminds me that since my discipline is communication and homiletics, I was actually dependent on the work of others in the field of hermeneutics. While every attempt was made to acknowledge the direct contribution of others, doubtless there are times when my work is influenced by others in more subtle ways, and for all these contributions I gratefully acknowledge my dependence on their work. Thanks also to many students along the way for their feedback on this content. Special thanks to the stellar students in my Ph.D. seminar, "Preaching the Genres of Scripture," who read early forms of these chapters and added helpful commentary along the way: Tim Fuller, Kyung Hun Lee, John Mann, Chris Osborne, Sunghoun Park, Z Seung, Immanuel Thomas, Paul Vacca, Ted Williams, and Hyung-Jae Yu.

Thanks also to Jason K. Lee with whom—though he might not claim me as his student—I bartered Mexican food for hermeneutical tutelage. He gave me the idea for the master graphic that expresses the macro-level understanding of genre, although I applied it slightly differently here. Special thanks to my brother Josh for giving me the idea for the title and for reminding me very often how great it is that he gave me the title that he gave me.

Finally, I am extremely grateful to my wife Ashley, who through some very daunting times gave me space to write, and to Jewell, Sidney, and Shepherd for their patience with Dad. I love you all very much.

INTRODUCTION

HONESTLY, I'M NOT ALWAYS CONFIDENT IN WHAT WE REFER TO AS "EXPOSITORY PREACHING."

Theologically, I'm a fan of exposition. I've given my life to teach expository preaching in the hopes that students will fall in love with the words of the Word and give their lives to explaining it. I unashamedly hope this book contributes to the work of those who want to explain the text. However, let's be honest; much of what we call expository preaching simply isn't. The word comes from a Latin root: we *ex* (remove) the *posit* (postulate) of truth that is in the text and show it to the people. Though the use of the word *exposition* has been well intended, I fear it has often become a referent for a tired, formulaic preaching template—so much so that when we say "exposition" we are using the word to refer to a *style* of structuring sermons. But I'm not willing to call students to give their lives to a style. That's nonsense since styles change with each generation. Expository, text-driven preaching is not a style but a theologically driven philosophy of preaching whose purpose is to get as close to the text as possible.

Don't get me wrong: a template to help us start preaching is not a bad thing; it's a helpful thing. But if we only have one template then eventually we will find that one template does not serve every text. The word is organically dynamic, not static. When a text does not fit a template we have to decide, will we preach the template or preach the text? This was my struggle for years.

It's not that I didn't have a formula, a template. The reality is that I was concerned that using my template on every text could misrepresent the text, as if I were trying to get it to fit my pre-determined outline. I thought there must be a better way, and I don't think I'm alone. But let's say for a minute that I am, and that every other preacher in the world is perfectly satisfied with his sermon structure. What is the justification of this book on the relationship of genre to sermon structure? Good question. The rationale for the book hangs on two axioms.

1. Preaching is re-presenting the Word of God. We are not making things up. This is a theology of preaching in one sentence: we speak for God because he has already revealed himself in his Son and his Son has revealed himself in his Word. This book is God's communication with us. Therefore, as my friend David Allen says, we are not preaching sermons, we are preaching texts. Preaching is more than explaining Scripture, but it is no less. So, when I sit down after the sermon, whatever else has happened, I must know that I have re-presented what God has already said to people. This is because in seeing the text they see Christ and in seeing Christ they see the Father. Therefore, to keep people from the Word is to keep them from Christ. We have an obligation to re-present what God has already said. So, we have to get at the meaning. Which leads us to our second axiom.

2. The structure of a text influences its meaning. Why does God speak through at least nine different genres? Why are they not all lectures, each with four points and three corresponding sub-points? An attempt to answer is ridiculous: that's in the mind of God. However, I'm so glad we have the robust poetry of the Psalms, the direct wisdom of Proverbs, the biting irony of Ecclesiastes, the shocking narratives of the Old Testament, the richness of the Gospel narratives, the personal nature of the epistles, and the glorious joy of kingdom consummation in Revelation. And each of those genres influences the meaning of the words that they communicate. While I don't like the word per se, they also influence the *feel* of the text—that is, the author-intended emotional design of the text. Since the Word of God is perfect, the respective genres were ordained to be conduits for particular texts. The question then is, do I have a sermon structure that allows me to re-present the text in the way it was originally presented? Which leads to our conclusion.

Therefore, we preach the Word of God as influenced by the voice of God. By "voice of God" we mean genre. This is saying what God says, the way God says it. The question is, how can I capture the voice of God while I am preaching the Word of God? To ignore the genre is to miss some of its meaning. The humble ambition of this book is to show a preacher or teacher how the genre influences the meaning of the text and give practical help for those who want to know how we can shape our sermons to reflect this meaning. This is genre-sensitive preaching. This raises two questions. Are we arguing for imitating the text? No, not imitation. We are not imitating but re-animating the text. In other words discovering the meaning imbedded in the genre and allowing it to influence the sermon. More on that later. Secondly, isn't it enough to preach the Bible verse by verse without any attention to genre? The problem is that could possibly lead to forcing texts into pre-determined forms, forms that do not allow the text to breathe and miss some of the meaning.

Not every preacher wants to be an expositor. I get that, but that is another discussion. For now one could wish that those of us who claim to be expositors would not mask the meaning of the text under the guise of explaining it. We can't suggest we are taking the homiletic high ground by preaching "exposition" when all we do is walk through a book serially while drawing points from a text with the same capriciousness that one would pick a topic at random and assign a text that had some semblance of that topic in it.

Perhaps this paper-thin veneer of "exposition" as a pre-made template laid over a text is the reason so many younger preachers are walking away from it.

Please hear my heart: I'm not implicating my brothers as much as expressing my own frustration and failure. For years, maintaining a homiletic form kept me further from the text, not closer. I was too naïve, and perhaps willful, to admit that the form of the sermon did not accurately re-present the form of the text.

There has to be a better way.

There is.

We should let Scripture breathe.

If Scripture gives life, then our sermon forms should be the open windows through which the breath of life blows. As preachers, we are conduits whose task is not to filter out what is unpalatable—as if God's Word was somehow too explicit for a modern world. To allow the text to breathe means that we allow the shape of the text to drive the shape of the sermon. This commitment flows from our doctrine of inspiration. If the content of the Word of God is inspired, and the shape of a text influences its content, should not our sermons be re-presentations of what God already presented? It is not the task of the preacher to flatten the literary genre in a quest to mine out theological truth. The structure of the text is actually part of the message, and we must pay attention to it.

For those of us who believe in inspiration, preaching really is a re-presentation of a text of Scripture. This truly is exposition. Our simple proposition is that the shape of the sermon should be influenced by the shape of the text. It is as simple as that. And since Scripture has many different genres, it is as complicated as that as well. If God is gracious, reading this will free you to let the text determine the sermon structure and be a primer to aid when the practice of genre-sensitive sermons gets complicated. And it does get complicated. So we will attempt to toggle between a work that is informed by recent scholarship yet has the daily application to the preacher in mind. Thus you can keep it at your elbow in the study when preaching through a specific genre. This is just an introduction so you will want to use the bibliography in the back for further study. Preaching, for me at least, is always daunting. This is written in the hope of washing the feet of other preachers.

I don't have all the answers. Later today I'm going to fight my flesh as I prepare the next sermon. I certainly don't know *the* way to preach each text. And this is part of the point. There is a thrill to being forced to think through each genre of Scripture on its own terms. However, I do want to stand on the shoulders of our predecessors who helped us with sermon form and enable us to get closer to the text. I do want to imitate Jesus, who was the exact voice of God. We are not perfect; we are weak prophets with a burning desire to get closer and to be clearer.

In an effort to get closer and clearer, we will study the genres of Scripture—their shape—so that the shape of the text informs the shape of the sermon. In this way we are recapturing the voice of God while we preach the Word of God. May he be gracious as we get closer and clearer.

Chapter 1

RECAPTURING THE VOICE OF GOD: PITCH, RATE, VOLUME

INTRODUCTION

SCRIPTURE IS THE WORD OF GOD PRESENTED IN THE VOICE OF GOD. Preaching is re-presenting the Word of God by recapturing the voice of God. Therefore to capture the meaning of God's words we must present the Word of God in the voice of God. To say it negatively, to capture the words of God without the voice of God is to miss the meaning of the text. Scripture is God's Word in God's voice. This book is about capturing the meaning of the text—the Word of God—in sermons influenced by the genre of the text—the voice God chose to speak his words.

I love the way my toddler runs. He flails his arms and runs with abandon. Our driveway leads down to a busy street, so when he comes near the street I muster up my deepest baritone, and raising the volume of my voice while lowering the tone of my voice at the same time, I bellow, "Shep!"

There are only three ways the voice can be adjusted. We can modify the volume, the pitch (think intensity), or the rate (the speed). I'm not thinking about all that at the moment. I don't have to. The emotions I am feeling simply emerge in a heightened pitch and volume. And it works. Shep has heard me say his name hundreds of times: in joy, in gratitude, or in playfulness. As a growing parent I am learning that variety in voice is a useful tool for discipline and for the demonstration of affection. I am motivated by love. And at this moment, I want to protect him; I am protecting him with my voice as much as my words. In fact, it's not the word that stops him; it's the tone of voice. To say his name in a soft way would misrepresent the way I feel. There are times I want to communicate all sorts of emotions, but in that moment I want to communicate fear, danger, and warning—for no other reason than that danger exists. I'm not being dramatic. It's real. Because I love my son I want him to fear what could cost him his life.

Scripture also has pitch, rate, and volume, nuances that are represented in the genre of the text. There is one Bible, many genres. There is one Word in many voices, all motivated by the love of the Father toward us.

The first question of the Bible, "Where are you?" is a haunting inquiry of paternal love and disappointment.[1] In the flood, God rains a word of judgment from a cloud of grace.[2] God screams a word of warning through the story of Israel so that we will obey.[3] The great people of faith in the Old Testament are not presented for our amusement. While stories of Old Testament heroes are legendary, that's not their purpose. Their lives represent the very voice of God cheering us to run well, to know that the very pain we are experiencing is the birthmark of a child of God.[4] The race is real, so the encouragement is real. The psalms express the range of human emotion, yet the psalms are not authored merely by a human, but by God. In the psalms, God expresses his love to us by telling us the ways we might respond to him. God loves us so completely that he speaks to us, and then gives us a voice when we don't know how to respond back to him.

God speaks triumphant hope in stories like Ruth and Esther. He pleads and argues with us in the prophets.[5]

The gospel story is the last word.[6] God has nothing more to say about the revelation of himself. Christ is the ultimate and fully expressive Word from God to us. The voice of God is so loud in the incarnate person of Christ that Christ does not have to scream. His presence is enough, the deafening roar of invitation spoken in the Son's humiliation. Christ concealed his glory so that the Father would be revealed at the right time.[7] This is why many did not recognize him. As Jesus spoke, it was God from heaven speaking to the world in a voice they had never heard before. It is the single most dramatic story of all time. But the message is not the drama; the message is the Word of God to us. Many miss the Word for sake of the story. They love the drama of death to life, but are not willing to die so they can live. They have heard the story; they have not heard the Word.[8] Yet the story is the vehicle for the spoken Word. God is condescending. And condescension brings accountability. To hear the story of Christ and not respond is to assume that he came for entertainment. Every story in Scripture awaits a response, especially the ultimate story of Christ. He humbled himself by taking a human form for one reason: to speak to us the right word in the right voice. He awaits a response.

He instructs us in the Epistles. The Epistles are the very words of Jesus explaining to us, through the voice of the apostles, how we are to live in light of the Gospels and Acts.[9] They are God's spoken commentary on his Son and his church.

In the last book, the book of Revelation, God ends the battle the same way he began the world. All things begin with one word. All things end with one word.[10] Revelation is Jesus-spoken. God the Father revealed to Jesus, who revealed to the angel, who revealed to John the encouraging word for the church, so that she might hope in the definite physical return of Jesus the Warrior Messiah to right every

---

1. Gen 3:9.
2. Gen 6–9.
3. Heb 10:26–39.
4. Heb 12:1–6.
5. Isa 1:18; Mic 6:8.
6. Heb 1:1–2.
7. Phil 2:8.
8. Matt 13:9.
9. John 14:25; 15:26; 16:12–13.
10. Gen 1:1; Rev 19:21.

wrong, redeem his bride, and bring justice on his enemies. It is a loud book for the reason that the encouragement is so needed. It is the last word on the last word. The Bible is one Word in many voices.

God, who knows every situation that we will ever encounter, uses a tremendous amount of vocal variety. To say it another way, God, who is unchangeable, varied his vocal approach out of a desire to communicate himself to us. This is why the Bible is not a flat one-dimensional book. It is a rich granular voice speaking to every condition in multiplied variety. There is pitch, rate, and volume in Scripture.

If God changes his voice, shouldn't we preachers change ours? People do not think God is boring from reading his Word. They think that God is boring because we have trained them to think such by monochromatic, flat, uniform, one-size-fits-all approach to preaching. This misrepresents the many variations in God's Word for the very reason that no one ever heard the voice of God and was bored. God is not boring. The work of boredom is not the work of God but the work of man. God has a voice and he uses it.

This book is an encouragement to identify the voice of God in the Word of God. This is not principally intended to teach you how to interpret the Word, nor is this book about how to craft sermons from beginning to end. It's not so much about mining what God is saying from the text, but help on identifying how God is speaking by study of the genre of Scripture and then to shape sermons that recapture that voice in his Word. Once captured, this voice determines the tone and structure of the sermon. This implies that meaning is found not only when we identify the substance of the text, but when we identify the structure and the tone of the text as well. God has a voice and he uses it. The question is how do we use our voices to re-capture the voice of God? In other words, how do we structure sermons influenced by the genre of the God-inspired text?

BEYOND THE BRIDGE

As preachers, we want to help people. Thus, historically, one of the most helpful metaphors for preaching is building a bridge, because we do in fact want to build a bridge from the biblical text to the modern world. We mine the Scriptures for truths to help our hearers, the end result being "biblical sermons." These are sermons in which the points come from the Bible. This is what we want. We observe something in the text and we identify it for our listener. Let's call this preaching by identification/observation. Much of what we call "expository preaching" is preaching by identification/observation. We observe something in the text and then identify it for our listener.

Yet, we actually want to do *more* than observe things in the text. Here in this short volume we are calling for something more in the same trajectory. Something slightly different. This is about preaching that not only identifies what is in the text, but re-presents it in the same way the text presented it. What God said. How God said it. To speak God's Word influenced by the way God said it, to re-present the Word of God by re-capturing the voice of God. Yes we do build bridges, but when we walk across that bridge we are to re-present God's Word by recapturing God's voice. The reason this is so critical is for the very reason that this is how God has chosen to communicate. Therefore we are after shaping sermons in God's voice. In this way, the shape of the text becomes the shape of the sermon.

THE SHAPE OF THE SERMON

The structure of a biblical text determines the structure of the sermon. This proposition is simple enough, but it's a challenge to execute. In fact, it's a radical departure from many approaches to sermon structure. However, the struggle to hear the voice in the Word and further re-present that word in God's voice is worth it. Personally, this truth has liberated my preaching from self-imposed expectations that my sermons must be shaped and structured like those of my favorite preacher. This book is about learning how to shape our sermons according to the shape of the biblical text, a conversation that is framed in the context of the history of preaching and a theology of preaching.

Closer: A Little History of Preaching

> Reduce your text to a simple proposition, and lay that down as the warp; and make the use of the text itself as the woof; illustrating the main idea by the various terms in which it is contained. Screw the words into the minds of your hearers. A screw is the strongest of all mechanical powers . . . when it has been turned a few times scarcely any power can pull it out.[11]

It is in the metaphor of the "Warp and Woof" that British Divine Charles Simeon (1739–1836) helps us understand the structure of the modern sermon. Simeon was a fellow at King's College in Cambridge and the pastor of Holy Trinity Church. Perhaps his greatest contribution was his influence on preaching and the shape of a propositional sermon. A propositional sermon is a sermon that advances certain axioms or truths, and may in fact be crafted around a central proposition. The word picture he uses above is textile in origin. A weaver lays down the thread in front of her vertically (warp). Then thread is woven through it horizontally (woof); ergo, the warp and woof in common vernacular is the "whole thing."

In the mind of Charles Simeon, this is the whole sermon. You lay down the main idea of what you want to say in the sermon then demonstrate from the text how that theme is woven throughout the text of Scripture. This is structured in a sermon with clear divisions. Simeon explains the idea of divisions around a main theme when he writes,

> Division ought to be restrained to a small number of parts: they should never exceed four or five at the most; the more admired sermons have only two or three parts. There are two sorts of divisions, the first is the division of the text into its parts; the other

---

11. Charles Hopkins, *Charles Simeon of Cambridge* (Eugene, OR: Wipf and Stock, 2012), 59. I'm indebted to the work of Denny Autry for finding this gem, as well as other insights regarding Simeon in his dissertation, *Factors Influencing the Sermonic Structure of Jean Claude and His Influence on Homiletics* (Ph.D. diss., Southwestern Baptist Theological Seminary, 2013). Autry notes that this illustration of the screw is borrowed from Huguenot pastor Jean Claude in Simeon's *Essay on the Composition of a Sermon*.

is of the discourse, or sermon itself, which is made of the text. The division of the discourse is proper when it gives light to a text. . . .[12]

When your parts are too closely connected with each other, place the most detached first, and endeavor to make that serve for a foundation to the explication of the second, and the second to the third; so that at the end of your explication the hearer may with a glance perceive, as it were, a perfect body, or a finished building; for one of the greatest excellences of a sermon is, the harmony of its component parts, that the first leads to the second, the second serves to introduce the third; that they which go before, excite the desire for those which are to follow: in a word, that the last has a special relation to all the others, in order to form in the hearers' minds a complete idea of the whole.[13]

From these brief quotes we get the fuller picture: the sermon should have a limited number of divisions, and those divisions should fit into a unified whole. What is implicit in this quote is that this sermon is built on one particular text, not several.

This propositional approach to preaching was not new, but Simeon, borrowing heavily from the French Protestant Jean Claude, said something more clearly than any of his contemporaries: a sermon should have a single text, a single theme, and multiple points to support that theme. Simeon demonstrated this method in his sermons printed in his *Horae Homiletica* (1832). His approach was represented later in the work of John Broadus, *On the Preparation and Delivery of Sermons* (1898). This was the most widely used preaching text for a generation and had tremendous impact on American preaching. Broadus, in turn, influenced many significant works in homiletics. Thus, the influence of Simeon, implicit or explicit, is hard to overstate.

So again, to Simeon a sermon was laying down the warp of a proposition. The woof of the text was woven through the proposition demonstrating how the text spoke to the proposition. Those of us who are committed to letting the text speak may want to say, more precisely, that we extract propositions from the text and then demonstrate how the text supports the one main idea of the text. Nevertheless, the principal is clear—you shape a sermon by having several points from one singular text, and you explain those points woven around a singular theme.

This is why, out of all the history of preaching, Simeon is a good place to begin this conversation. He was not the fountainhead of expository preaching. To understand a careful history of the expository sermon one would have to, at the very least, look beside Simeon to the Puritans, and behind Simeon to the Reformers, and further behind him to Augustine, Chrysostom, Jerome, and ultimately back to the New Testament church who, borrowing from the model of the synagogue, read and explained Scripture in early Christian worship. However, it is more than the need to keep this brief that takes us to Simeon. He is important. Simeon's model is a clear early representation of what we understand as the modern sermon—a sermon

12. Jean Claude, *Essay on the Composition of the Sermon, with Notes and Illustrations and One Hundred Sermon Skeletons by Charles Simeon* (Grand Rapids: Baker, 1979), 1:43.
13. Charles Simeon, *Expository Outlines* (Grand Rapids, MI: Zondervan, 1956), 21:311.

derived from a single text, driven by one main idea, and structured around several points.[14]

So, if you walk into an evangelical church on a Sunday morning, you will most likely hear a sermon structured in ways that reflect the ancient models with an introduction, a body, and a conclusion. You might hear a hint of Simeon with the propositions coming from a general topic, or a truth exposed and then applied to life. Again, there is more to the history of preaching. But most of the offshoots of contemporary biblical preaching, expositional preaching, can trace themselves to the immediate roots here; the contribution showed preachers how their sermons can be closer to the text. And this is what we want—to be closer in re-presenting what God has already said. Anything that detracts from this is an enemy to the sermon. Simeon's model was not perfect, but it was getting preachers closer to the text.

Now a question: What if a model of preaching is good for some texts but not all texts? When this happens we have a tendency to hold on to the homiletic form, even if we have to manipulate the biblical text to fit our sermon form. If we are not careful imitating the model that Simeon gave us, multiple points around a proposition often becomes the goal of preaching. Let me be clear. The goal of preaching is not to develop points, nor is the goal to develop a narrative, nor is the goal to preach without points. The goal is to re-present what God has already said. This is the goal. In order to re-present what God has said, the sermon must not prescribe form to the text, but represent the form that is already in the text. The form is given to facilitate the preaching of the text. The form is the means, not the end. The end of preaching is not to sound like preaching. The end of preaching is to sound like God's Word.[15] So now we find ourselves in an odd position. Simeon helped us get closer to the text by giving us a method that would serve that goal. However, now we are tempted to serve the method instead of letting the method serve us. If we do this, what Simeon

---

14. Charles Simeon's approach is similar to another major contribution to homiletics, the Puritan William Perkins, who also had a high view of Scripture. In his *Art of Prophesying*, Perkins advocated what has come to be known as the Puritan Plain Style. The method was simple enough. The preacher extracted a doctrine from the text, explained the doctrine, and then applied the doctrine. Unlike the Puritan plain style, Simeon had more divisions in the sermon and was not holding to the text-doctrine-uses trichotomy Perkins advocated in his work, *The Art of Prophesying*. While both Simeon and Perkins were in the tradition of the Protestant Plain Style of preaching, the difference between the two is that Perkins followed a template of seeing text, doctrine, and uses (application). This model was perfect for one of the goals of the Puritan sermon: to extract doctrine from the text and explain the doctrine. So, while there is overlap in their approaches such that definitions tend to be reductionist, generally Perkins was aiming toward a method that extracted a singular doctrine from the text, and applications were made from the doctrine. Simeon, on the other hand, was extracting "points" from the text itself. Thus, it is in Simeon that we have the structure of much evangelical preaching today. A proposition is identified from a singular text, and then woven throughout a particular text in a sermon built on "points." While this sounds like Preaching 101, in Simeon's day this was a fairly radical idea.

15. One could rightly point to the movement of narrative preaching, most often thought of synonymously with the New Homiletic, as an attempt to correct this problem. However, a criticism of the New Homiletic is that while it challenged the notion that all sermons had to be deductive propositions, it replaced it with the notion that all sermons must be inductive narratives. If this is true, then it is still a form that is exalted above the text. For a critique of the New Homiletic, see David Allen's "A Tale of Two Roads," *JETS* 43 (2000): 489–515.

used to get closer to the text becomes a distraction that gets us further from the text. The user is now a servant to the means.[16]

We have inherited some forms of preaching. This is good. When those forms are found to be wanting, and we still use them, that is bad. All of us have inherited some good and bad preaching forms. So, the preacher who wants to protect himself from holding a form above the text must understand fundamentally what preaching is, which is something to reflect on for a moment. In the way that Simeon left old forms to help us get closer, we must now leave old form to get closer to the text. It's time. The question is, will you treat preaching as a borrowed template forced upon a text, or will you help the next generation get closer to what God is saying? Let me say it stronger: in the history of preaching there have always been those in each generation who have tried to get closer to the text. Our history compels us to get closer to the text, and, likewise, our theology calls us to be clearer.

Clearer: A Little Theology of Preaching

In Hebrews 1:1, God spoke in "various ways" through the prophets. The author does not elaborate on this, but he need not do so. We know the many ways the prophets spoke. And to expand on the trajectory of this verse, the Scripture is filled with variety. So God's perfect Word has variety. To say it another way, it is the nature of his perfection not to be uniform. This is mind blowing. The perfectly consistent, logical, cogent propositions in Scripture are woven through a multi-colored text. The reason we would go to such lengths to re-present what God said the way God said it is because God's communication is perfect. Preaching is an act of communication that we borrow from the source of communication, God. So before we talk about our communication, think about how perfect God's communication is.

After the writer of Hebrews discusses the many ways in which God has spoken, he now asserts that in these last days, "he has spoken to us by his Son . . . the exact imprint of his nature" (Heb 1:2–3). Christ is the exact representation of the Father. This thought is so pregnant with meaning it's difficult to fathom. This at least means that whatever the Father said, the Son said, and whatever the Father wanted him to do, the Son did (John 5:19–46). Whatever the Father would do had he a physical form, the Son did. This was ultimate communication because it was ultimate representation. The Son exactly re-presented the Father. Thus, there is nothing the Father wanted to say to us through Jesus that was left unsaid. It was complete. When Christ said, "It is finished" (John 19:30), he referred to his atoning work. No more sacrifice was needed. There is a sense of completion there. All that God wants to say has been said in Christ. All. This idea of completion is also resonate in the provocative description of Christ's nature and work in Colossians 1:15–10.

---

16. Preaching is principally learned through imitation. One caution: when imitation alone is our teacher we will replicate a form without a theology behind it. Imitation is the initial tutor for all of us. However, eventually the training wheels of imitation must be removed. The love for sounding like someone else must be replaced with a love for Scripture. The desire to get the text right must swell over the desire to sound right. If not, preaching will be managing our adherence to a form and not re-presenting God's Word.

The Greek πάς, "all," is used nine times, in various forms, in Colossians 1:15–20.

Christ is before *all* creation. (v. 15)
By him, through him, and for him *all* things were created. (v. 16)
In him *all* things hold together. (v. 17)
In him *all* the fullness of God was pleased to dwell. (v. 19)
He reconciles *all* things to himself. (v. 20)

When Scripture discusses the perfect communication of Christ, the emphasis is not so much on perfection as freedom from error (though he certainly was free from it), but the emphasis is on perfection as completion. This "all" includes the communication of Christ. All that Christ wanted to say about the Father was said. It was indeed finished.

That same sense of completion is hinted at in John 14:25–26. Note the completeness of Jesus' words when he says to his disciples,

These things I have spoken to you while I am still with you. But the Helper, the Holy Spirit, whom the Father will send in my name, he will teach you all things and bring to your remembrance all that I have said to you.

Christ told his disciples he was leaving them. This was a problem because of the previous verses (14:23–24). "If anyone loves me, he will keep my word, and the Father will love him, and we will come to him and make our home with him. Whoever does not love me does not keep my words. And the word that you hear is not mine but the Father's who sent me." Access to the Father is granted through the Son; access to the Son is granted through his words.[17] How then could they keep his words if he was leaving them? How could they be in Christ and therefore in the Father? The answer is that the Helper, the Holy Spirit, would come and reveal all things that Jesus said. The "things" refers to everything Jesus taught them.[18] We can imply from that statement that it includes everything we have witness of in the Gospels, and maybe even things that Jesus said that were not written down, but later influenced the writing of the Epistles through the apostolic tradition. Now, how do we know the things that Christ taught them, that later the Holy Spirit revealed to

---

17. It is interesting that this is the same relationship that is expressed in 2 Cor 4:4, ". . . the light of the gospel of the glory of Christ, who is the image of God," and later in 4:6, ". . . the light of the knowledge of the glory of God in the face of Christ." There is an intrinsic relationship between God the Father's communication of himself in the Word, and the Holy Spirit's communication of Christ in the Word, the Scriptures.

18. William Hendriksen writes, *"These things*, in view of *while still remaining with you*, which is surely very general, cannot be restricted to the words spoken that night, but obviously indicate *all* his teaching up to this very moment. Now Jesus draws a *distinction*—notice, he does not present a *contrast*; δε should here be translated *moreover* or *and* or *now*, not *but*—between his own teaching during the days of his humiliation, on the one hand, and his own teaching through the Spirit in the glory of his exaltation, on the other. The central idea of verses 25, 26 may be summarized as follows: 'While yet abiding physically with you I have given you certain teachings which after my physical departure from you I, through the Spirit, will make much clearer to you (cf. 1 Cor 2:13). Moreover, I will then teach you *everything* which you need to know in order to perform the work of witnessing which is assigned to you.'" William Hendriksen, *Exposition of the Gospel According to John*, Baker New Testament Commentary (Grand Rapids: Baker, 1953), 285–86.

them? The answer is of course the Word. The Word of God is the written witness to Christ. Thus, when the Word of God is preached, John 14:26 is being fulfilled. The Holy Spirit revealed to the disciples all things they needed. We, therefore, can fulfill John 14:23–24: we can know the words of Christ, we can be in Christ, and therefore in the Father.

In the same way that God is completely/perfectly represented in the Son, the Son is completely/perfectly represented in Scripture. It is odd when someone says that we don't need the propositions of Scripture, what we need is just Jesus. How would we know who Jesus is without the propositions of Scripture? The revelation of Christ is given through Scripture, and it is perfect.

Now we see how God communicates—perfectly: with exactness or completeness. And this is our ambition for preaching. In preaching we imperfectly attempt to re-present the Word as completely as the Spirit has re-presented Christ in the Word, and as completely as Christ has re-presented the Father by his words. We may fairly ask "What would Jesus do?" but we can never ask, "What would Jesus say?" We have the perfectly complete revelation of Christ in his Word. If Christ were to show up in our churches, we know exactly what he would say. He already said it. So we preach that. This is not drawing points out of a text; this is showing the text just as it is. This is preaching that is Scripture re-imaged. This is the Word re-presented.

However, it was not only the words of Christ that communicated the Father, but the very life of Christ as well. Let's make one more visit to Colossians 1:15–22 before we make our application to preaching.

The reason Christ perfectly communicated the Father was that the very presence of Christ in the world is itself communication. He is the image of God (Col 1:15; 2 Corinthians 4). The word translated image is the Greek word *eikōn*, from which we get our English word "icon." In Greek, an *eikōn*, or image, made visible the invisible reality that it represented. Today, in English, an icon functions much the same way. For example, the Eifel Tower is an "iconic" image. You see a structure, but you think Paris, France. You see the Great Wall of China, but you think of the country of China. You see the Hollywood Sign and you think Los Angeles and the Golden Age of Cinema. These are all iconic images. The icon is the visual/visible symbol that surfaces a reality that is invisible/mental. There is a wide sense in which this is true of Christ. Christ was the visible image that allows us to see an invisible God. However, there is much more to Christ as the image of God than this. Christ is the image of the invisible God. However, Christ is not a symbol for God: Christ is God. To understand the nature of Christ one has to look beyond the physicality of Christ, the fact that he was God incarnate, and one must listen to Christ. Christ was not just a visible image; he was re-presenting exactly what God wanted to say.

The word "image," *eikōn*, in Paul's use means representation, but it means more than this. It means an exact image. Precise. A mirror image. Christ is not just a visual symbol that makes us think of an invisible God. Christ is a re-presentation of the thoughts of the Father; and thus, he helps us think of the Father more precisely. Christ is the exact visible expression of a God we cannot see. When we engage Christ we know exactly what the Father would say or do because Christ, in a physical form, is the perfect re-presentation of the Father. And this is how we understand the sermon. Yes, preaching is making observations from the text and building bridges to people's lives, but we are sketch artists first and bridge builders second. In other words, we make sure we have the Word of God captured in the voice of God before we walk across the bridge. Preaching is re-presenting God. We say what God has already said, and re-present it exactly as he said it. Yes, preaching is drawing things from the text, but it is more: preaching is re-imaging the text. In this way we stand in the trajectory of how God has chosen to reveal himself. Think of it in this reverse chronological way:

1. We re-present the text.
2. The text re-presents Christ
3. Christ re-presents the Father.[19]

We share truth to people in an attempt to get them to see the Word. When they see the Word, the Holy Spirit will communicate Jesus; and if they see Jesus, Jesus will communicate the Father. Then, it ends. The Father communicates no one. The Father represents no one. He speaks for no one but himself. The Father has never been told anything that needs to be communicated to others. He is the source of all. He has given everything and been given nothing. The Father is the beginning and end of communication. The Greek word is *telos*—that is, "end" or "goal." Thus, he is the source and the completion. All communication initiated in the Godhead and all communication has as its end to bring people back to the Father.

So what you began, dear Lord, may I wield as a weapon to win people to your Word, which will lead them to Christ, who will lead them to the Father. This is the end.

There is more to preaching, but there is at least the fact that a Christian preacher aims to re-present the Word, which re-presents Christ, who re-presents the Father. This is iconic preaching. We attempt to re-present exactly the Word, knowing that the Word will exactly represent Christ and that Christ exactly represents the Father. A preacher is not striving for perfection; he is striving for precision and completion. Are we saying what God wants us to say, the way God wants us to say it? This is the question. The answer to the question has many implications, but this book is primarily about sermon structure. Let's now make an application of this theology to sermon structure.

If the structure of a biblical text influences its meaning, and we want the sermon to mean what the text means, doesn't it make sense that we can borrow the form of the text as the form of the sermon? Can we not use the voice of God to re-present the Word of God? I don't want to say that all observational preaching is bad. Rather, we want more in the same trajectory. Let a generation stand on the shoulders of the great preachers who went before us and be careful to explain the Word while recapturing the voice. It's a question of theological trajectory. If the Word is right, then it is sufficient; if the Word is sufficient, then we must say that what it said was influenced by the way it is said. There is meaning at the structural level of a text; should we not pay attention to the structure of the text and how it influences meaning? That is an argument from the doctrine of Scripture, and we have been arguing from the nature of Christ. So, let's say it another way.

The issue with sermon form is not right versus wrong. Again, the issue is that of trajectory. God has communicated perfectly in Christ; Christ communicated the

19. 2 Cor 4:4, 6.

Father perfectly; and the Holy Spirit communicates the Son perfectly in Scripture. So what sermon form continues the trajectory of completeness? The point is that the next step in that same trajectory is to shape sermons like Scripture. To say what God says in the voice that he said it. Sermons are sculptures modeled after the Master Communicator. Therefore I have the freedom to shape my sermons like the text! What sweet liberty. This leads to the application of our premise: the structure of the biblical text determines the structure of the sermon. Knowing that God inspired the structure of the text, and that the structure of the text influences meaning, this book is intended to help us shape our sermons like Scripture. This is driven by the fact that Christ exactly re-presented the Father, and I want to exactly re-present the text. I am imitating the method of Christ.

If the structure of the sermon is the goal of preaching; if the end game is adherence to a homiletic form; then the inevitable temptation will be to consider ourselves faithful when we have kept the form. However, when a means of preaching the Word is more visible than the Word, then it is no longer a means to preaching the Word. The end of the medium is not the medium. Sermon structure should serve the text.

So before we talk about the genre of Scripture, it's important to see this in its theological trajectory. God is revealed in Christ; Christ is revealed in the Word. Understanding the genre, the structure of a biblical text, helps us understand how to communicate the Word. Therefore, learning how to preach sermons that consider the genre in which God chose to reveal them is a means toward greater faithfulness when re-presenting that Word. So this book has a theological premise: God is revealed in Christ, and Christ in the Word. And this book has one plea: let's consider how the genre of each text helps us be more faithful to that Word. So, all that we will discuss about methodology has one aim: to more faithfully re-represent the text.

CONCLUSION

So, let's sum this up. From the history of preaching we learn that we have inherited a sermon structure; this is good, but becomes bad when we force a sermon structure that does not help explain the text. From a theology of preaching we learn to evaluate sermon structure by how clearly and transparently it allows the text to show through it so that in the text we can see Christ, and in Christ we can see the Father.

All of this presents a compelling case that we cannot ignore the shape of the text and resign ourselves to a life of predictable preaching forms. Not only is it amazingly boring, it misrepresents the dynamic nature of Scripture by making it something flat and predictable.

The question remains then, if we cannot preach with inherited forms because left alone they might rob the text of its full beauty, then how do we preach? The answer is to find a sermon structure that is so simple that it does not suffocate the text. The Holy Spirit of God has life giving power through the Word of God. So we use a homiletical method that allows the text to breathe; a method that helps us re-present what the text has said; and a method that is driven by the nature of the text itself. This is text-driven preaching.

Chapter 2

TEXT-DRIVEN PREACHING:
SUBSTANCE, STRUCTURE, SPIRIT

Text-driven preaching is
   the interpretation and
   communication of a biblical text in a sermon that re-presents
      the substance,
      structure, and
      the spirit of the text.

LET'S TALK ABOUT THIS DEFINITION.

INTERPRETATION: HEARING THE VOICE OF THE TEXT

In the process of interpretation we answer the question, what does this text mean? This is the process by which we study the text from the original languages, using all the exegetical tools at our disposal to understand what the text means. Theoretically, this would be one half of the pastor's week; however, this is not always the case. Some sermons demand more time on interpretation and others on communication.

The temptation, of course, is to shortcut this process, to try to figure out how to say it before we know what it says. The danger is that we can do that easily. We can figure out exactly what we want to say before we figure out what the text says. Remember however, we are not preaching sermons, we are preaching texts. We are re-presenting what God said. Speech making is not difficult. Re-presenting the Word of God is. The secret of "great" preaching is often little more than staying at it until the meaning of the text is clear. So the first part is the interpretation of the text. The end result of this process is an exegetical outline—the raw structural ingredients of the sermon, but not yet ready to preach.

Zooming In—Panning Out

While the nature of the book is not to cover basic interpretive strategies, let me mention a strategy that has helped me tremendously in interpretation and one we will turn to as we discuss the various genres of Scripture. Often in trying to interpret a text, I get stuck. For the life of me, I do not understand what a text means.

This could be because I have not spent enough time in the Scripture. When this is the case, it makes perfect sense. Of course I would know it better if I studied it longer. However, there are times when I study a text for a long time and still do not feel I have the meaning. I zoom in the lens as tight as possible to see every nuance in focus, and still cannot feel confident that I know what the text means. The reason for this is that sometimes the meaning of the text is not in the text. In other words, the meaning of the text may be around it on a macro level, not in it on a micro level.

This was driven home to me while trying to interpret the difficult parable of the Rich Man and Lazarus of Luke 16:19–31. I studied the text but could not for the life of me get a good handle on what the text was saying. Granted, the parable can seem complicated. So I drilled down to study the semantic structure of the sentences and the meaning of the individual words. And yet, the more I drilled down, the further I got from the meaning of the text. What I needed was to pan out.

If you pan out to the next chapter you see that the parable fits as the last of five parables all dealing with lostness (15:1–16:31). The first four are positive examples of how Jesus deals with lostness, and the last is a negative example. In the first four Jesus paints a picture of how he views lostness—he seeks people, and loves them more than this world. Then he chastises the Pharisees for loving money and tampering with the Word of God (16:14–18). So then Jesus tells a story of a man who loves money more than people (16:20, 24) and has a low view of Scripture (16:27–31).

In other words, this provocative parable that includes a scene in hell, is not really about hell. In fact, there is no new information about hell that is not affirmed other places in Scripture. He did not have to defend hell; his audience assumed its reality. The reason is that Jesus is not trying to describe hell; he is trying to describe the kind of people who go there: people who love things more than people and have a low view of Scripture are the kind of people who go to hell. If you pan out to the book level, you can see that this fits with Luke's overall theme of Christ reaching out to those who are weak and marginalized. The meaning is not in the micro level of exegesis, but the macro level.

Imagine you are in the Louvre in Paris. Imagine you have full access, all by yourself, to study the Mona Lisa. You stand 25 feet away and realize you don't really understand the painting. So, you move closer, and with every step you appreciate it more. Then, you move your eyes so near the canvas that you can see the brush strokes. This close perspective is interesting, but you realize there is a limitation to this view as well. There is a temptation in interpretation to stand so far from the text that we don't understand it. There is also an equally dangerous temptation to get so close to the nuances of verb tense and sentence structure that we miss what is going on at the macro level. Both perspectives are needed so they should be held in dynamic tension. The process of interpretation involves systematically "zooming in" to the micro level of the text, but we also "pan out" to the surrounding context. Both the macro view and the micro view are essential to determining meaning.

So the interpretive process is the exegetical process. This is the process by which we read the text many times and then use all the exegetical tools we have to discover the meaning of the text. Once we know what the text says, then we try to figure out how to say it. In the chapters that follow the "Interpretation Section" we will not cover all areas of interpretation, but only those limited to issues related to the genre of the text. So now that we know what the text means (interpretation), we will turn to how to say it (communication).

COMMUNICATION: RECAPTURING THE VOICE OF THE TEXT

Now that we know what the text says, we answer the question, how do we say it? This is when we work out of us in preaching what has been worked into us by study. This refers to the delivery, yes, but for our conversation the process of communication specifically refers to the process of composing a sermon that represents the text.

Here lies another temptation. Once the exegetical work is complete and we know what the text says, the temptation is to take the meaning of the text and present it in any homiletical form we like the best. However, we want to argue here that the shape of the sermon is not arbitrary. As we said above, the shape of the sermon should be determined by the structure of the text. Specifically, a text-driven sermon is based on the substance, structure, and spirit of the text.

Substance

By "substance" we mean the meaning of the text. Thus the exegetical process of interpretation yields an exegetical idea—the text in a sentence. The process of communication yields a main idea—the sermon's thrust summarized in a sentence. Thus, the main idea of the text is to be represented by the main idea of the sermon. The example I often cite in class of how not to do this is the sermon I heard on tithing from John 3:16. The idea is that God so loved the world that he gave—so dig deep. Someone might argue that the concept of giving was in the text, so why not apply it to financial giving? After all, God gave, and we should give. Both of those things are in fact true. The problem is not what is said, but what is not said. Everything we say in the pulpit we say to the exclusion of something else. So the problem is not that there is not a corollary between the two ideas, the problem is that what is actually in this text, the richness of the atonement, is missed for the sake of a misplaced application. Preaching that makes "points" from a text, but avoids the meaning of the text makes our people vulnerable. In other words, a sermon such as this takes the pressure off the preacher to understand and communicate the incredible grace of God in the atoning work of Christ. Sitting under this preaching, people may never grow to maturity in their understanding of the faith and thus become vulnerable. This is the real problem. Avoiding the meaning of the text is not lying to people, but it prepares our people to accept lies. People can sit under our preaching for years and not know basic Bible doctrine because we have reduced difficult, rich, meaningful texts to a compilation of practical points for living. Our sheep are vulnerable because our people do not know the Word, sitting under preachers who extract "points" from one text, call it exposition, but never deal with the text in context. So what's worse, the preacher who tells lies, or the preacher who will not preach the truth? The former is a false prophet; the latter is a negligent shepherd.

There is in fact a relationship between tithing and the atonement, and it is a strong relationship; however, it is found in 2 Corinthians 8:7–15, not John 3:16. So, when we preach a text, the substance of the text must be the substance of the sermon.

There is, on the other hand, another temptation. While there are those who never deal with the substance of the text, there are those who tend to *only* deal with the substance of the text. Those of us who really want to get the text right can spend all of our time in the substance. We tend to the exegetical nuances of the text but forget that meaning is not found at the substance level only; it is found at the level of structure and spirit. There are many excellent texts that address finding the meaning of the text from the exegetical study of the text. Since, on balance, most preaching books deal more with the substance, this work will deal with the structure and the spirit of the text. However, let's not set up a strict, misleading trichotomy. When one understands the structure of the text (the semantic shape of the passage), and the spirit of the text (the author intended emotive design of the text), it influences the substance of the text. In other words, we are not after what the text says: we are after what the text means. And there is meaning at the substance and spirit level of a text. This is the voice of the Word.

What follows is not so much exegetical help, in the technical sense of the word, but a discussion of how the genre shapes the meaning; more attention will be given to how we shape the words of the Word in a way that is faithful to the voice of the Word. Again the ultimate objective is not creativity; it is closeness. We want to get closer to what the text says so that we find the right voice for the right words.

Structure

There is meaning in the structure of the text. If we do not understand the history of preaching, we might think that any sermon form will serve any text equally. If we do not understand theology, we might not think this is a bad thing as long as we tend to the form of the sermon. However, even without history and theology we should consider some basic linguistic theory: there is meaning in the structure of the text.

If we ignore the structure of the text, we may not get the meaning of the text. God could have simply told us to have faith in God alone for our salvation because God always keeps his covenant promises. However, instead of a lesson he presents us with the stories of David, Daniel, and Abraham. The difference is not just in how the message is translated, but in the "content." The meaning of the message is deeper because it is embedded in the form of narrative.

God could have given us 176 reasons why we should love the Word of God, but instead he gave us the amazing poem of Psalm 119. We will discuss this in the following chapters, but for now it is enough to say that the Word of God is not a flat instruction manual. It is richer than that. It is a rich nuanced book in which the variance of genre makes the text come to life. To present it as flat and one-dimensional is to misrepresent the book. And this is the point of this book: sermon shape is determined by text shape.

This simple truth has given me more freedom in preaching than anything else I can imagine. If a text has four points, I preach a sermon with four points. When I preach a narrative that has no easily discernable points, my sermon has no points.[1] When I preach a parable that has three scenes and a warning of Christ at the end, my sermon does the same. For the rest of my life, how to structure a sermon will always be a secondary question. The primary question is always, How is the text structured? If I

---

1. This is not to say the sermon has no structure. The scenes of the story become the structure of the sermon. The scenes of the story may be communicating points themselves, or, more likely, they will lead to one major point.

answer that question, then I have my sermon structure. This does not mean there is not some thinking time involved. The mystery of text shape is fascinating. However in wrestling with the structure of the text, I find the structure of the sermon.

By the way, as an aside, this protects us from two extremes: (1) the slavish adherence to a fixed homiletic template and (2) a line-by-line commentary on the text. The former misrepresents the text by an imposed structure, and the second misrepresents the text by ignoring the structure. Both extremes miss the fact that there is meaning in the structure of the text. So be liberated. Let the text breathe. You are free. You don't have to construct a sermon that sounds like anyone else. The structure of the text determines the structure of the sermon.

At this point it might be good to clarify what we mean about the structure of the text informing the structure of the sermon. We are not trading one set of rules for another. We are not trading in an old homiletic stricture for another one. We are not, as someone said, "form-fundamentalists." And, most importantly we are not suggesting that the sermon can exactly mimic the text. Structuring a sermon like the paragraph unit of a letter is natural: observe the verbs in the text, note the coordinating and subordinate clauses, and build a structure around the form. Yet, lifting the form of poetry, Wisdom literature, and Law and using it as the sermon form may be challenging if the preacher uses the same approach to all genres as he does to Epistles. What we are after is not imitation, but re-animation. This I believe is on a continuum: at the most the sermon will have the exact same structure as the text; at the very least, the preacher understands how the structure influences meaning and re-presents the text in a way that considers the meaning provided by the structure. Thus, sometimes we borrow the sermon structure from the text; other times the text informs the sermon structure. Regardless, we are taking our cue for sermon structure from the structure of the text. This has the effect of re-animation, meaning the intended effect on the ancient listener/reader is recast for the modern listener.

As an aside, this approach to preaching does not limit the amount of text one can take for a sermon. In theory a text-driven sermon is not bound by length of text. There are exegetical concerns (e.g., identifying the natural divisions of the text) and pastoral concerns (e.g., identifying the receptivity level of an audience to the text) that will determine the length of text chosen.

Spirit

By spirit we mean the author-intended emotional design of the text. (We do not mean the Holy Spirit; notice the lower case "s.") The spirit of the text comes through in many ways. The most obvious way is the genre. A poem simply "feels" different than a letter. A prophetic voice is different than the Wisdom literature. So we learn something from the genre. However, the genre alone does not dictate the mood of the text. Sometimes genres do the unexpected: in the Prophets poetry warns; the Epistles encourage and threaten; the parables both encourage and challenge. So the genre helps us understand the tone of the text, but each genre is not strictly limited to communicate one particular tone. Rather, each unit of Scripture has its own mood.

For example, the letter of Paul to the Galatians is filled with in-your-face warnings. The letter of 1 Thessalonians is filled with warm paternal metaphors, a different mood for a different occasion. The parable of the Sower (Matt 13:1–23) gives great hope that despite initial rejection the kingdom will find exponential growth. The parable of the Dragnet (Matt 13:47–50) warns that those who reject the kingdom will be thrown out! In the same chapter the mood of encouragement and warning are both present. We could go on, but the idea is clear enough. Some texts of Scripture simply feel different than others. The spirit of the text, then, becomes the spirit of the sermon.

When preaching, we are trying to get the meaning right through interpretation, structure the sermon like the text, communicate the sermon in a way that re-presents the meaning or substance of the text, and then deliver it in the same spirit of the text. This is a text-driven sermon. At this point I am tempted to spell out the procedure for developing a text-driven sermon. However, in this volume we will not deal with each aspect of sermon development—i.e., illustrations, applications, delivery. That has been done well in many great texts on expository preaching. For now I want to point out the broad macro categories of interpretation and then communication: developing an exegetical outline of the text and a communication outline for preaching; hearing the voice of God and recapturing the voice of God for preaching. We will, of course, focus on the part of communication that helps us understand the structure and the spirit of the text. Again, our focus is the voice given to the Word. This seems like a daunting process, and it is. So let me anticipate a question that someone might ask: is biblical preaching warranted? Can't a pastor be committed to simply being a great communicator and helping people via scintillating speeches? Is it really necessary that he take pains to make the Scripture clear? Is text-driven preaching explicitly mentioned in the Bible?

Is Text-Driven Preaching Biblical?

This is the question I was asked in class: "Where in the Bible does it say that we have to preach expository, text-driven, sermons?" Great question. Where exactly is that verse in the Bible? In other words, give us the text in Scripture that defends this method. That's fair enough. We are tempted to reference Paul's simple admonition to preach the Word (2 Tim 4:2). However, while Paul's admonition to Timothy is clear enough, it is more of an admonition to faithfulness to explaining Christ from all of Scripture than it is advocating a philosophy of preaching. This is an incredible passage of Scripture, but this is not a defense for text-driven preaching. To use this text as such is to ignore all the magnificent things it is saying. The truth of the matter is that the one proof text does not exist. There is not, in my mind, one single verse that advocates text-driven preaching as the right way to preach. The reason we wave that banner of text-driven preaching is not from one single text, but for another reason. And before we spend time talking about the influence of genre, perhaps it is necessary to give some rationale for our approach.

The reason text-driven preaching is so compelling does not come from one single verse, but it is found in answering another question: Is it the pastor's responsibility to explain Scripture to his congregation? This is a simple, critical question, but it's fair enough. When a pastor discharges his duties, is he responsible for explaining Scripture? Perhaps you have already answered this question. I certainly don't want to insult anyone's intelligence. However, the truth of the matter is that by listening to most preaching, we find the jury is still out on this question. Many pastors are not yet convinced that it is their responsibility to explain Scripture to their congregations. We could look at several places in Scripture for an answer to the question; however, let's limit our answer to Paul's words to Timothy and Titus in the pastoral Epistles since they most explicitly deal with the function of a pastor. Look at this limited collection of verses from 1 and 2 Timothy and Titus:

> Remain in Ephesus, so that you may instruct certain people not to teach other doctrine. (1 Tim 1:1)

> For the overseer must be . . . skillful in teaching. (1 Tim 3:2)

> By teaching these things to the brothers, you will be a good servant of Christ Jesus, trained in the words of faith and of the good teaching that you have followed faithfully. (1 Tim 4:6)

> Command these things and teach them . . . (1 Tim 4:11)

> Until I come pay attention to the public reading, to exhortation, to teaching. (1 Tim 4:13)

> Fix your attention on yourself and on your teaching. Continue in them, for by doing this you will save both yourself and those who hear you. (1 Tim 4:16)

> And command these things, in order that they may be irreproachable. (1 Tim 5:7)

> Reprove those who sin in the presence of all, in order that the rest also may experience fear. (1 Tim 5:20)

> Teach and encourage these things. If anyone teaches other doctrine and does not devote himself to the sound words of our Lord Jesus Christ and the teaching that is in accordance with godliness, he is conceited, understanding nothing, but having a morbid interest concerning controversies and disputes about words, from which come envy, strife, slanders, evil suspicion, constant wrangling by people of depraved mind and deprived of the truth, who consider godliness to be a means of gain. (1 Tim 6:2–5)

> Hold fast to the pattern of sound words that you have heard from me. (2 Tim 1:13)

> Entrust these things to faithful people who will be competent to teach others also. (2 Tim 2:2)

> Remind people of these things, solemnly urging them before the Lord. (2 Tim 2:14)

> Make every effort to present yourself approved to God, a worker having no need to be ashamed, guiding the word of truth along a straight path. (2 Tim 2:15)

> And the slave of the Lord must be . . . skillful in teaching, tolerant, correcting those who are opposed with gentleness. (2 Tim 2:21)

> But you continue in the things which you have learned and are convinced of . . . the holy writings. (2 Tim 3:14)

> All Scripture is breathed out by God and profitable for teaching, for reproof, for correction, for training in righteousness . . . (2 Tim 3:16)

> I solemnly charge you before God and Christ Jesus, who is going to judge the living and the dead, and by his appearing and his kingdom, preach the word, be ready in season and out of season, reprove, rebuke, exhort, with all patience and instruction. For there will be a time when they will not endure sound teaching . . . (2 Tim 4:1–2)

> Holding fast to the faithful message according to the teaching, in order that he may be able both to exhort with sound instruction and to reprove those who speak against it. (Titus 1:9)

> Speak the things which are fitting for sound instruction. (Titus 2:1)

These texts seem clear enough. Whatever else Paul expected Timothy and Titus to do, he at least expected them to teach the Word of God to people.[2] These seem to be clear exhortations to explain the truth of Scripture to people. And, this admonition, on balance, could be the heaviest of all. Add to this the implicit commands to protect revealed truth (1 Tim 1:11; 6:20; 2 Tim 1:12, 14), and the case is pretty strong that it is the responsibility of the pastor to explain revealed truth to the people. No need to belabor this. The point is clear enough: there is someone who is responsible for the explanation of the Word to the people.

The question is not should pastors teach the Scripture? That is clear enough from the above text. It has been answered for us. We must teach our people Scripture. The question now is, what method best facilitates the pastoral mandate to explain Scripture to the congregation? From this question we get the answer of text-driven preaching. Text-driven preaching is not a style; it is a theologically driven philosophy of preaching. It is a method that facilitates the mandate God gives for a pastor to explain and proclaim Scripture to the congregation. The emphasis is on the indefinite article—it is *a* method. While I don't plan on leaving the text-driven preaching approach, what that means for me is constantly being tweaked as I seek God for the best way to get closer to the text. The mandate drives the method.

---

2. I'm aware of the temptation to transcribe "Scripture" for "gospel instruction" in some of the texts on teaching whose referent for "message" or "word" is simply the gospel or gospel instruction.

Conclusion

At some point in recent times evangelical preachers decided they are not preachers as much as communicators. It's true that in the past pulpits have been filled with those who could sound like preachers but did not communicate. What being a "communicator" means, at least, is that we are not beholden to a sermon form. No formal clothes. No formal alliterated outlines. Casual atmosphere with casual preaching. No formal points are needed since the sermon is a conversation. However, what is not always but often missing from this approach is a theological center.

We are indeed communicators, but we are more than communicators. We are re-presenters. We are not just communicators who have a loose connection to an ancient text that we go to so we can pepper the conversation with an authoritative vibe. Nor are we taking a text and making observations from the text. Rather, we are standing before the people answering the question, What did God say? We are re-presenting what God has already said. This is iconic preaching. We are pointing people to another reality while imitating the rhetorical strategy of Christ.

Now that we know what we're after, let's look at the raw material of preaching: namely, the genres themselves. Since the idea of studying the biblical genre can be overwhelming, let's begin with some good news.

Chapter 3

PREACHING AND THE GENRE OF SCRIPTURE: STORY, POEM, LETTER

Everything in Scripture is a story, a poem, or a letter.[1]

WE HAVE ARGUED THAT THE SHAPE OF THE TEXT DETERMINES THE SHAPE OF THE SERMON AND, FURTHER, THAT THE GENRE DETER-MINES THE SHAPE OF THE TEXT. Therefore, shaping sermons like Scripture demands an understanding of the genres that shape the Scripture. The chapters that follow are brief primers on preaching genres—the genres we must under-stand in order to shape our sermons accordingly. So before we dive in, let's look at three critical features of genre: genres are limited; genres are situational; and genres are moving.

GENRES ARE LIMITED

The Bible can be a complicated book. And sometimes it intimidates me. There, I said it. The sweet simplicity of God's love for me is communicated in a book so masterfully complex we will never exhaust its meaning or beauty. And yet what makes it inexhaustible can make it exhaustingly difficult to understand. So perhaps it is wise to move from the simple to the complex, from lesser to greater.

There are arguably nine discernable genres of Scripture: Old Testament Narrative, Law, Psalms, Prophecy, Wisdom Literature, Gospels/Acts, Parables, Epistles, and Revelation (Apocalyptic).[2] This is some really good news: there is not an infinite number of genres. The number is limited. There is further good news: broadly speaking, all of these genres are expressions of only three basic structural forms.

---

1. The bulk of this chapter is a modified form of the author's article, "The Gospel in Genre," presented to the Evangelical Homiletics Society, October 2013.

2. There are many potential ways to categorize the genres of Scripture. For example, Thomas G. Long, in *Preaching and the Literary Forms of the Bible*, deals with five; Jeffrey Arthurs, *Preaching with Variety: How to Re-create the Dynamics of Biblical Genres*, deals with six (see bibliography). The list here pro-vides some sub-genres, of which there are sub-sub genres. The purpose of this book is to demonstrate how text structure influences sermon structure; thus, the categories are developed around these forms.

The nine genres listed above fit under three macro structures: Story, Poem, and Letter.

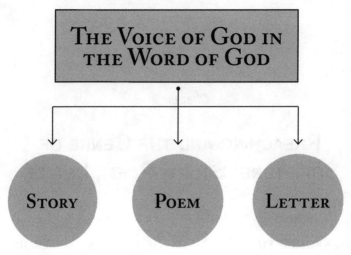

Everything in Scripture is story, poem, or letter. Further, the genres can all fit under these three categories.

1. Story (Narrative): Old Testament Narrative, Law, Gospels/Acts, Parables
2. Poem: Psalms, Prophecy, Wisdom literature
3. Letter: Epistles, Revelation

There is a lot to understand about genre. However, one must at least understand narratives and their scene structure, Epistles with their paragraph structure, and Hebrew poetry and its strophe structure (a strophe is to poetry what a paragraph is to prose—a contained unit of thought, much like a verse in a song). Therefore, if the sermon reflects the text, at least three different sermon forms are needed: one that recognizes the flow of stories, one that reflects the verve of poetry, and one that can communicate with the directness of letters.

These axioms undergird this work: (1) the sermon structure should reflect the genre, (2) there are at least nine discernable genres, but (3) preaching those genres may be facilitated by mastering three basic templates.

This is indeed, and may I add intentionally, reductionist. Admittedly, preaching the poetry of the prophecy of Ezekiel is different than preaching the poetry of Ecclesiastes. However, understanding the structure of Hebrew poetry provides the student the macro template by which to preach both Psalms and the Prophets. Understanding narrative can help one preach both Genesis and Acts. Understanding the epistolary genre helps one preach both Titus and Revelation. At the same time, a macro-level understanding of the genres allows the preacher to realize the differences in the types of genre. In the spirit of having a starting point, we will consider macro-level genre (Story, Poem, Letter), genre (OT Narrative, Law, Psalms, Wisdom Literature, Prophecy, Gospels, Parables, Epistles, and Revelation) and further subgenres within the genres (e.g., types of Psalms, Sermons in Acts, types of Parables, procedural texts). So we will work from the macro level to the sub-genre level.

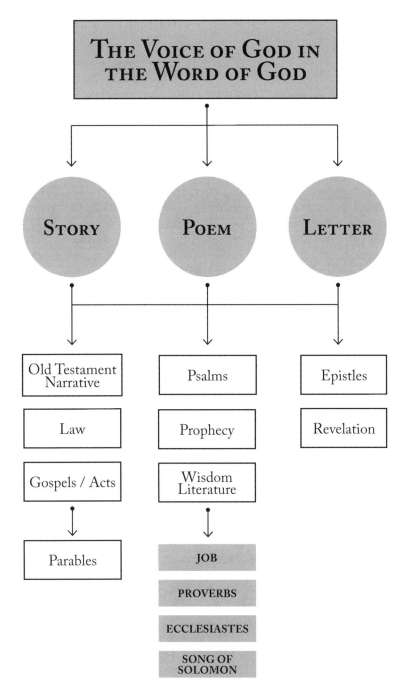

The multiplicity of genres may be limited to at least three macro-level genres. One may fairly ask why God used these specific literary genres and why he used them in this measure. Of course, this is in the mind of God, but asking the question leads to the second important feature of the genres, namely that genres themselves are situational.

GENRES ARE SITUATIONAL

Humanly speaking, the use of literary genres emerges from the needs of specific situations. The situation of angst and complaint calls for a psalm. The situation of a struggling church calls for an epistle. The situation of the grand movement of God calls for a narrative. Clearly understanding the situation to which, or from which, a text is written helps us understand its meaning. When Paul understood how far the young Galatian believers were from Christ, he did not sing a song or give them a law. Rather, he gave them a stinging rebuke in the form of a letter (Gal 1:6–10). The situation drove the genre. The situation of the writing of the text is helpful to understanding its meaning.

However, the knowledge of the situation can also be a distraction away from its meaning. This is because the knowledge of the situation can produce the latent temptation to preach the situation and not the text.

This temptation to preach the situation and not the text is especially acute in the Psalms. Take for example David's psalm of contrition in Psalm 51. The psalmist is lamenting his sin. His contrition is deep ("for I know my transgressions," v. 3) and wide ("and my sin is ever before me," v. 3). The poem is the perfect medium for David's loathing. The strophe structure allows the heartache and pain to seep through his porous soul in waves of theologically nuanced suffering. The medium is perfectly situated for the message. And herein lies the problem. The temptation in such a psalm is to reach back to the story and preach the story and not the psalm. The narrative of 2 Samuel 11–12 is fascinating, provocative, and heartbreaking. The natural temptation is to take as one's text Psalm 51, but use most of the time preaching the narrative of the sin and ignore the psalm. In other words, instead of preaching the meaning of the text to the immediate audience, we preach the situation of the text. Instead of preaching the text and its implications for today, the bulk of the sermon is what is behind the text.[3]

While this temptation is especially acute in the Psalms, the temptation can be equally as great while preaching the words of Paul to the people of Galatia, the Sermon on the Mount from Jesus to the people, or the Revelation to John from Jesus to the seven churches. All of these texts are situational, and the situations are fascinating (at least to the inner nerd within every Bible student). The situation is in fact helpful. However, it is helpful as an interpretive guide to the text at hand. The preacher wants to avoid preaching the text that is behind the text (the situation) instead of preaching the text itself.

This is our theology of Scripture. We are not preaching the situations; we are preaching texts. Preaching the situation that is behind the text to the exclusion of the text at hand misrepresents the nature of Scripture. The message of Scripture "trans-historically"[4] transcends time and speaks to our situation. While we must pay attention to the situation in which it was originally given, a sermon that deals

---

3. See Abraham Kuruvilla, *Privilege the Text! A Theological Hermeneutic for Preaching* (Chicago: Moody, 2013).

4. Ibid., 44.

too much with the historical situation moves the preacher further from dealing with the situation in which people find themselves: the need to be aware of sin. This is the most important aspect of the situational nature of the genre: it is situational in an anticipatory way. The genres exist not just to facilitate the ancient situation, but as facility for our situations. The point is not that the genres capture the limited numbers of ways God chose to communicate, rather that the genres speak to the unlimited number of situations of all believers of all time. Genres are situational, but in a trans-historical way.[5] In order to allow the text to meet the current situation, we must preach it in a way that addresses immediate needs.

Tending to a study of individual genres should make us more sensitive to present needs, not desensitized against present needs while being sensitive to the ancient situation. Understanding the ancient situation is an aid to understanding the text, a text that, by the power of the Holy Spirit, is able to speak to the present situation.

This then leads to a question. Why exactly are the genres able to meet the current situation? Or more precisely, what makes an ancient text relevant in our situation today? After all, this deference to ancient literature as absolutely trustworthy has little modern equivalent. In a day when baccalaureate science textbooks go out of date by the time they are printed and reach the market, it is a significant challenge for the evangelical to present an ancient text as the answer for contemporary problems. However, the reason that they are able to meet current needs is because they themselves have never been static, but have always been moving.

GENRES ARE MOVING

The reason the text from any genre can speak to a contemporary need is because the genres are themselves moving. More precisely: they are still situational because they are not static. Therefore they are still relevant to a new situation. Further, the moving nature of the genres should help one understand them as moving toward a very specific end goal.

The genres are literary devices. That is the way they function. However, if only viewed as literary devices, they may be errantly treated as either flat or static. Both of these aberrant understandings of the text manifest themselves in the pulpit. Let's briefly look at both flat and static homiletic approaches to the text.

Flat

The flat approach assumes that a text is a text is a text. The preacher is predisposed to a universal homiletic template, which is then transposed over any text regardless of the genre. In this way, the genres themselves have no consequence on the sermon. In this scenario, the preacher chooses the homiletic template first. The sermon is a demonstration of how neatly a text can fit into this pre-chosen form.

The problem is that when genres are viewed arbitrarily, communication is itself flat. No life, no texture, no nuance, no color in the text. Just a monochromatic lecture. This is tragic for the reason that it does not re-present the text. What often happens as a result is that the text is presented as flat and "creativity" (i.e., supplementary material, visuals) is then needed to make the text compelling. Creativity

---

5. Ibid.

is essential, and multi-sensory communication can be compelling. However, the breadth of the creativity should come from the depth of exegesis. In other words, we are not bringing creative elements to the text as much as we are showing the creativity that is already embedded within the text. We are letting the text breathe. We are not suffocating it with our own thoughts. Exegetical work is mining the life that is already embedded in the text.

The deeper problem, as established above, is that the form of a text can influence the meaning. To ignore the shape is to risk missing a part of the meaning. So while suggesting that the communication will be flat may seem like a rant against creativity, one is pressed further to see that not paying attention to the genre is a matter of interpretation first, and communication second. There is meaning in the structure of a text.

Static

Like the flat approach, the static approach perceives that the genres are nonmoving literary devices. In this way the genres, and the pericopes within the genres, function like a rhetorical artifact that can be studied independent of their setting within the cannon. It's as if the pericope is an isolated artifact. Each sermon from such a pericope is a one-volume short story influenced by nothing outside of the homiletic binding of the introduction and conclusion of the sermon. But that approach belies the canonical relationship of each text with the whole of Scripture.

The multiplicity of genres in Scripture not only gives witness to the many situations to which it was written, but to the many situations to which Scripture is able to speak. In other words, the many genres speak not only to its variety, but to its direction. The genres by their nature are situational. Therefore, they are as applicable in the twenty-first century as they were when they were written. They are limited genres speaking to unlimited situations.

Perhaps the best way to understand this is to look at the book of Revelation. Revelation is the most intertextual of all the books, and necessarily so. As the climactic book in the canon it comprises many genres. Here we see multiple genres alive in one book.

Revelation is an apocalyptic narrative. Revelation begins with a vision of Christ, his word to the churches, and a sense of direction as to where these things are all headed. Most commentators see an outline to the book in 1:19, "the things that you have seen, those that are and those that are to take place after this." This outline is the movement of a story, especially the narrative flow of the last section, or bulk of the book, where things move from a scene of worship in heaven (4–5) moving toward a great battle (16:10–19:21) to the new heaven and the new earth and the descent of the new city (21–22) leaving John in breathless wonder to cry "Come, Lord Jesus." The book is one dramatic narrative.

However, this narrative also contains the genre of prophecy, meaning it is both predicting the future and proclaiming who Christ is against the background of the current situation.[6] The bulk of chapter 18 is structured with the Hebrew parallelism

---

6. See Paige Patterson's conclusion that the genre of Revelation is "a prophetic circular letter which not infrequently makes use of apocalyptic imagery and device" in *Revelation*, New American Commentary (Nashville: B&H, 2012), 24.

that is found in the Old Testament Prophets. And the prophets, of course, use the genre of poetry. So in Revelation 18 one finds the strophe structure of Hebrew parallelism that is found throughout Scripture.[7] Added to this is the genre proper of Revelation, which is apocalyptic—meaning that it brings all of salvation history to a climax.

All of this revelation is wrapped in a situation. The situation is that John is writing an epistle to the seven churches, a specific author writing to a specific audience. So the epistle of the Revelation of John contains narrative, prophecy, poetry, and apocalyptic. These individual genres are alive and they are indeed going somewhere. They are moving to a very definitive ending. The quick pace of the book of Revelation, and its use of the genres to accomplish that pace are, in many ways, metaphorical devices for the whole of Scripture: many genres used for one purpose, to move us to one end.

So against the flat or static approaches, the genres are themselves intentionally vibrant, and they are dynamic. In other words, God desired for a limited number of macro-structures—story, poem, and letter—to speak to an unlimited number of situations. Therefore, they are intentional in their placement and they are intentional in their movement toward a destination. That destination, once understood, helps us to know what to do with them when we preach them.

CONCLUSION

The text is not static; it is moving like a train. Like a train, it is composed of individual cars whose shapes are determined by the cargo they carry. In the same way the shape of the genres of Scripture are not things that need to be willfully bent toward Christ by the preacher; rather, they exist like they do *because* of the gospel message.[8] The commonality is the destination. They are each moving individual, car-specific cargo to the final destination of God's plan in redemptive history.

The genres are limited and there are a finite number of them. The genres are situational and speak to every contemporary situation. The genres are also moving. They are carriers of a message that is complete, but a story that is not yet complete. Thus, the limited genres speak to unlimited situations that are all reaching their climax through the message of the gospel.

This is one reason the preacher can make the gospel explicit from any text. It is warranted in any situation, because the nature of Scripture demands it. In other words, the composition of Scripture begs for the explanation of the gospel from it.

If this is the case, then the genres are carrying us as well. We are studying the genre, but the genre is also studying us. Preaching is explaining to people how God is reading them. It is our situation to which *they* speak; therefore, it is to the present situation that *we* must speak. And that situation demands the gospel. So, before we jump in, let me give one last encouragement for considering the genre when we preach.

---

7. See Leland Ryken, *Words of Delight: A Literary Introduction to the Bible* (Grand Rapids: Baker, 1987), 477.

8. While not the subject of this book, this argument from the nature of Scripture gives warrant to the idea of preaching Christ from any Scripture—or more precisely, showing how all Scripture advances the plan of the gospel of which Christ is operative and through which he will be exalted.

Preaching Is the Act by Which I Die So That Others May Live

The best metaphor for preaching the gospel is the gospel.[9] This is summed up best in 2 Corinthians 4:12 when Paul describes his ministry this way, "So death is at work in us, but life in you." Applied to preaching, this describes the preacher who is willing to die in the pulpit, so that there may be life in the pew. In this way, there can be no cross from the pulpit, unless there is first a cross in the pulpit. This, I believe, is on a continuum. The more I act on my desire to be liked—my desire to be thought of as hip, entertaining, or a strong leader—the less the Word can seep through. Fleshly desires are to preaching what asthma is to lungs: they constrict the breath of the Word from the pulpit to the pew by slowly shrinking the circumference of the conduit of truth. My desire to become known as a great preacher can be a great impediment to the Word flowing through. It's like a conduit.[10] It can either be clear that light can pour through, or it can be all junked up so that no light gets through. Clogged. Dammed. We are not containers, we are conduits. The highest ambition in preaching is not to get in the way of the flow of God's Spirit to people. The greatest preacher is the one not trying to be great. The conduit is free of self, and, in that death, the Word lives.

This brings us to a strange irony. Sometimes the very means of communication of Scripture can be an impediment to people hearing it. To put it bluntly, our sermon structures can suffocate the hearing of Scripture. Are we so committed to a homiletic form that we impose it on the text? Are we so committed not to having any homiletic form that the Word of God is not clear? This volume is not arguing for a homiletic form. Rather we are arguing that Scripture shape dictates sermon form. It is arguing that our high view of Scripture demands that the text itself determines the shape of the sermon. We do not pick homiletic forms. We simply preach texts and allow the form of the text to be the form of the sermon.

In this way we are dying to our desires, and we are allowing the living Word to breathe through our approach. Imagine the liberation of allowing the text to determine our sermon structure. Preaching sermons that honor the genre is the choice to die and let the genre of the text live. It is an extension of a high view of Scripture.

Chapter Structure

Each chapter will be structured according to our definition of text-driven preaching. The first section is "Interpretation: Hearing the Voice in the Literary Features of the Genre." This section deals with matters of interpretation with a focus on the individual genre. This is not exhaustive like a text on hermeneutics, but highlights features that will help you understand how the specific biblical genre works. Our goal is to provide a short primer on the genre and then point you to the best resources to a discussion of each genre.

---

9. This section quotes freely from the author's *Dying to Preach: Embracing the Cross in the Pulpit* (Grand Rapids: Kregel, 2008).

10. As a result this also becomes the same metaphor by which we understand what to do with sermon compliments. If we are clear conduits through which God's praise flows then when someone compliments the sermon, it is sent right back to the Father through this clear conduit. See the author's article, "Re-Send: What do you do with the post-sermon compliment?" http://theologicalmatters. com/2013/05/30/ re-send-what-do-you-do-with-the-post-sermon-compliment.

The second section of each chapter, "Communication: Recapturing the Voice of the Genre" will be sermon tips for crafting a sermon that recaptures the voice of the Word in a manner specific to the genre. However, our focus here is on sermon structure, so we will have a short final section that deals just with the issue of shaping sermons like the text: "Structure: Structuring a Sermon from This Genre." This last section is necessarily short since the conclusions should be clear by that point. A sermon sample will then be given. These are not perfect, but simple attempts to offer a sample of the approach. The sample will be followed by some questions for reflection and some resources for further study.

The purpose of looking at genre is not slavish imitation. Rather the purpose is to get at meaning. The idea is reanimation, not imitation. We are asking, what about this genre influences the meaning of this text? In order to preach with accuracy we must tend to the meaning of the text as given through the spirit of the text as influenced by the genre. Think of the work of Bible translators. They must get the meaning of the original languages precisely. Yet, the word order of Greek and Hebrew is different than what modern English readers would expect. They must translate in a way that communicates the sense of meaning. In other words, in order for the words to have the intended impact, they must translate the sense as well as the words. Translators refer to this as the difference between "formal equivalence" and "dynamic equivalence." In the same way, we are not in pure imitation of the genre. The idea rather is to look at how the genre of the text shapes meaning and then try to capture that meaning. This is why, when possible, we allow the structure of the text to dictate the structure of the sermon.

The genres of Scripture are important not because the form is sacred but because the Word of God is sacred, and it is in a certain form. Therefore, tending to the form allows us to get at the meaning. And we are further arguing that there are aspects of the meaning that will never be understood clearly without wrestling with the genre. And wrestling is a good metaphor. The meanings are not superficial. Scripture simply does not work that way. They have to be wrought out with hard work if they are going to be declared with faithfulness. Therefore, to preach the Word of God in the voice of God we must first listen carefully to hear the voice ourselves.

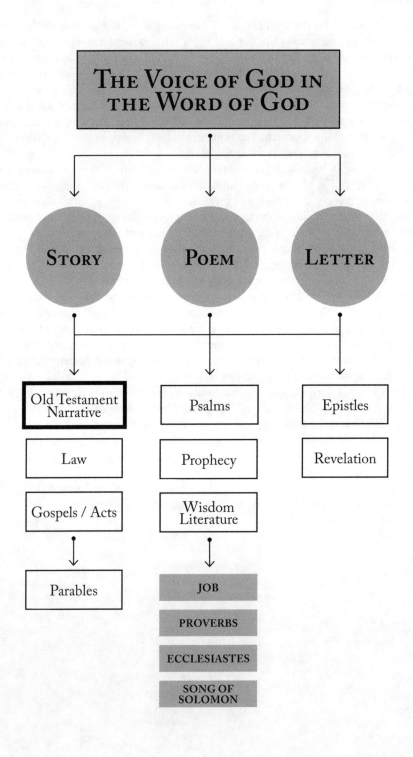

Chapter 4

RECAPTURING THE VOICE OF GOD IN OLD TESTAMENT NARRATIVE

THE SETTING

As I walked in, I could tell the guy was seasoned. The jewelry salesman had this look of a polished gentleman that made me want to give him my money. Eventually I did. I said "Hello," and introduced him to my very nervous girl-friend. I said we wanted to look at rings, which was at least half true. I know I did. He looked at Ashley and said, "I think I have something you would like." We walked to another part of the store; he pulled back the glass from behind the counter and produced a ring that was perfect for her. She's still wearing it. This beautiful ring had everything. Everything, that is, except a diamond. That was another purchase. I have heard of girls wanting a band without a diamond. However, I've never heard of a girl wanting a diamond without a band. The setting, the part that makes it look like a wedding ring, says something. In this way the setting and the stone both reveal things about a relationship.

We preachers sometimes treat stories as if we stumbled upon a diamond on the ground. That would be an amazing thing, right? We are walking outside and find glistening on the ground a chunk of stone that seems unusual. We research it and realize that our discovery is potentially a five-carat diamond. This thing is going to be worth thousands of dollars. We call friends; we post it on social media. We do all kinds of things to let people know of our great find. But this diamond is just a rough stone. It needs to be cut and polished, and then it needs a setting. A setting will show off the beauty of the diamond even more brilliantly.

The text we are to preach is a set stone, not a rough diamond. If we find a story that doesn't appear to be influenced by its context, then we need to look closer. We need to look around the text as much as we do within the text. The author of Scripture has designed it so that each of the smaller narratives contributes to the larger narrative. Within the canon of Scripture, the individual books are designed the same way. The process of understanding the biblical text is the process of understanding how this little gem of text fits into the larger whole. This will make the story even more glorious. This is how Jesus used the stories of the Old Testament. The individual parts fit into the larger whole.

How Stories Work

When we think of Jesus' use of stories, we think of the parables. Jesus made up stories. However, in the Gospels we also see Christ regularly using the stories of the Old Testament. Moses is mentioned almost 200 times in the four Gospels. Many of these are references to the law of Moses. There are also more explicit references, such as Moses lifting up the serpent in the wilderness (John 3:14) and the manna from heaven (John 6:14). In fact, when Matthew tells the story of the transfiguration of Christ (Matt 17:1–13), it is clear that he wants us to understand it in light of the story of Moses descending from the mount after receiving the Ten Commandments.[1] Jesus used other stories such as the story of the flood (Matthew 24; Luke 17) and the stories of Elijah and Elisha (Luke 4). As we look at the stories Jesus used, the important thing to notice is how he used them, but more on that later.

Why did Jesus use stories so much? The reason is that he came to a story-telling culture. We often separate "facts" from stories. By facts we mean information, raw data, and pure objectivity. In our culture, stories have the connotation of subjectivity at best and fairy tales at worst. However, the audience Jesus was talking to made no such internal bifurcation. The stories *were* truths. The facts, or the details, were only a part of the stories. The truths were part of a larger story. That stories are from a particular point of view or for a specific reason has no bearing on their truthfulness and the truth they contain.

Some argue that there was no such thing as a "fact" before the invention of the printing press.[2] Think about it. A fact is a piece of information that is detached from any other referent. A fact is just information. That is all. Information on a page. It's not that "truths" did not exist; it's just that they did not exist independent from stories. And so, in order to give truth, Jesus told stories, and his stories were dependent on stories.

The writers of the New Testament did the same thing. The New Testament writers spun out their teaching in the framework of a much larger story. This is why it is only possible to understand the New Testament in light of the stories of the Old Testament. They used stories for their foundation, as we will discuss later in the chapter on the Epistles. Perhaps the best example of this is the book of Hebrews. So much of this book is dependent on story. The prime example is chapter 11, the great chapter on faith where 16 Old Testament characters are mentioned. Preaching Hebrews 11 then comes with a challenge—we want to encourage our people to be people of faith, but the whole argument is contingent upon them knowing the Old Testament stories.

After the incredible roll call of faith in Hebrews 11, the author then gets to the application, the reason he told the narrative to begin with. He writes,

> Therefore, since we are surrounded by so great a cloud of witnesses, let us also lay aside every weight, and sin which clings so

---

1. See D. A. Carson, "Matthew," in *Matthew, Mark, Luke,* ed. Frank E. Gaebelein, vol. 8 in The Expositor's Bible Commentary (Grand Rapids: Zondervan, 1984), 383–86.

2. This is represented in the works of many communication scholars. For an accessible discussion of how the art of writing changed the shape of communication, see the staple communication text by David Crowley and Paul Heyer, *Communication in History: Technology, Culture, Society* (New York: Longman, 1999).

> closely, and let us run with endurance the race that is set before
> us, looking to Jesus, the founder and perfecter of our faith, who
> for the joy that was set before him endured the cross, despising
> the shame, and is seated at the right hand of the throne of God.
> (Heb 12:1–2)

The purpose of the list of the great people of faith was not simply to encourage us in our faith. The purpose was to encourage us to run like Jesus. The author is using stories to accomplish a purpose in the book. So, when we preach Hebrews 11, we cannot do so honestly without taking it to the application of Hebrews 12:1–2. And similarly, when we teach the Old Testament narratives, we must always place them in the larger context. In this case, the larger context is the whole of salvation history. These stories exist, the author of Hebrews shows, to make us appreciate their ultimate act of faith even more! In fact, he sets up his argument at the end of chapter 11 in just this way. He writes, "And all these, though commended through their faith, did not receive what was promised, since God had provided something better for us, that apart from us they should not be made perfect" (Heb 11:39–40).

The people of the Old Testament narratives ran the race of faith well. However, they still did not receive what was promised. In other words, they still did not see the Messiah come and bring salvation. However, we have. So, run in such a way that completes, or brings full circle, their sacrifice.

Therefore the application of the story is not, "These people ran well, so you run well." No. The logic is, "These people ran well without seeing Christ. You have seen Christ. In light of their sacrifice, looking to the model, namely Christ, you too must run well." The stories serve a larger purpose. We understand the stories in light of their larger purpose in salvation history. Understanding where stories fit in salvation history, and in the canonical context, is the model we must follow for all the stories.

So, both Jesus and the New Testament writers have a unique strategy they employ when using Old Testament stories; they always put them in their setting.

BIBLICALLY FAITHFUL

As we approach the features of Old Testament narratives, one more thought is in order. If our goal is to create people who are biblically faithful, people who make life decisions based on their understanding of Scripture, then it stands to reason that we must be biblically faithful as well. The preacher that has a grasp of the way Scripture relates to itself will be best equipped to lead his people to love the Word. The reason I bring this up now is threefold. First, slogging through the material of the Old Testament can be a daunting proposition. There are times when we really will think that finding a gem in the pages of the Old Testament really is like finding a diamond since we have to do so much mining. The difference is that the Old Testament is not the stuff we haul out in rail carts so we can mine out the one little gem of truth. Rather, all of it is the inspired revelation of God. We might whine and wince, but we need to get over it. God, in his omnipotence, is perfectly capable of giving us any kind of word. The "modern" needs of people are not new to him. We must have the ingenuity and tenacity needed to mine out the gems. Of course, this does not mean that we will spend equal time with each text. After all, Jesus privileges some stories over others by his use of them. All of Scripture is diamond, but some stories have a more central place in the setting. All are equally inspired, but some play more dominant roles. So digging in is the only way to find the diamonds. When we start to saturate ourselves with Scripture, we see the big canonical picture, and then we begin to change in our thinking.

Second, we are trying to shape a mind not a moment. When we are preaching, there is more at stake than that moment. We want our people to think differently, more completely, more wholly about Scripture. We want to arrest their minds with biblical thinking. In order to do this, we have to preach in that way. In order to do that, we have to think in those ways.

Finally, this "big picture" way of viewing the narratives not only teaches people to think biblically, it teaches them biblical thinking about the Bible. The first implies the application of the Bible to life. The second implies understanding how the Bible relates to itself. They are not different; in fact, they are concomitant. They serve each other. To get people to apply the Bible to themselves we begin with applying the Bible to itself. Show them the wholeness of the Bible, and then connect it to them. Connect the internal dots, and then connect the external dots. Show how Scripture is one cohesive unit, then apply it to their lives. To do only the first is faith without practice. To do only the last is practice without faith. Either extreme is horribly bankrupt.

INTERPRETATION: HEARING THE VOICE IN OLD TESTAMENT NARRATIVES

Old Testament Narratives Are Parts of the Larger Whole

To risk stating the obvious, Old Testament narratives are units of thought that fit within the larger framework of a book.[3] Each book fits within the framework of the Old Testament, and the Old Testament fits within the framework of the entire Bible. Unless we understand that each of the narratives fit into a larger whole, we will treat them as isolated stories detached from their original purpose or authorial intent. The fallout of such an approach is immense. First, if we treat the stories as stand-alone units of thought we will not see the beauty of the canon of Scripture. We will miss how Scripture informs Scripture and, we may miss a key doctrine as seen below. Our people are then robbed of seeing the tapestry of the whole of Scripture. Yet, that is not the worst fallout of this practice.

When the stories of the Old Testament are treated as individual, stand-alone units, without attention to the macro structure,[4] moralism will eventually reign. If we do not understand how a story fits into the story around the story, then we are forced to bridge the gap to the present with the applications that seem obvious to us, (e.g., David was repentant—so you should be repentant). Yet, when this story is used in 2 Samuel, there is so much more going on than repentance. There is the way David avoided repentance despite multiple warnings. On the other side of his repentance,

---

3. See Dale Ralph Davis, *The Word Became Fresh* (Boss-Shire, Scotland: Christian Focus, 2006), for a great discussion on the macro structure of a book in his chapter "Macroscope."

4. Perhaps the best example of this is the nature of the Pentateuch that is itself a book. When the first five books of the OT are understood as a singular literary unit, the individual stories can be read, and therefore preached, in light of this whole. See John Sailhamer, *The Pentateuch as Narrative* (Grand Rapids: Zondervan, 1992), 1–78.

there was tremendous cost. If someone is caught in the vices of devastating sin, they cannot so quickly appeal to David as an example of someone who slipped up, repented, and went on with life. Not at all. David sinned in a huge, presumptuous, ugly way. It cost him greatly (i.e., evil against his house, mistreatment of his wives, even the life of his child).[5] And the similar sin manifested in his son, Solomon, cost him the division of the kingdom. There is no way to overestimate the effect of his sin. Yet, you only get that picture when you see the story of David's repentance in the light of the broader context. When you zoom out and look at the whole of the book, you see Israel's search for a king can only be met in the Messiah because only he is able to make them different than the nations around them.

New Testament Text and Theology Are Built on Old Testament Narratives

One of the most provocative features of the Old Testament Narratives is the way they inform the rest of Scripture. Obvious examples come to mind: Jonah (Matt 12:39–41; 16:4–17; Luke 11:29–32), the flood (Matt 24:37–38; Luke 3:26; 17:26–27; Heb 11:7; 1 Pet 3:20; 2 Pet 2:5), and the story of Sarah and Hagar (Gal 4:24–25). The list is incredible. So much of what the New Testament teaches about theology is dependent upon Old Testament narratives. Therefore, when we come to an Old Testament text that is mentioned in the New Testament, we must allow the New Testament to interpret this text for us.

Stories Have Structure

The most important discovery the preacher can make is the scene structure of the narrative because it is in this discovery that the structure of the sermon emerges. Walter Kaiser observes that "Each scene represents something that took place at some particular time or place. In this regard, then, the scene acts much as the paragraph does in regular prose writing, usually supplying one main idea for each scene."[6] Every story is unique, yet narratives each have some common scene structure. This is the structure of the biblical text, and thus this is the structure of the text-driven sermon that is built on a narrative.

Leland Ryken identifies four other elements of narrative: setting, plot, characters, and narration.[7] Let's discuss each of these briefly.

Setting.[8] The setting gives the story a place to begin, and it is crucial to show this if we want the listener to be engaged. However, the temptation in preaching may be to deal too much with the setting. The theological setting—where this text fits

---

5. See 2 Sam 12:11–14.

6. Walter Kaiser Jr., *Preaching and Teaching from the Old Testament: A Guide for the Church* (Grand Rapids: Baker, 2003), 64.

7. Leland Ryken, *Words of Delight: A Literary Introduction to the Bible* (Grand Rapids: Baker, 1987), 53–90.

8. Leland Ryken, borrowing from the language of Kenneth Burke, refers to the setting as the "container" of the narrative. The metaphor is helpful as long as the metaphor is not pressed. Preaching the setting given at the front of the sermon will not contain all the action, but merely give a place for the action to begin. Ryken, *Words of Delight*, 54. For a fuller application of Burke and the dramatistic pentad specifically, see "Pentadic Criticism" in Sonya Foss, *Rhetorical Criticism* (Prospect Heights, IL: Waveland, 1996), 455–72.

in the history of redemption—is something that can generally be dealt with later in the sermon or as the conclusion. At the start of a sermon, the minimalist approach is best. How much of this setting is necessary to get the people into the narrative? Too little and they are lost, too much and they get off the bus mentally. Again, the right amount of setting is as much as is necessary to get safely into the first scene.

Plot. J. P. Fokkelman refers to the plot simply as "the main organizing principle of a story."[9] "The plot provides the head and the tail we need to hold on to, and thus determines the boundaries of the story as a meaningful whole."[10] In this way the plot of the story will emerge from the structure of the scenes. Therefore, the secret to effectiveness in preaching narratives is not to give away the plot line too soon in telling the story. This is not a rhetorical trick; this is in fact what the text is doing. It is unwrapping the story. We are not diagnosticians with X-rays getting to the point as quickly as possible; rather, we are provocateurs re-presenting the way the text allows the story to simmer.

The plot of each story is unique. However, the plots generally follow the rule of setting, tension, rising tension, release of tension, and the final situation.[11] We will discuss the fact that the release of tension is not always there in Hebrew narratives; however, generally these basic elements can be seen in the scene structure of the plot.[12]

Remember, the plot is the story line and not the theme. The plot facilitates the end of the story, which leads to the theme. The plot is the action followed through to resolution. The spiritual principles are not the plot; they will be derived from the plot.

Characters. Character development does not take place through direct description. We deduce that Joseph was impetuous because he told his dream, and we know that he was full of faith because of his patience under abuse and neglect. The narrator did not tell us this directly; we are able to deduce it from the action. In this way there is a strong relationship between plot development and character development.[13]

While character development is essential to the story, it can be communicated in the same way that the biblical authors do so, through use of plot development. In the sermon, allow the characters to emerge as the story emerges. Thus, as when reading a good story, you may not know the true character of a person until the story is over.

Narration.[14] Narration is extremely helpful in narrative since the narrator is telling us, out of all the details that exist, the ones that especially need our attention. This is

---

9. J. P. Fokkelman, *Reading Biblical Narrative* (Louisville: Westminster John Knox, 1999), 76.

10. Ibid.

11. Jeffery D. Arthurs identifies the typical elements of plot as background, conflict, rising action, climax, and resolution. See his chapter, "Preaching the Old Testament Narratives" in *Preaching the Old Testament*, ed. Scott Gibson (Grand Rapids: Baker, 2006), 76. Mathewson explains plot structure as exposition, crisis, resolution, and conclusion in Steven Mathewson, *The Art of Preaching Old Testament Narrative* (Grand Rapids: Baker, 2002), 44.

12. See the helpful chapter by Laurence A. Turner, "Preaching Plot" in *Reclaiming the Old Testament for Christian Preaching* (Downers Grove: InterVarsity Academic, 2010), 13–29.

13. Leland Ryken, *Words of Delight: A Literary Introduction to the Bible* (Grand Rapids: Baker), 72.

14. Andreas J. Köstenburger and Richard Patterson identify four types of narration (repetition, highlighting, irony, and satire) in *Invitation to Biblical Interpretation: Exploring the Hermeneutical Triad of History, Literature, and Theology* (Grand Rapids: Kregel, 2011), 251–52.

helpful in biblical narrative for the reason that the biblical narrators are inspired by God.[15] While these inspired narrators "do not make up events or characters, they do select, arrange, and depict them with skill."[16]

When preaching a story there is a temptation to fixate on a detail or an interesting nuance of the story we may especially like. However, ignoring the narrator is like ignoring the theological context of the story; it becomes a breeding ground for reading our own ideas into the text.[17] If we are to preach the text, we must let the narrators be our guides.[18] They tell us what details are important. While we may be surprised by what they highlight and what they neglect, they are our tour guides through the story.[19]

These Are Jewish Narratives

A classic narrative has a classic set up. There is a setting, several scenes that move toward rising tension, and then there is release of tension. This is simply how narratives work. Each of these components is essential. There must be some sense of where the action is taking place, (i.e., its geography and context). There must be movement in the story, whether it is a simple plot or a complex plot with multiple plot twists and subplots. And at some point, there must be a problem. It can come early, or it can come late. But in order for the problem to function as it should, there needs to be some resolution at the end. And, in order for there to be resolution, there must be a problem. A good story can be lost if there is not enough dramatic tension to make the resolution of the tension interesting. All these characteristics about classic narrative are almost always true about Jewish narrative. There will be a setting, there will be a plot with character development to move it along, and there will be rising tension. However, there is a unique feature about Jewish narrative that is different. Jewish narrative does not always resolve the tension.[20]

Perhaps the best example of this is the book of Jonah. The setting of Jonah is the rebellious heart of the prophet. The prophet has heard from God to go preach against the most dominant city state in the world, Nineveh. This city was so massive that it took three days to walk across.[21] The city was so wicked that it evoked the anger of God. No doubt this was a huge assignment. But Jonah ran. He ran hard. He disobeyed God's command (character development). Then comes the ship, the

---

15. This causes us to stop and consider why authors used such strategies as repetition. See "The Techniques of Repetition" in Robert Alter, *The Art of Biblical Narrative* (New York: Basic, 2011), 111–41.

16. Jeffrey Athurs, *Preaching with Variety: How to Re-create the Dynamics of Biblical Genres* (Grand Rapids: Kregel, 2007), 64.

17. Terry G. Carter, J. Scott Duvall, and J. Daniel Hays, *Preaching God's Word: A Hands-On Approach to Preparing, Developing, and Delivering the Sermon* (Grand Rapids: Zondervan, 2011), 231–32.

18. Clearly the narrators have a "point of view" that is guiding their commentary. See Meir Sternberg "Viewpoints and Interpretations" in *The Poetics of Biblical Narrative: Ideological Literature and the Drama of Reading* (Bloomfield, IN: Indiana University Press, 1985).

19. See helpful discussion on story details in Jeffrey Arthurs, *Preaching with Variety: How to Re-Create the Dynamics of Biblical Genres* (Grand Rapids: Kregel, 2007), 80.

20. For a helpful insight into Judaism and narrative, see the classic Abraham Heschel, *Between God and Man: An Interpretation of Judaism* (New York: Harper, 1959).

21. The size and influence of Nineveh in the Assyrian Empire is profound. See Frank Page and Billy K. Smith, *Amos, Obadiah, Jonah*, New American Commentary on the Old Testament (Nashville: B&H, 1995), 203.

storm, the fish, and the vomit (rising tension). Jonah finally relents and preaches to Nineveh. And the city repents (release of tension). But there is more tension still. As the story comes to a close, we are back in the same setting, the heart of a disobedient prophet. The same self-righteousness that kept him from going to Nineveh in the first place is now exposed in his anger over a worm. A worm. This worm was actually sent by God. The reason God would worry about a worm is because he had to expose the heart of a man who cared more about plants than he did about people. He loved comfort more than effectiveness in his call. And the commissioned worm was on assignment from his Creator to expose the wickedness of Jonah's heart. So the story, and the book, ends with a question: "And should not I pity Nineveh, that great city, in which there are more than 120,000 persons who do not know their right hand from their left, and also much cattle?" (Jonah 4:11).

This question did not need an answer. The answer was obvious. Here God spared the lives of thousands of people, and thousands of animals, but Jonah could not care less about either. He was too obsessed with the worm that stole his comfort. In many ways it is a sad exposure of a heart that is not given to God. When obedience is reluctant, it will be exposed at some point. And this sadness, this tragedy, is how the story ends. So, the people repented, but did Jonah? God gave Jonah a second chance, but did God give Jonah a third chance? We just don't know. For those of us longing for resolution, this story is mildly irritating, if not frustrating. What exactly did happen? The answer is that this is just how Jewish narrative "works." While we do not know what happened, the resolution of the story is not necessary for the story to be effective. This is the main point we need to grasp about Old Testament narrative. The point of the story is in the telling of God's activity, not in the resolution. From the telling of the story we learn that God is incredibly huge. He is sovereign over creation, and he has a massive love for the people who have rejected him. God could not be larger, and Jonah could not be smaller. The smallness of Jonah's vision and compassion makes God's love and greatness even more pronounced. This idea becomes very clear when the story is not resolved.

The Facts Serve the Themes

Similarly, it is also true that the authors of Old Testament narratives have a theme that transcends the historical details. As we read a text, we may really want to know how the details of the text are reconciled with the rest of the story, with the rest of the Bible, or with what we know of ancient history. One must keep in mind that the author's ambition is not always to reconcile every detail of a story. Rather, the satisfaction for the student of the Scriptures lies in finding how the author was using these details to accomplish his purposes. This is not to suggest that the details are unimportant. They are. Nor should we draw from the previous statement that the accuracy of facts is irrelevant because God can speak to us regardless of whether the Bible is relevant. (This kind of thinking has tentacles deep in the religious academy and has practically found its way in the church.)[22] However, we worship a God who

---

22. A familiar expression of this idea in the late twentieth century appeared in the work of Jack Rogers and Donald McKim, *Authority and Interpretation of the Bible: An Historical Approach* (Eugene, OR: Wipf and Stock, 1999), the idea being that the Scripture did not have to be complete in all historical detail to be of practical use for the believer. For a critique, see John D. Woodbridge, *Biblical Authority: A Critique of the Rogers/McKim Proposal* (Grand Rapids, Zondervan, 1992).

is perfectly capable of delivering to us a perfect revelation of himself. That is hardly a challenge for God. He can, and he did, do just that. Scripture is perfect in its historicity. However, in the re-telling of ancient stories, we find this to be true: what was most important in the telling of stories was not the great details, but the great God.

If I tell you the story of how my dad rescued me from a burning building—he didn't, but only because he was not given the opportunity—then my attention to the details serves a purpose. The purpose it serves is that it shows how great my dad is. In fact, to tell this story accurately would not leave you feeling as if you were watching the events unfold live, like the grainy video footage of a security camera. No. That would be so one-dimensional. It would be flat. You would have the exact facts, but it would be an inaccurate view of the story because the truth of the story was not in "seeing" the events, but in understanding the human dimension. The love, bravery, and self-sacrifice are the truth of the story. If those things are not told, then the story is not told. So, a true storyteller will highlight those things. The facts will be there. However, the facts serve the themes.

Narratives Are Inductive

This is obvious. You do not know the point of a story until the story is over. Stories do not state their intention immediately. This is one of the things that make them great. The sermon strategy is equally as simple. Since we do not know the point of a story until the story is over, we are not compelled to resolve the story at the beginning. In fact, no one wants this. They want to see the story develop and then have the resolution brought to them at the end of the story. We know this to be true, and we may have even been taught this. However, saving the main idea of the story until the end of the story can be more difficult than it seems. Let's deal with this in the communication section that follows.

The Gospel Is in the Old Testament

How do you preach the Gospel from the Old Testament? This is a significant issue that has received a lot of attention in recent years. The most unsatisfying approach is to take whatever text we are preaching, and then mention Jesus at the end. Of course such an approach is better than not mentioning Jesus. But is there a better way? Let's begin by asking some questions about the nature of the Scripture itself.

First, is the Old Testament a Christian book? The answer to this seems obvious— of course it is. But there are millions of people who would disagree. To many, this is a Jewish book that has been absconded by Christians. Many Jewish people would disagree with the terminology, "Old Testament." To them it is the only Testament, the only Covenant. However, this is in fact a Christian book. Paul made this most clear in 1 Corinthians 3 in his discussion of the superior nature of the new covenant over the old covenant. Without a doubt this is a Christian book. And, as we said earlier, the Old Testament Scriptures lead us to Christ (2 Tim 3:14–17).

Secondly, if this is a Christian book, can we see Christ in the Old Testament? The answer here is affirmative as well. Think of the words of Paul, "For I delivered to you as of first importance what I also received: that Christ died for our sins *in accordance with the Scriptures*, that he was buried, that he was raised on the third day *in accordance with the Scriptures*" (1 Cor 15:3–4).[23]

The question, again, is, are Christian preachers to see the Old Testament as valuable in preaching Christ? Let's consider the words of Christ, and the first Christian sermon.

The OT Points to and Is Fulfilled in Christ. Christ was passionate about the Old Testament. Most explicitly in Matthew 5:17–19 he stated,

> Do not think that I have come to abolish the Law or the Prophets; I have not come to abolish them but to fulfill them. For truly, I say to you, until heaven and earth pass away, not an iota, not a dot, will pass from the Law until all is accomplished. Therefore whoever relaxes one of the least of these commandments and teaches others to do the same will be called least in the kingdom of heaven, but whoever does them and teaches them will be called great in the kingdom of heaven.

In John 5:39 Jesus said, "You search the Scriptures because you think that in them you have eternal life; and it is they that bear witness about me."

By far the most provocative of all the texts is Luke 24:13–27. Jesus is walking with his disciples on the Emmaus road. They were discouraged because Christ had died and they did not know what would happen next. Verses 25–27 are incredible,

> And he said to them, "O foolish ones, and slow of heart to believe all that the prophets have spoken! Was it not necessary that the Christ should suffer these things and enter into his glory?" And beginning with Moses and all the Prophets, he interpreted to them in all the Scriptures the things concerning himself.

Jesus condemned his own disciples for not understanding how all that had happened was in fulfillment of Scripture. Then, he takes them through a tour of the Old Testament and shows them that the Old Testament Scriptures point to him. Later, in the upper room, he takes the rest of the disciples on the same tour.

> Then he said to them, "These are my words that I spoke to you while I was still with you, that everything written about me in the Law of Moses and the Prophets and the Psalms must be fulfilled." Then he opened their minds to understand the Scriptures, and said to them, "Thus it is written, that the Christ should suffer and on the third day rise from the dead, and that repentance and forgiveness of sins should be proclaimed in his name to all nations, beginning from Jerusalem. You are witnesses of these things." (Luke 24:44–48)

They were witnesses to the very things that Scripture prophesied. Jesus essentially said, "You read about these things," and "now you have witnessed these things."

---

23. Emphasis added.

They had two sources of revelation: the Old Testament Scriptures and the fulfillment of the Scriptures right before them in Jesus, the Son of God. This is nothing short of miraculous.

Given these texts of Scripture, it would be impossible to conclude anything other than the fact that Jesus Christ is the direct fulfillment of the Old Testament. The Old Testament is a book about Christ; thus, all of Scripture points to Christ and is fulfilled in Christ. This is a truth that becomes clear when we notice how the earliest Christians understood and applied the Old Testament.

The First Christian Sermon Was an Exposition of the OT. The disciples certainly got this message. We know this by the events that followed. Christ ascended into heaven, immediately followed by Pentecost. Then, in Acts 2:14–41, Peter preached the first Christian sermon. What he did is interesting. First, he took the immediate question on the mind of the listeners who were curious about the resurrection, then he preached Christ from the Old Testament. The first Christian sermon was an exposition of Old Testament texts.

> But Peter, standing with the eleven, lifted up his voice and addressed them: "Men of Judea and all who dwell in Jerusalem, let this be known to you, and give ear to my words. For these people are not drunk, as you suppose, since it is only the third hour of the day." (Acts 2:14–15)

The people are trying to understand this incredible phenomenon of people speaking in one language but other people understanding in their own language, and Peter tries to explain this phenomenon by giving a biblical explanation.[24] He begins with the prophet Joel. In verses 17–18 Peter says,

> And in the last days it shall be, God declares, that I will pour out my Spirit on all flesh, and your sons and your daughters shall prophesy, and your young men shall see visions, and your old men shall dream dreams; even on my male servants and female servants in those days I will pour out my Spirit, and they shall prophesy.

Peter isn't just reaching back and choosing some obscure passage. He has reached back and chosen the exact passage of all the Prophets that speaks especially to that moment. God is saying that there is a time coming when he would pour out his Spirit in an unprecedented way. Male and female, young and old—all God's people would receive his Spirit.

You take some cultural phenomenon that doesn't have some other explanation and you run to Scripture and show how Scripture addresses it. We can do this easily because everything we deal with is either directly or indirectly, explicitly or implicitly, addressed in Scripture; we just have to find it. This is, in my mind, one of the best arguments for being a text-driven preacher. If you commit your life to only preaching about the pressing application of the moment, when bigger needs arise

---

24. There are, of course, varying interpretations, different than the one assumed above, on the events of Pentecost. For a helpful treatment, see John B. Pohill, *Acts*, New American Commentary (Nashville: B&H, 1992), 95–122.

you probably won't have anything to say about them. In other words, preaching for immediate life change only, may leave you in the position of mining Scripture for application alone. This robs one of the ability to see, or rather to listen to, what God is doing in the bigger picture across the swath of salvation history. On the other hand, if you commit yourself to explaining texts of Scripture, you will then begin to interpret culture in light of Scripture.

But Peter doesn't stop here. He begins with biblical explanation but then he moves to gospel confrontation. Now he gets to the bulk of his sermon: the presentation of the gospel. Look at the progression of his argument.

> Men of Israel, hear these words: Jesus of Nazareth, a man attested to you by God with mighty works and wonders and signs that God did through him in your midst, as you yourselves know—this Jesus, delivered up according to the definite plan and foreknowledge of God, you crucified and killed by the hands of lawless men. God raised him up, loosing the pangs of death, because it was not possible for him to be held by it. (Acts 2:22–24)

His point is that this is a part of God's plan. In verse 22 he says that "this Jesus, [who was] delivered up according to the definite plan and foreknowledge of God, you crucified and killed." There is a real sense in which their disobedience didn't thwart the plan of God, but rather they became a part of the plan of God by their own disobedience. Peter has referred to Joel 9 and now he references Psalm 16, both for the purpose of trying to explain the resurrection. That is why he begins in verse 24 saying,

> God raised him up, loosing the pangs of death, because it was not possible for him to be held by it. For David says concerning him,
> "'I saw the Lord always before me,
>   for he is at my right hand that I may not be shaken;
> therefore my heart was glad, and my tongue rejoiced;
>   my flesh also will dwell in hope.
> For you will not abandon my soul to Hades,
>   or let your Holy One see corruption.
> You have made known to me the paths of life;
>   you will make me full of gladness with your presence.'" (Acts 2:24–28)

Everything in verses 25–26 is true of David, but verse 27 is not true of David. And so he continues in verse 29,

> Brothers, I may say to you with confidence about the patriarch David that he both died and was buried, and his tomb is with us to this day. Being therefore a prophet, and knowing that God had sworn with an oath to him that he would set one of his descendants on his throne, he foresaw and spoke about the resurrection of the Christ, that he was not abandoned to Hades, nor did his flesh see corruption. This Jesus God raised up, and of that we all are witnesses. Being therefore exalted at the right hand of God,

and having received from the Father the promise of the Holy Spirit, he has poured out this that you yourselves are seeing and hearing. For David did not ascend into the heavens, but he himself says, "The Lord said to my Lord, 'Sit at my right hand, until I make your enemies your footstool.'" Let all the house of Israel therefore know for certain that God has made him both Lord and Christ, this Jesus whom you crucified. (Acts 2:29–36)

The exegetical idea that Peter is pushing in his quotation of Psalm 110 is that the kingdom has come. Jesus Christ is the Lord, and this One whom they crucified is now the One whom God has exalted.

This is a remarkable sermon on many levels, but the point is simple: the first sermon ever preached after the resurrection was an Old Testament exposition. If there was any doubt in your mind, in theory or in practice, allow the passionate words and philosophy of the first sermon to put the doubts to rest. We can preach the gospel faithfully from the Old Testament! So, again, how are we to do this? How is Christ to be preached from the Old Testament? We will address this below.

COMMUNICATION: RECAPTURING THE VOICE IN OLD TESTAMENT NARRATIVES

Avoid Moralism

All too often the temptation is to open a book of the Old Testament as if it is a collection of short stories. Our motivations are pure enough. We want our people to be encouraged in their faith and drawn closer to God. We see the stories of the Old Testament as the greatest source of such inspiration. So we draw from these stories the inspiration that people need to finish the task. This is commendable, and right. After all, we have a model for this in the New Testament. Jesus referred to many stories in the Old Testament, and the writer of Hebrews used multiple examples in Hebrews 11. So there is value, and biblical warrant, in using the Old Testament characters as examples. However, if our preaching of Old Testament narratives only advances the moral lesson of a story, then it stops short of bringing the listener to Christ and can simply become a lesson in how to be better.

So, how do we avoid treating the Old Testament narratives like moralistic fables?

First, understand the individual story in light of the author's purpose. In order to do this, we must read the book over and over again. Reading the introductory material in good commentaries will help here, but only after someone has spent a tremendous amount of time reading the individual book. This is the most important work that someone can do.

Second, once we see the individual story in light of the author's purpose, we should frame it that way in the sermon. Use the introduction to show how this fits into the larger portion of the book, or highlight this at some point in the sermon. For some texts this will not be necessary. For example, if you are preaching through Genesis, you will not need to do this at every turn, but only when the occasion calls for it in order to bring it back to the attention of the people because it sheds light on the story.

Take, for example, the flood narrative of Genesis 6–9. The author uses this narrative to help us understand the need for redemption throughout the rest of the book. He also uses the narrative to set up two of the most important themes in all of Scripture: sacrifice and covenant. This is not the first time that sacrifice is used in the Old Testament. We see Cain and Abel bringing sacrifices. However, this time we see the sacrifices as a part of God's covenant that he makes with Noah. The union of covenant and sacrifice is a theme that will be reiterated throughout the book of Genesis and the rest of the Pentateuch. Armed with this information, what do I do? Well, when I get to chapter nine, if I have enough time to preach it all, I show them the power of God's covenant and even have them look briefly at the Abrahamic covenant, or even look back to the Adamic covenant. I could even pan out further and have them look at the Mosaic and Davidic covenants. These are possibilities. If I am preaching the whole flood narrative, Genesis 6–9, then at least I mention that this is a hint at the sacrificial system that will be seen explicitly throughout the Pentateuch.

How much I actually say in the sermon is a pastoral concern. It will vary from sermon to sermon. The real point of the strategy is our understanding. So again understanding the author's purpose, and setting the purpose in the sermon will allow the sermon to recapitulate the author's purpose and protect the sermon from moralism.

Find the Connection and Then Show the Connection

Sometimes we preachers feel we need to protect people from the Bible, when it is the Bible that gives them life. We feel as if we can either be engaging or teach the Bible. Of course, this is a false dichotomy. Showing the dynamic interdependence of the Scriptures is one way to engage our people as we teach the Bible.

When preaching an Old Testament narrative that has a New Testament referent, take the people to the New Testament and show them the connection. One might contend, "But isn't this somewhat adrift from the meaning of the Old Testament in its context?" The response is simple; we are preaching what the author of the text had in mind when the cannon was completed. The New Testament is the most immediate, and therefore the most important, commentary on the Old Testament. As preachers, we are not seeing whether an Old Testament narrative is mentioned in the New Testament as an interesting aside. Rather, we are running to the New Testament first to see if God has commented on his own work. He is in the best position to interpret what he wrote. Find the connection and then show the connection.

See the Whole

Above we discussed elements of narrative: setting, plot, character, and narration. As you read the story, take note of how these four elements emerge. However, we are about re-presenting the text. So the purpose of preaching is not to say, "Look at this plot . . ." Though we very well may do this, the point is to have them feel the plot emerge in our sermon as it does in the biblical text. The same is true of character development and setting. We want to set the scene and let the characters emerge the way they do in the story. Thus, our emphasis here is more on the scene structure of the story.

Don't Resolve the Unresolved

When preaching an Old Testament narrative, do not feel compelled to reconcile each story in a tight, Hollywood-like, ending. The resolution of many stories is simply not that clean. While some stories do have great endings—such as David and Goliath or the book of Esther—there are plenty that have partially resolved endings—like the book of Nehemiah, many of the stories in Kings and Chronicles, and the story of Job. When approaching one of these texts, be sure to preach what is there and do not feel compelled to resolve something that has no immediate resolution.

The reason for this is simple: if we spend time trying to resolve plots that do not need to be resolved, then we take time away from what the text is saying. Why spend more time on what God could have told us, but didn't, than on what he did in fact tell us? Time wasted with speculation is time taken from exhortation. Therefore, preach the text before you.

If, in this pursuit, there happens to be a nagging question, we can always address it. However, sometimes our response will be that we simply do not know. We do not always know why God allowed events to turn out the way they did. God has left some issues unresolved. And we have the freedom to leave them unresolved as well.

Let the Flow of the Story Determine the Flow of Your Sermon

Let's discuss different ways a sermon can be structured around an Old Testament Narrative. We will borrow loosely from Haddon Robinson's helpful designations of deductive, inductive, and inductive-deductive.[25]

First, consider inductive/deductive approach. Deduction is where we begin the sermon with the main idea and work from it. This is how many New Testament Epistles develop. An idea is stated and then the sermon flows from the main idea. On the other hand, an inductive sermon flows to the main idea. The idea is developed throughout the sermon, but not explicitly stated until the end of the sermon. This is how stories develop. You usually do not know the point of the story until it is over.

When preaching an Old Testament Narrative, it makes sense that we would preach it inductively. Tell the story and then get to the main idea at the end. The narratives are stories, and we often do not know the point until the end of the story. However, once the idea is made clear, we must press the idea, make applications, and call for decision. Therefore the combining the two approaches into an inductive, then deductive approach works well. So for an OT Narrative we want to work to the main idea through story development, then work from the main idea for application. The example below should clarify this.

Second, consider giving the subject without the complement. One of the questions that often arise is, "If they do not know the main idea up front, how will they know where the sermon is going?" The answer is simple: they will know where the sermon is going because they have *some* of the main idea, but not all of it. The best way to understand this is to look at the parts of a main idea.

A main idea has a subject. This is the content of the sermon. The main idea has a complement—what we are saying about the subject. So, borrowing from the sermon

---

25. Haddon Robinson, *Biblical Preaching: The Development and Delivery of Expository Messages* (Grand Rapids: Baker, 2001), 17, Figure 1.

sample below, if my main idea is "God gives grace for those who need it," we may break this main idea into two parts:

1. Subject: Who receives grace from God?
2. Complement: Those who know they need it.

So again, the subject is the topic; the complement is what we are saying about it. The complement is the answer to the question the subject of the text is raising. Preaching is raising the question the text is raising, and then using the text to answer the question. Developing a main idea is distilling the subject and complement into one memorable statement. This is a challenging practice but one that pays huge dividends.[26]

In the example below we use the introduction and first parts of the sermon to raise the question, "Who gets grace?" This seems to be the question that is being raised in the text. Then we work through the text in the sermon highlighting the scenes, and the application from the scenes, as we go. Then more toward the end we pull it all together by saying, "God gives grace to those who know they need it." In this way the sermon has structure, but the full main idea is not given until the end. Sermons from narratives are neither incoherent ramblings, nor are they simply recasting the story. We are, in fact, preaching the narrative. However, what is sermonic about all this—what makes us want to exhort, apply, challenge, and equip—usually comes after the main idea. So we structure the sermon around scenes, the main idea, then the application. Which leads to a very important point.

Third, remember, you do not need to apply each scene. We will use the flood narrative of Genesis 6–9 as our example. Telling the whole story dictates that I take a big chunk of text. Surely you could take a smaller section, or preach the story as a series, but I want the listener to grapple with the whole story, so I am going to take the whole section. On the broadest possible level, I will divide the scenes of the story. There are many ways to divide the story, but there are at least three scenes: the call of Noah, the flood, and the covenant.

Stepping back and looking from a distance, the scenes of the story help me see what this text is about. There is something there about the mercy of God toward Noah and the wrath of God toward the rest of humanity. This is the main thing I want to communicate. And I will use the scene structure to carry the weight of this main idea in the story.

Now, there are several interesting things in this story. Noah took care of his family. Noah was diligent in building. Noah had a God-infused vision and did not stop. Noah was a great man of faith! All of these are interesting features and have varying levels of importance. However, I am not going to stop and mention each one. In fact, I will leave some out. Why? The answer is that I am after the one driving idea of the text. There are other ideas, good ideas, but they might compete with the main idea. When preaching a larger narrative, it is important to allow the central idea to come to the surface. Other ideas may be in the text. If they are highlighted in the sermon, they need to be done so as to show how they build to a larger theme.

---

26. In this section, I'm indebted to the understanding of the main idea of a sermon explained in Robinson, *Biblical Preaching*, 33–50.

Back to the example below. The smaller themes are building to the larger theme of God's grace. This is what I believe the author is doing, and so this is what I am doing. To put it specifically, I am asking, "What is the driving idea of the text?" and then, "How do the scenes get to this idea?" Once I answer those questions, I have arrived at the substance and the structure of the sermon. I may bring in details from the text, hopefully some interesting ones. However, the only details I bring in are ones that carry the sermon along to its main idea.

Now imagine this story preached with an obligation to make a practical application with each scene. It might look like this:

1. Scene One: Noah Listens to God: We should listen to God.
2. Scene Two: Noah Obeyed: When the Lord speaks, we should obey.
3. Scene Three: Noah Worshipped: We should worship God.[27]

These are all true statements, but they miss the macro-level idea of the text. Now, let me be quick to say that you could apply each scene. Theoretically, it may be possible, and sometimes it may be preferred. However, you should not feel the obligation to apply each scene. If that is our default position we may find ourselves making small applications in the text but missing the bigger point of the text. The reason is that stories are more clearly understood from a distance. Don't think of rows of wheat; think of crop circles. You need to stand way above them to understand them. So we tell the story, get to the main idea, and then apply the main idea. There may be application along the way, but it is in service to a bigger application that will come later.

Highlight the Facts You Are Given

At some point in preaching an Old Testament Narrative, you will come across great miracles. There might be a temptation to ignore those. But God is there. He is not bound to the natural. And, despite what someone in the academy might say, your people want God to be that big. All around them, forces work to supplant their belief that God is big enough to work miracles. Affirm their faith by dealing with the miracles with tenacity. This includes doing the hard work of reconciling apparent inconsistencies in the biblical record.

Determine How to Point to Christ

If, as Jesus stated, the Scriptures point to Christ, then we must understand that centrality as not only an interesting novelty of God's construction of the text, but as the hermeneutical framework for interpreting Scripture. So, let's begin with three things to avoid.

Avoid allegorizing. An allegory is a story that has a one to one relationship with something outside the story. Allegory makes the story less significant, and its

---

27. Again, there are many micro stories within the larger story. There is the story of the familial relations, the work of building the ark, and the antagonism against such. However, my implicit argument is that we often try to mine the details of the story for application and miss the beauty of the story on the macro level.

application more significant.[28] Preachers have seen the wood of the ark as representative of the wood of the cross of Christ, or the fine nuances of the priestly garments as representative of the character of Christ. Why should we avoid this approach? The answer is simply that doing so would be putting our words into God's mouth. Allegorizing is misleading and falls short of our goal of preaching in a way that teaches people how to read the Bible. There are ways to explicitly and overtly preach Christ from the Old Testament texts without suggesting something that is not clear from the text.

Avoid spiritualizing. While this is a broad concept, what we mean is a hermeneutical approach that ignores the plain meaning of a text while looking for an inspiring meaning behind the text. When preaching the narrative of the wise men, one might observe that the wise men were led to Christ by a star, and that we should all be stars leading people to Christ. Both statements in the previous sentence are true. The problem is not what is being said, but what is not being said. Every time we say something in the pulpit, we say it to the exclusion of something else. So, when we discuss the stars leading people to Christ, we are taking time away from the richness of what is actually in the text. For example, God divinely orchestrated a star to draw Gentiles to the birth of Jesus, the King of the Jews, while Herod—"king" of the Jews—and all Jerusalem, had to inquire where the birth of the Christ was to take place. How could his own people miss the fact that their King had come?

Avoid moralizing. Moralizing is when we reduce the message of an Old Testament narrative to whatever moral lesson can be gained. An example would be preaching on the depression of Jeremiah, and then saying, "Don't get depressed." The problem is that the text of Jeremiah has a bigger message than the psyche of the prophet. Jeremiah is depressed because he has a message to tell. The message is that there is a new covenant coming. This is fulfilled in Christ. So the message to us is not, "Stop being depressed," but rather, "There is hope in Christ!" The latter is a far better message.

One test of moralizing is to ask ourselves if we are saying something that only a Christian preacher could say. I can tell people to be brave, be full of faith, or be trusting, and base these moral lessons on the foundation of the stories of Daniel, David, and Ruth respectively. Those truths are there. However, if this is all I am saying, then this is not a Christian message. A Jewish priest or a Muslim Imam could say those same things.[29]

The message of Christianity is not, "Here are examples of how you can be a better person." Rather, the message of Christianity is, "You can never be better on your own. You need Christ." So a Christian reading of the story of Daniel's confrontation with death at the jaws of lions, one that reads it in light of Christ's sanctifying work in our lives, flows more like this: "Daniel was brave. You can't be brave. Therefore you must throw yourself at the mercy of Christ." If Christ is expressed in the Old Testament the way the disciples understood him to be, the way Christ taught them,

---

28. See the discussion of the history of allegory and preaching Old Testament texts in Walter Kaiser, *Preaching and Teaching from the Old Testament* (Grand Rapids: Baker, 2003), 43, 45.

29. See the discussion of "exhortations without the Gospel" in Graeme Goldsworthy, *Preaching the Whole Bible as Christian Scripture* (Grand Rapids: Eerdmans, 2000), 18.

then the messages from the Old Testament texts must express the gospel; namely our inability to succeed, and Christ's ability to give grace to those who need it. My nothingness, his all. This is the message of the gospel from the Old Testament.[30] So, what are some strategies that will help us preach Christ from the Old Testament?

Find the New Testament explanatory parallel. As mentioned above, many Old Testament stories have explanations in the New Testament. Some examples are

> Jonah 1:17 mentioned in Matthew 12:39–40
> Genesis 6–9 mentioned in Hebrews 11:7[31]
> Genesis 3 mentioned in Romans 5:12

These are fairly well known examples. However, we might think this is pretty rare. After all, what are the chances that the Old Testament text you want to preach is actually mentioned in the New Testament? You might be surprised. Look at the following chart. Notice there are over 3,000 mentions of the top 10 Old Testament books in the New Testament. This is absolutely fascinating. It is likely that a story you are preaching in the Old Testament has a mention, if not an allusion, in a New Testament book.

Most Referenced OT Books in the New Testament[*]
1. Isaiah, 419 times in 23 New Testament books
2. Psalms, 414 times in 23 books
3. Genesis, 260 times in 21 books
4. Exodus, 250 times in 19 books
5. Deuteronomy, 208 times in 21 books
6. Ezekiel, 141 times in 15 books
7. Daniel, 133 times in 17 books
8. Jeremiah, 125 times in 17 books
9. Leviticus, 107 times in 15 books
10. Numbers, 73 times in 4 books
* Harold L. Willmington, *The Complete Book of Bible List*s (Wheaton: Tyndale, 1987), 36.

But what if we are preaching a narrative not mentioned in the New Testament?

Find how the individual passage fits within salvation history. We have already established that Christ understood the Old Testament as a witness to himself. And, the New Testament begins this way. Matthew begins with a genealogy. However, this is not just any genealogy. The genealogy is based on the generations from Abraham to Christ (Matt 1:1–17). Interestingly, Matthew bases his understanding of

---

30. See Sidney Greidanus, *Preaching Christ from the Old Testament: A Contemporary Hermeneutical Method* (Grand Rapids: Eerdmans, 1991), for a historical treatment and seven strategies for preaching Christ from the Old Testament.

31. Noah is mentioned eight times in the NT.

these events around two major figures and one event leading up to Christ: Abraham, David, the deportation to Babylon, and then Christ.

Another way to understand this would be to look at the covenants represented by these people: God's covenant with Abraham, God's covenant with David, and God's new covenant in Christ. So Matthew begins the New Testament with a review of the Old Testament. This was his way of saying, "We are moving on, but I want to give you a way to understand all the events in the Old Testament: Abraham—David—Christ."[32]

Of course, there is a little more to the Old Testament than that, but Matthew is hinting at something that Jesus would spell out explicitly in Matthew 26:27–28; "And he took a cup, and when he had given thanks he gave it to them, saying, 'Drink of it, all of you, for this is my blood of the covenant which is poured out for many for the forgiveness of sins.'"

The connection of the old covenant to the new covenant is an idea that was introduced in the Old Testament in places like Jeremiah 31:31, "'Behold, the days are coming,' declares the LORD, 'when I will make a new covenant with the house of Israel and the house of Judah.'" It was an idea affirmed by Christ. Therefore, this is an idea that should be used as an approach to preaching Old Testament texts. Now that we know what to avoid and what to connect, let's look at a strategy for preaching Old Testament narratives.[33]

A STEP-BY-STEP APPROACH TO PREACHING OLD TESTAMENT NARRATIVES[34]

STEP 1: Locate the Structure of the Story[35]

Remember, this is a story so it does not have "points," rather it has "scenes." The default position for preachers is to rush to find the points of the story. However, remember that narratives do not have points. They may have multiple applications, and they will have one driving idea, but they do not necessarily have multiple points.

You are trying to get behind the narrative and determine its structure. This means you are looking at setting and scenes. At its most basic level, the setting and scenes are the structure of the text. So, as you prepare, write these out as an outline for the sermon as you would the textual divisions of an epistle. For example, your document may look like this:

---

32. Graeme Goldsworthy uses Matthew 1 as a homiletical approach to connecting each Old Testament text to the Abrahamic of Davidic covenant, and therefore to Christ in Goldsworthy, *Preaching the Whole Bible*, 4ff.

33. The chapters that follow will not have the same step-by-step template. However, the insertion of this template here provides a template for chapters on narrative that remain.

34. See also Sidney Greidanus "Steps from Text to Sermon," in *Preaching Christ from the Old Testament* (Grand Rapids: Eerdmans, 1999), 347–48.

35. This chapter does not address the fact that there are sub-types of Old Testament Narratives. William Klein, Craig Blomberg, and Robert Hubbard identify five types of OT Narratives as Report, Heroic Narrative Prophet Story, Comedy, and Farewell Speech. That notwithstanding, the scene structure will accommodate the genre proper. When other things are embedded in the narrative (poem, speech, etc.), the principles for communicating that particular genre would apply. See Klein, Blomberg, and Hubbard, *Introduction to Biblical Interpretation*, 261–71.

Setting

        Scene One (v. ___)
        Scene Two (v. ___)
        Scene Three (v. ___)

Don't worry about the flow of the story yet; we are just going after structure. Remember, the structure will support the main idea. Also, keep in mind that each scene will develop inductively in itself, meaning you will state the point after you have developed it from the text of Scripture. Doing so shows the listener what they saw. In other words, you show the story then explain to them what they saw. In this way the sermon is inductive as are the individual parts of the story.[36]

STEP 2: Do Exegetical Work on Each Scene by Asking Three Questions

1. Is There a Unique Semantic Structure to This Passage? Is the author using a specific structure to this passage that makes us stand up and take notice? When Abraham is about to sacrifice Isaac (Genesis 22), the wording of the narrative shifts. In the middle of the scene, the verbs intensify at a faster rate than before: Abraham built the altar, laid the wood, bound Isaac, laid him on the altar, reached for the knife. All this action occurs in two verses (22:9–10). The semantic structure of the passage influences the way it is preached.[37]

2. How Does This Passage Fit in the Larger Theme of the Book? Often the meaning of a story is not in the story. The meaning of a story may be in how the author uses it to accomplish his purposes. A good example of this is the giving of the Ten Commandments to God's people in Exodus 20:1–21. The giving of the Law looks back to how God delivered them (v. 2). So they are delivered to represent their covenant relationship by keeping his Law. The narrative of Exodus 20 draws the reader into the trajectory of the book.

3. Does the Author Use Key Words as Rhetorical Clues to the Meaning? Sometimes the author will use key words that tie the story into the larger theme of the book. You will notice that in Ruth 1, the central figure is not Ruth, but Naomi. So the idea in the first chapter relates to God's sovereignty in Naomi's life. It is a theme that is more dominant, or the backdrop, for the faithfulness of Ruth in verses 6–18. This is a clue to the interpretation of the book. Naomi is driving the action in chapters 2 and 3, and the book ends with a reconciliation of chapter one: Naomi, who lost her husband and therefore the opportunity to have a lineage, has a daughter-in-law who is more than seven sons (v. 15). The use of Naomi as a central character in the early chapter sets this up.

---

36. See Steven Mathewson, *The Art of Preaching Old Testament Narrative* (Grand Rapids: Baker, 2002), 112–21, regarding shaping the sermon.

37. David Allen has made this observation in the Hebrew when teaching on the influence of linguistics in preaching narratives.

STEP 3: Develop the Main Idea

The main idea of the sermon, as discussed above, is encapsulating the idea of the text in one memorable sentence. It is important that we do so in this part of the process. We are not forming an idea and then imposing it on a text. We are simply identifying the way the author tells the story. Once the story has been told, then we see a theme emerging.

Just one hint here. As we are telling the story, we will often wonder how much material to leave in and how much to leave out. There are some details we will not be able to cover. However, we do know that we must at least deal with the main idea of the passage. If we cover everything and miss that, then we have missed everything! So identify the main idea, then look back over the story and ask, "How do the scenes of this story develop the idea?" As I tell the story, I am making choices on what to include or exclude depending on how they carry along the idea of the text. For example, in the sermon below, three chapters are taken, yet with only three scenes. This is because whatever else can be gleaned from this story, at the very least the message of the grace of God and the wrath of God must be carried along. The three scenes are not everything that could be said; rather, they represent the tips of mountains that carry the message along. These are not mines; they are vistas. The priority is that the listener sees the big picture of the story. That is more important than the fine details. Or, more precisely, the details given must all ultimately contribute to the movement of the larger idea.

STEP 4: Develop Application from the Story

As discussed above, the application may be woven throughout the story, or placed at the end of the story. The most natural place to put an application in any sermon is the place where the truth that we need to apply emerges. Thus, in preaching Epistles, we often pepper the entire sermon with application. However, in the narrative, we really do not know the truth that the author wants to communicate until the end of the story. It just moves along and we see it in retrospect.

Thus, the nature of narrative lends itself to application that comes after the bulk of the narrative. This is simply because it's here when we finally know what the truth is that we want to apply. Of course, there are exceptions, and this is a principle not a rule. However, if you do include application throughout the sermon, make sure it is not "forced." Remember, you do not have to apply the text all the way through the story. The best approach is to hint at application, and then give the big application at the end.

STEP 5: Develop Your Conclusion

If you follow the inductive/deductive model suggested earlier, the conclusion is a natural extension of the applications. So it will flow like this: setting, scenes, main idea, applications, conclusion. Your conclusion may be your applications. At the very least, a conclusion will be a reaffirmation of the main idea you already introduced. This is one reason Old Testament narratives are so compelling. They give you the chance to drive home the main point of the sermon not long after you made it. This is a great value to preaching Old Testament Narrative.

STEP 6: Develop Your Introduction

What makes introductions unique in preaching Old Testament Narratives is that you can just start telling the story. In this way, the setting or the first scene becomes the content of the introduction. This is a compelling way to do it. But this must be used with the following caution: it can be boring if you are not good at using words to thrust people into the ancient world quickly.

If you are splitting the main idea, introducing the subject at the beginning and the complement later, then you are just setting up the topic of the sermon without the full idea. This is a set up. But your hearers do not know it's a set up. That of course, is why it's a set up. They think they are getting what the sermon is about. An introduction that does this well will leave the listeners with a question in mind. A question they want the text to answer for them.

STEP 7: Look for the Gospel in the Narrative

In the ways that we discussed above, locate the gospel in the narrative. Or, more precisely, look at how this story fits into the overall picture of the redemptive story. It fits. It fits hand in glove. The problem is not in determining whether or not the connection exists, but finding how to go about communicating it.

In the method given above, we discussed locating the narrative in the larger context of salvation history. One reason I like this method is that every story fits into salvation history, so the method applies to all texts. However, it is possible to find parallel themes. In other words, there might be a story of redemption or sacrifice, and we might want to make the connection of redemption and sacrifice to Christ. Such connections might be explicit in some texts, but not in all, nor even in most. If this is our only option, then the connection to the gospel will feel forced. So, we can find thematic relationships with our story and the gospel. However, those connections are subservient to the larger purposes of the book, which serve the larger purpose of the Old Testament, i.e., to show how the promises made in the Old Testament are fulfilled in Christ. Thus, the salvation history method proves a better alternative when the thematic relationship method feels forced.

STRUCTURING A SERMON FROM AN OLD TESTAMENT NARRATIVE

1. Follow the Scene Structure

This has been discussed above in some detail. If you are exclusively a "point by point" preacher, this scene type of structure may seem daunting. However, remember the sermon structure exists to serve the text, not the other way around. If we compromise the text for a structure then we are practicing a form of idolatry that suggests that a sermon form is more important than the Scriptures.[38] After you read the story over and over again, a scene structure will begin to emerge. You will see the scenes become clear. These are divisions of the sermon.

---

38. See a parallel idea in Dale Ralph Davis, *The Word Became Fresh* (Ross-shire, Scotland: Mentor, 2011), 2.

2. Use Induction on Individual Scenes

An inductive sermon works to a main idea—not from it. So you really don't know what the story is about until it's over. This is the point of a good story. It is a little unpredictable until the very end. What is true of the whole story is true of the whole sermon is true of the scenes. So describe the scene first, then give the idea of the scene.

3. Consider Induction/Deduction

If you don't know the main idea of a sermon until the end of the sermon, this raises the question of how to find application. First, by induction we do not mean that the main idea will be the very last thing out of your mouth. We only mean that it comes toward the end. In a deductive sermon the idea usually comes after the introduction. In an inductive sermon the idea usually comes before the conclusion. Once you state the main idea, then make application from the idea. In this way, most of the application will come at the end.

Sample Sermon

Uncommon Grace (Genesis 6–9)

> **PREACHING STRATEGY**
>
> It seems that the question the text is raising is, What does God do when people abuse his grace?

Introduction

> **INTRODUCTION**
>
> In the introduction I am trying to set up the idea of grace by explaining the difference between common grace and saving grace.

When I was in junior high, after some seeking and confusion, I gave my life completely to Christ. Before doing so I was, for the most part, a good kid. No major violations of the law. However, if I died before giving my life to Christ, I would have faced the full wrath of God. This sounds extreme, but I was guilty of sin that warranted such punishment, especially one sin: I abused the grace of God.

You see, God gave me a great family, a wonderful home, a church that would nurture me spiritually, and I felt as if all of these blessings were owed to me. So, even though I knew I should repent, I continued in my sin, walking over the very grace God provided me.

In fact, all people who live are experiencing a life that God has provided and in that sense they are all under the grace of God. We would distinguish between God's common grace that is given to all who ever live, and his saving grace that is given to those who come to faith in him. So, those who have not given their lives to Christ are all experiencing his grace, but they are abusing it by enjoying all that God provides while assuming he owes it to them and that they have no need to repent.

Imagine that the entire world was abusing the grace of God. That is what is happening in Genesis 6. Everyone is a grace abuser. So, the question is, What does God do when people abuse his grace?

> This is the question that sets up the sermon.

SETTING: Noah

TRANSITION: People are Abusing Grace. What Is God Going to Do?

Scene 1—God Told Noah to Build a Boat (Gen 6:13–22)

> **SCENES**
>
> The narrative is presented as three macro-level scenes. After each scene there is an "observation." This is like a point but notice that it is inductive—the observation is made at the end of the explanation. After the observation there is more application, illustration, etc.

God told Noah to build an ark, a boat. The interesting thing is that the boat took 120 years to build. So in one breath God declares that he will destroy the earth, and then he takes 120 years to do so. In other words, God gives people more opportunities to repent!

Observation 1: When people abuse grace, God extends more grace!

Scene 2—Noah Boards the Ark and the Floods Come (Gen 7:1–16)

Even though God extended grace, eventually the grace expired and justice came.

Observation 2: God's grace has a limit!

The question is now, why did God save Noah? Genesis 6:8 tells us that Noah found favor that clearly he did not deserve. Noah seems to find favor for the reason that he knew he did not deserve it.

Main Idea: God extends common grace to all, but he only extends saving grace to those who understand common grace.

> **MAIN IDEA**
>
> The main idea of the sermon is placed after the third point. It seems to fit naturally here. Thus, the sermon is inductive, working to a main idea that is not clear until this point.

Scene 3—God Makes a Covenant with Noah and All the Earth (Gen 9:1–17)

> **FINAL SCENE**
>
> Notice the final scene jumps to the covenant. There is a lot that is missed taking three chapters, but the events of the flood make sense in light of the covenant. The covenant here points toward the new covenant in Christ.

The sacrifice was a sweet aroma to God. This language and structure hint at the sacrificial system that will come, a system that points to Christ.

Observation 3: God is satisfied with the sacrifice that points to the sacrifice of Christ.

Conclusion

> **CONCLUSION**
>
> Most all the application is saved to the conclusion. This makes sense because the application is not intended to follow each scene. We are not forced to apply each scene, but we are at least compelled to apply the one main idea of the text.

Three Applications

1. Compassion

This story brings a word of compassion. God had so much compassion for people, giving them every opportunity to repent and come to him.

2. Security

There is some encouragement in this story. If God would give that much mercy to those who abused his grace, how much more will he give to those who embrace his grace?

3. Warning

There is a word of warning here. No one deserves God's mercy, but he will have mercy on those who know they need it, and repent in faith, and return.

REFLECTION

1. How did Jesus use the stories of the Old Testament?
2. Do Jewish narratives always resolve the plot line neatly?
3. Why would you identify the structure of the narrative before deciding on the main point?
4. Do narratives have points?
5. Is it necessary to make an application from each scene of a narrative?

RECOMMENDED RESOURCES

Alexander, T. D. *From Paradise to the Promised Land: An Introduction to the Pentateuch*. Grand Rapids: Baker, 2002.

Alter, Robert. *The Art of Biblical Narrative*. New York: Basic, 2011.

Davis, Dale Ralph. *The Word Became Fresh*. Ross-shire, Scotland: Mentor. 2011.

Fokkelman, J. P. *Reading Biblical Narrative*. Leiderdrop, The Netherlands: Deo, 1999.

Mathewson, Steven. *The Art of Preaching Old Testament Narrative*. Grand Rapids: Baker, 2002.

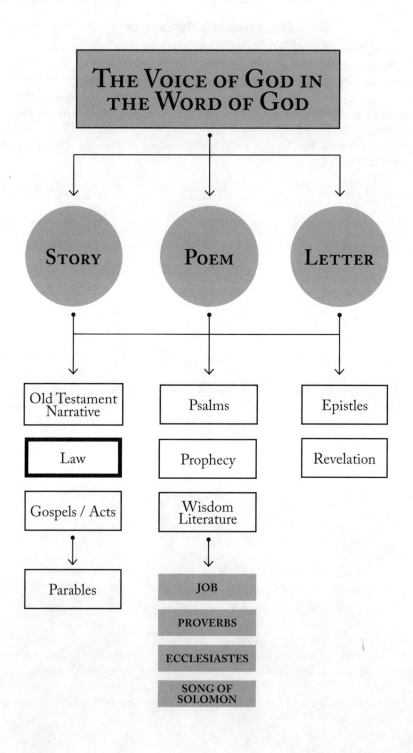

THE VOICE OF GOD IN
THE WORD OF GOD

STORY

POEM

LETTER

Old Testament Narrative

Law

Gospels / Acts

Parables

Psalms

Prophecy

Wisdom Literature

JOB

PROVERBS

ECCLESIASTES

SONG OF SOLOMON

Epistles

Revelation

Chapter 5

RECAPTURING THE VOICE OF GOD IN THE LAW

If a prophet or a dreamer of dreams arises among you and gives
you a sign or a wonder, and the sign or wonder that he tells you
comes to pass, and if he says, "Let us go after other gods," which
you have not known, "and let us serve them," you shall not listen
to the words of that prophet or that dreamer of dreams. For the
LORD your God is testing you, to know whether you love the LORD
your God with all your heart and with all your soul. You shall walk
after the LORD your God and fear him and keep his commandments and obey his voice, and you shall serve him and hold fast
to him. (Deut 13:1–4)

WHY PREACH THE LAW?

THE ABOVE SCRIPTURE IS PROVOCATIVE. Think of the implication: the Lord
their God was going to test the Israelites with the presence of a false prophet. This
may seem tricky, but it wasn't at all. It was a test, not a trick. A trick intends to
deceive. A test from God is intended to build our faith as we follow his commands.
And this is why it was not deceitful—they knew the commands.

God had specifically given Moses the law (Exod 19–20; 34:1–28). Moses wrote
the law down (Exod 34:28). Moses taught it to leaders who were to teach it to the
people (Deut 1:9–18). The fathers taught it to their families (Deut 6:4–9). From the
mouth of God to the smallest child the people knew the law of God. They understood his commands. They knew how God felt about the issues. So, when a false
prophet emerged spewing lies and tempting people away from God, they were on
him. They knew he was no good because they knew the law. People stray spiritually
because they do now know the law. Sheep are easy prey when they cannot defend
themselves. And so it is with the contemporary church. The only way to protect
people spiritually is to make them strong in the Word. So an understanding of the
law was critical then and it is critical now for the same reason: if our people do not
understand the place of the Old Testament law in the biblical narrative, then they are
vulnerable to believe that which is false.

Charles Spurgeon told the story of a minister who went to call on a poor lady to
help her financially. She would not come to the door, and he assumed she was gone.

When she later said he never came by he explained that he did, but that she was not at home, to which she replied that she was at home but didn't answer because she thought he was someone coming to collect the rent. We think of the law as God taking our freedom, when in reality it is actually God's gift of grace to us.[1]

In our minds the law is only negative; we think the only purpose the law serves is to govern those who cannot govern themselves. It is true that the law is for the lawless, but it is also a guide for the lawful. Think of Psalm 78:5–8 (emphasis mine) when the psalmist writes,

> He established a testimony in Jacob and appointed *a law* in Israel,
>> which he commanded our fathers
> to teach their children,
>> that the next generation might know them,
> the children yet unborn,
>> and arise and tell them to their children,
> so that they should set their hope in God and not forget the works of God,
>> but keep his commandments;
> and that they should not be like their fathers,
>> a stubborn and rebellious generation,
> a generation whose heart was not steadfast,
>> whose spirit was not faithful to God.

In knowing the law, the next generation would set their hope in God and they would not commit the sins of their fathers. In fact, the whole law reflects the covenant that God made with Israel through Moses on Mt. Sinai, a covenant initiated by God and intended to protect his people.[2]

Perhaps this is one reason that not one part of the law could be relaxed for fear that the one doing so would be called least in the kingdom (Matt 5:17–19). We preach the law under the fear of Christ and are motivated to lead people to the relationship to God that it brings.[3]

We must re-think the purpose of the law as governance and think of it as guidance; in doing so, we will love God's law because we are grateful for the love of the lawgiver.[4] Think of the strangeness of Psalm 119:18 "Open my eyes that I may behold wonderful things from your law." And even more strange is Psalm 119:20, "My soul is consumed with longing for your righteous rules at all times." Clearly the psalmist is not thinking of obsessing over obscure regulations. The answer is found throughout this incredible psalm, but summed up well in verse 105–6 when he writes, "Your word is a lamp unto my feet and a light to my path. I have sworn an

---

1. Charles Spurgeon, *All of Grace*, from The Spurgeon Archive, accessed December 4, 2013, http://www.spurgeon.org/all_of_g.htm.

2. David Dorsey, *The Literary Structure of the Old Testament: A Commentary on Genesis–Malachi* (Grand Rapids: Baker, 1999), 47.

3. Christopher J. H. Stuart, "Preaching from the Law," in *Reclaiming the Old Testament for Christian Preaching* (Downer's Grove: InterVarsity, 2010), 99.

4. See Walter Kaiser Jr., *Preaching and Teaching from the Old Testament: A Guide for the Church* (Grand Rapids: Baker, 2003), 139–41, for helpful discussion on the relationship of the believer to the law.

oath and confirmed it, to keep your righteous rules." The idea, similar to Psalm 78, is that the law has value because of its ability to guide.

This is the great irony of the law. In the law, God demands strict adherence to a moral code, and yet he gives one the means to propitiate for disobedience. The law is not a composition of rules. The same law that gives the rules is the same law that provides the details of the tabernacle and sacrificial system. God's law is at once guidance and provision.[5]

Again, the law is in fact for the lawless, but it is a guide for the lawful. It is there for guidance as much as for governance. Therefore, it is a treasure.[6] The challenge before the preacher is to show the beauty, majesty, and practicality of the law. Clearly you do not need motivation to preach the law; otherwise, you would not be reading this. The Word of God does not need to be defended, but sometimes *we* need encouragement. Why should we take the time to preach the law? Well, besides the guidance it provides, here are four other reasons.

The Law Leads Us to Christ

There can be no grace without law. The law established the norm that calls us to beg for grace. Paul calls the law a schoolmaster (Gal 3:23–24) that leads us to Christ. Don't read "taskmaster" for "schoolmaster." The point is that a willingness to keep the law is the greatest form of self-awareness in that it demonstrates we know that we have nothing and we are nothing. Christ saves us from ourselves.[7]

The Law Helps Us Understand God's Character

God is overwhelming in his loving-kindness. It is incredible. One could debate that attribute of God is expressed most clearly in Scripture, but in a sense the argument is nonsensical. In the end, God's love is modified by his perfection. He is perfect love. This is an overwhelming thought. God said to Moses,

> The LORD, the LORD, a God merciful and gracious, slow to anger, and abounding in steadfast love and faithfulness, keeping steadfast love for thousands, forgiving iniquity and transgression and sin, but who will by no means clear the guilty, visiting the iniquity of the fathers on the children and the children's children, to the third and fourth generation. (Exod 34:6–7)

---

5. Graeme Goldsworthy, *Preaching the Whole Bible as Christian Scripture: The Application of Biblical Theology to Expository Preaching* (Grand Rapids: Eerdmans, 2000), 155.

6. Douglas Stuart makes the point that the rules were the foundation to a relationship with God. He writes, "In any preaching from the law it is important to get across early and often the following simple but crucial concept: No rules, no relationship. That's the essence of what people need to understand about the value of laws for them as they seek to follow Christ . . . Biblical laws are covenant stipulations: a means of connecting two parties (God and his people) with all the benefits that the connection provides," Douglas Stuart, "Preaching from the Law," in *Preaching the Old Testament*, ed. Scott M. Gibson (Grand Rapids, Baker, 2006), 90.

7. For a sample sermon on the law leading to Christ, see Walter Kaiser Jr., "God Can Forgive All Our Sin," in *Preaching and Teaching from the Old Testament: A Guide for the Church* (Grand Rapids: Baker, 2003), 146–51.

We learn a great deal about God's character from these lines. First, he is a God of magnificent love and a God who cannot tolerate sin. In every situation I need to know that God is a God of love. And when I feel the need to sin, I can be assured that he will not tolerate it. It is good to know that this is what he wanted the Israelites to know before giving them the law. Why? Because the law of God speaks to the character of God. His holy inability to tolerate sin and his gracious forgiveness of sinners is the perfect entre into the giving of the law. It is seen in these verses. The law extends loving protection. We need to be protected from others and from ourselves. The law does this. And, ultimately, if we reject the law, we need to be protected from God. The law lovingly shows us the character of God. We want to ask, how can we love God without all this law? The real question is, can we know God apart from his law?

The Law Protects Us from Evil in All Its Forms

This brings us back to the false prophets. No one has walked into my town and tried to publicly dissuade me from following God. We don't have those kinds of false prophets; we have other kinds. We have the marketing machine demanding I consume things as if it is my individual right. We have preachers that distort the gospel. We have preachers who do not understand the gospel. And the biggest enemy I have is myself. I try to tell myself not to trust God. He's not that loving. I try to tell myself I can sin and get away with it. He is not that severe. The false prophet I have to identify today is the one living inside me.

This is deadly serious. So, in Deuteronomy 13:5 the LORD said, "But that prophet or that dreamer of dreams shall be put to death. . . . So you shall purge the evil from your midst." The law has the power to do this. But this still does not make it easy to preach the law. So how do we tackle the major portions of Exodus, Leviticus, Numbers, and Deuteronomy that are filled with law? Let's deal with matters related to the interpretation of the law, matters of communication, and then how to structure a sermon on the law.

INTERPRETATION: HEARING THE VOICE OF GOD IN THE LAW

The Laws Fit within the Larger Story

When the laws seem difficult to apply, remember that they fit within the larger framework of the story of God's people. Perhaps the best example is the Ten Commandments. Think of the context. The Israelites had just been delivered from the bondage of the Egyptians. God is returning them to their land. However, this time they are a large people living among other large nations. God is going to distinguish them from among the other peoples. Thus, he precedes the giving of the commandments with, "I am the LORD your God, who brought you out of the land of Egypt, out of the house of slavery" (Exod 20:1). The context was their deliverance. So the Ten Commandments should be preached in that context.

The example below is built around a narrative, but all of the laws have a surrounding narrative. And all of those narratives fit into the macro narrative of the book. So the smaller stories, the laws, are swallowed up in the large story of the book. This fact will redeem the law from seeming dull. We will return to this in a moment.

Carter, Duvall, and Hays give four excellent interpretive keys to help us understand the law.[8] As with all the genres, there is a hermeneutical discussion that goes beyond the scope of this book. However, these interpretive keys are a helpful framework to guide us as we approach the sermon process. They are paraphrased loosely below.

1. Recognize the limitations of categorizing the laws as civil, ceremonial, or moral. As we approach the Torah, we are struck with the fact that some laws do not seem to apply today. What are we to do about mixed fabrics and meat mixed with milk? What is one to make of the laws concerning worship in the Levitical code? One approach is to see some laws as ceremonial, others as civil, and others as moral. The reasoning is that moral laws transcend time and are still applicable today, while the ceremonial laws and civil laws do not transcend time and are therefore no longer applicable, at least in a straightforward manner. This idea has everything going for it except that the laws are not explicitly classified this way in Scripture.

2. Recognize that the law is not presented in the Bible by itself as some sort of timeless universal legal code, but rather as part of the theological story that describes how God delivered his people from Egypt and established them in the promised land. This is why we will take the approach of Old Testament Narrative, as a rule, when we preach the law. The law is a part of the larger story of the deliverance of Israel and her relationship with a covenant-making, covenant-keeping God. "Indeed, our methodology of interpreting Old Testament law should be similar to our methodology of interpreting Old Testament narrative, for the law is contextually part of the narrative."[9]

3. The law is an integral part of the Mosaic covenant and should be interpreted accordingly. The Mosaic law was closely tied to Israel's conquest and occupation of the land. The blessings of the Mosaic law were conditional, and the old covenant has been surpassed by the glory of the new covenant (1 Corinthians 3). Therefore the Old Testament laws are no longer applicable to New Testament believers as law.

4. Interpret the Old Testament law through the grid of the New Testament. The law is a part of the "all Scripture" that Paul references in 2 Timothy 3:16 and is therefore "God-breathed and is useful for teaching, rebuking, correcting and training in righteousness." However, the law no longer functions as a binding code of our covenant relationship with God. Christ came to fulfill the law (Matt 5:17)—to bring its function to completion.

How then is the law to be applied? Again, the interpretive process begins by understanding that the law fits into the larger story of God's deliverance of Israel. The giving of the Ten Commandments begins with "And God spoke all these words, saying, 'I am the LORD your God, who brought you out of the house of slavery.'" Everything God would command them to do was framed by the narrative of his deliverance.

When we preach the law, the same principle applies. We are not Israelites delivered from Egypt; we are new covenant Christians delivered from sin. Therefore, the law is not binding on us in the same way it was the Israelites.

---

8. Terry Carter, Scott Duvall, and Daniel Hays, *Preaching God's Word: A Hands-on Approach to Preparing, Developing, and Delivering the Sermon* (Grand Rapids: Zondervan, 2005), 238–42.

9. Ibid, 239.

All the Laws Are Applicable

We wonder how in the world we can apply these laws. The irony is that these were direct commands—they were application—to the original hearers. Some have suggested that the way to apply them is to distinguish between civil, ceremonial, and moral law. However, this is unhelpful if we understand the distinction to mean that *some* laws are for us, but not all.[10] It makes it appear as if some laws have more value to us than others. However, all of the Scripture is a means to lead us to Christ (2 Tim 3:15–16). This does not mean that the laws are equally applicable. The truth is that some are not. However, the ceremonial and civil laws point to a God who engenders people to be distinct, unique, and protected. The law was, after all, for the people; the people did not exist for the law.[11] Therefore we can take the ceremonial law and the civil law and determine what they teach us about God and about ourselves. From this vantage point there is application to be preached.

The Laws Point to Christ

Jesus came, not to abolish the law, but to fulfill it (Matt 5:17). Thus, some understanding of the law is necessary to appreciate Christ's fulfillment of it. We addressed this briefly above, but we need to remember the function of the laws. They serve to show us the disparity between God's standard of holiness and our ungodliness, and to distinguish the Israelites from the nations that surrounded them. However, it is one thing to know this theological connection; it's another to apply it. The question is, "How do you actually do this when you preach?" See the section on pointing to Christ below.

Remember, the law was given in the context of sin. As Goldsworthy notes,

> The incident of Aaron's golden calf illustrates the point that the lust for autonomy for the word of God still characterizes the human heart even in the aftermath of the most amazing demonstration of grace and the instruction concerning the shape of graced life.[12]

As mentioned above, the same God who gave the law gave the means to deal with disobedience to the law. God, knowing the law would expose sin as much as motivate righteousness, gave the tabernacle and its attending sacrificial system as a means of mediating fellowship between a perfect God and a perfectly sinful people.

The Gospel According to Abraham

Perhaps you have heard it preached that in the Old Testament the Israelites were saved by keeping God's law, but in the New Testament we are saved by grace. We read John 1:17, "For the law was given through Moses; grace and truth came through Jesus Christ" and we intimate a dichotomy that is not there. The truth is that no one is saved without grace. As we noted above, the law was for the people who already

10. See ibid., 328–36.
11. Christopher J. H. Wright, "Preaching from the Law," in *Reclaiming the Old Testament for Christian Preaching*, ed Grenville J. R. Kent, Paul J. Kissling, and Laurence A. Turner (Downer's Grove: InterVarsity, 2010), 55.
12. Goldsworthy, *Preaching*, 157.

had a covenant relationship with God. This is why Paul says, "And the Scripture, foreseeing that God would justify the Gentiles by faith, preached the gospel before-hand to Abraham, saying, 'In you shall all the nations be blessed.'" (Gal 3:8). Of course we should never preach the law without the gospel, but we must also remem-ber that the gospel of saving faith preceded the New Testament.[13]

If it is the case that the gospel of faith preceded Christ, then why is Christ always challenging the religious establishment? Christ is not reacting to their keeping the law; he is reacting to their abuse of the law. This is why in the Sermon on the Mount, Christ begins by affirming the law by saying that he had come to fulfill it, and not one accent mark of the law would pass away (Matt 5:17–18). Then, he clarifies the meaning of the law with this formula, "You have heard it said . . . but I say to you" (5:21–22, 27–28, 31–34, 38–39, 43–44). As God, Christ is the preexistent source of the law; the Pharisees were the ones who had twisted it. So, if they distorted the law, and Christ needed to correct their understanding of it, then surely there was some-thing in the law worth restoring. So, how do we preach the law in a way that shows it is a means of grace?

COMMUNICATION: RECAPTURING THE VOICE IN THE LAW

Preach Law in the Story

Context is not inconsequential. Think about the giving of the Ten Commandments. The people had just been delivered from bondage. The laws, the Ten Commandments and those that follow, are shaped by this story. The Israelites are no longer slaves—they are now free to worship God. So God tells them how a free people worship him. The laws that are given are nuanced by their structure in this story. When we preach them today, we are preaching to a church who is free to worship God; the command-ments tell us how to worship God as free people. It was true then, and it is true now. So, preach the laws in their immediate context.

Then, point to the larger story of the book. This will lead to the covenant that the laws represent, which will ultimately lead to the gospel. The laws come out of a relationship with God and represent the stipulations of the Mosaic covenant. That relationship with God was inaugurated by a covenant with Abraham. According to 1 Corinthians 3, we are ministers of a new covenant: "God . . . has made us sufficient to be ministers of a new covenant, not of the letter but of the spirit, for the letter kills, but the spirit gives life" (v. 5). Since the law exists to take us to the new covenant, then go there. When preaching, get from the law to the gospel.

Preach the Transferable Principle

Behind each law is a principle about the character and nature of God. Identify this principle and preach it in light of New Testament theology. Think of the won-derful narrative of Moses descending the mountain with his face shining in Exodus 34:29–35. The following verses are a seemingly obscure group of commands on how workmen should honor the Sabbath day that is "holy to the Lord" (35:1–3). From this, we see a God who asks for time to be given just to him, that is separate (holy) from all other time. Jesus helps us understand that this is not meant to hold us in legalistic

---

13. See Wright, "Preaching," 49.

bondage. Christ would later clarify that man was not created for rules, but rather the rules were created to help man, and that he is the Lord of the Sabbath (Mark 2:27–28).

There have been many who have waived the caution flag against moralism.[14] The warning is well heeded not to take a passage of Scripture, given to affirm and encourage the covenant, and reduce it to a moral lesson. However, finding a relationship between what was expected of the listener receiving the law, and what is expected in us in response to the law is not in and of itself moralism. It becomes so when not expressed in covenant terms, but it is not inherently so.

Take for example the law to honor the Sabbath rest given in Exodus 31:12–17. This has much immediate application and is dealt with in the New Testament. The preacher can discuss what Christ did with this law (Matt 12:1–8), and the relationship between our need for physical rest and spiritual rest in Christ (Matt 11:25–30). However, if one is preaching Deuteronomy 19:1–13, on the cities of refuge, the application seems less obvious. However, the passage is rich with application. Remember the law teaches us about the character of God. In Deuteronomy 19 God makes it clear that he is a God of compassion; he is a God who does not want innocent blood to be shed; and he is a God of the practical need.

The way to protect our application of the text from moral instruction alone is to teach what the passage teaches about God. However, the second way to protect it from being about moralism is to teach what it teaches about the covenant. Any mention of the covenant is a way to explain how this points to the future revelation of the new covenant. In this case the motivation God gives them for establishing the cities of refuge is "lest innocent blood be shed in your land that the LORD your God is giving you for an inheritance . . . " The land was sacred because it was inherited land. Standing on the promised soil was the inescapable reminder that God keeps his promises. The ultimate fulfillment of this promise was the incarnation of Jesus Christ.

So when extracting from the law a transferable principle, be sure and show what the law teaches about God, and show how the law points to Christ. These two rails will serve to steer the application to a place that is safe and productive theologically.

Note Any Explicit Connection in the New Testament

There are some laws that are directly dealt with in the New Testament. Remember Jesus' interaction with the rich young ruler in Luke 18:18? He wanted to know what he could do to inherit eternal life. Jesus responds that he must keep the commandments. However, Jesus only gives him a select group of commandments. Why the Lord did this is a mystery, but it had a telling effect. Christ exposed the fact that one could keep the law and still have a wicked heart. Furthermore, in Matthew 12:1–8, Jesus redefined the Sabbath law, and in Matthew 22:37–40, Jesus sums up the entire law. Therefore when we come to a text with an explicit mention in the New Testament, we should preach it in light of its connection.

Show How the Law Fits into Salvation History

If there is no explicit connection between the law section you are preaching and the gospel, then show how the law fits into salvation history. This is a way of pointing to Christ, who came after the law. For example, Jesus explains why the law exists in

---

14. See Goldsworthy, *"Preaching,"* 118, for discussion of "exhortations without the gospel."

Matthew 22:37–40. If all the law and the prophets "hang" on loving the Lord your God with all your heart, soul, and mind (Deut 6:5), and loving your neighbor as yourself (Lev 19:18), then keeping the whole law is an expression of these two. Preaching the law provides a wonderful opportunity to exalt Jesus. The law no longer carries the purpose that it did in the Old Testament. Since Christ has fulfilled the law, we are no longer under its authority. Again, this does not mean that we ignore the law, but rather this means that we preach the law and then allow it to lead us to Christ.

Preach the Law in a Spirit of Grace

The premise of our work is that we are taking the rhetorical clues of communication from the text, in no less than its substance, structure, and spirit. It may seem natural that the laws would be delivered, well, legally. However, if laws are an expression of grace, then this is not the case. So, how do you deliver it as such?

The laws represent a timeless principle—one that is often mirrored in the New Testament. Grace-shaped preaching on passages that contain law identifies the timeless truth represented by the law and then preaches it in the same grace. Think of it this way. The fact that God gave Israel law is itself grace. The law is a window into the character of God and a means by which we can express our gratitude to the God who has saved us. The very existence of the law was grace based.[15] Therefore, under the new covenant, we preach law in that tone. The best way to preach with a tone of grace is to take the listener to a corollary New Testament passage. This will be illustrated in the sermon example below.

Show Them the Witness of the Law

The idea of obedience as a witness is also a New Testament idea. We are to have such good works that people see us and glorify God (Matt 5:16); all people who see our love should associate us with Christ (John 13:35); and our obedience should adorn the gospel (Titus 2:10). When preaching the law, illustrate the transferable principle to the lives of your people. Then teach them, just like Israel, that the whole law functions to allow us to praise God, and that it proves a caring witness to the world around us.

STRUCTURING A SERMON FROM THE LAW

1. Look to the Narrative

When you want to develop the sermon structure for a sermon on the law, look first for the narrative feel of the law. There will need to be attention given to the narrative. You might even find that the narrative can drive the sermon so that the sermon moves around scenes, not points.

---

15. Christopher Wright makes the wonderful observation that the Old Testament saints were not saved by keeping the law. They too were saved by God's grace. He stresses Exod 19:4–6 where God points to his deliverance of the people from Egypt before giving them the law. In other words, the law was given to an already redeemed people. Thus, obedience to the law was a way of expressing recognition of salvation, not earning salvation. See Wright, "Preaching," 48.

2. Consider Micro-Exposition

If you are preaching through the Ten Commandments individually, you will find yourself doing micro-exposition. This means that you will spend the sermon trying to explain what it means to covet, why we should not covet, etc. Perhaps the best advice is to pan out from what the text says, to what it means in its immediate context, to what it means in its canonical context. The admonition not to covet has a trajectory throughout Scripture. The law was broken famously by Israel who wanted a king like other nations. Against God's admonition they secured a king; the destruction of Israel followed.

So what is the difference between a "micro-exposition" and a topical sermon? Typically a topical sermon is a collection of texts on a particular subject. A good topical sermon will answer the question, "What does the Bible say about this topic?" However, to continue our example, a micro exposition will answer the question, "What does this text say about coveting?" The answer, within the text, is "not much." Don't covet. However, there is more to it than just the prohibition. The careful exegete moves from the immediate context in an ever expanding circle to get a fuller meaning of what that verse means. So, a micro exposition may cover more verses, but they are all in service of unpacking the meaning in that one verse. The goal is to show the meaning in a way that demonstrates a trajectory of the theme across Scripture. And this is the difference: micro-exposition is not teaching a topic, it is showing a trajectory.

3. Consider Macro-Exposition

In the example below, the sermon covers the text from a larger perspective, noting where the main themes lie. Extracting points from every few verses, in a text that describes the priestly duties, for example, would force the preacher to make illustration and application from points that were never intended to be used that way. The text needs to be understood as a whole and then, as a general rule, the functions of preaching (application, argumentation, illustration, exhortation) can be applied to the whole idea of the text. This may lend itself to having points of application that come at the end of the sermon after the explanation of the text.

Sermon Sample

Worthy of Respect (Exod 20:7–11)

> PREACHING STRATEGY
>
> The text is the third and fourth commandments and was in a series through the Ten Commandments. The text is answering, what does it mean to honor the Sabbath Day and to not take the Lord's name in vain?

Introduction

We used to live near Washington, DC and would often visit the changing of the guard at the Tomb of the Unknown Soldier. The ceremony is fascinating to watch, but the core gesture of the entire ceremony is the salute. The hand is raised in respect of another. The salute communicates at least two things: belonging and respect for authority. As Israel is receiving the Ten Commandments, listen to how they are prefaced with a sense of belonging in Exodus 20:2, "I am the LORD your God, who brought you out of the land of Egypt, out of the house of slavery." The idea was that based on the fact that God delivered them (belonging) they should live in a way to respect his authority over their lives. This is still true, but it is important to note that in the New Testament, Christ fulfilled the law (Matt 5:17). We do not keep the Ten Commandments to please God. Rather, Christ makes us pleasing to the Father so that we can keep his laws. So the keeping of the Ten Commandments is not me trying to please God; rather, it is because Christ made us pleasing. We are not working for God's pleasure, but from God's pleasure. With that in mind, let's look at the third and fourth commandments.

> The introduction is simply setting up the idea of respect. However, since the role of the law in the new covenant is such a big mental hurdle, time was spent dealing with this in the introduction. This allows the sermon to tie back to Christ at other points later on.

1. Respect the Name of God: Honoring the Reputation of God (v. 7)

Not taking God's name is vain is refusing to evoke the name of God in a way that is meaningless. God is adamant that his reputation be stellar to those who are watching.

2. Respect the Day of God: Honoring the Rest of God (vv. 8–11)

This is the only command not affirmed in the NT. However, we still celebrate a day where there is an absence of work and a presence of worship. Keeping the NT pattern, we do so in celebration of Christ's victory over the power of death.

> In both points above time was taken for necessary practical application. The need for this application seems more pointed in light of the assumed obscurity of OT law. However, the necessary application must be subservient to clear explanation of the relationship of the law and grace. Practical application without the gospel helps no one.

Conclusion

It is interesting that Israel celebrates rest at the end of the week, but Christians at the beginning of the week. This is symbolic. They were serving God in anticipation of what would come; we are celebrating what Christ has already done. They were to look for the hope; we are celebrating the rest of Christ that has already come. Christ finished his work and then rested; now we rest in his finished work.

REFLECTION

1. What is our motivation to preach the law?
2. In what way is the giving of the law a means to keep the law?
3. How can laws be applied when they were given to one specific context?
4. In what respect is the law for the world?
5. What is the difference between macro and micro exposition? Why are these approaches helpful for preaching law?

RECOMMENDED RESOURCES

Kaiser, Walter, Jr. *Preaching and Teaching from the Old Testament*. Grand Rapids: Baker, 2003.

Klein, William, Craig L. Blomberg, and Robert L. Hubbard Jr. *Introduction to Biblical Interpretation*. Dallas: Word, 1993.

Ryken, Phillip Graham. *Exodus*. Preaching the Word. Wheaton: Crossway, 2005.

Stuart, Douglas. "Preaching from the Law." In *Preaching the Old Testament*, edited by Scott M. Gibson. Grand Rapids: Baker, 2006.

Wright, Christopher J. H. "Preaching from the Law." In *Reclaiming the Old Testament for Christian Preaching*, edited by Grenville J. R. Kent, Paul J. Kissling, and Laurence A. Turner. Downer's Grove, IL: InterVarsity, 2010.

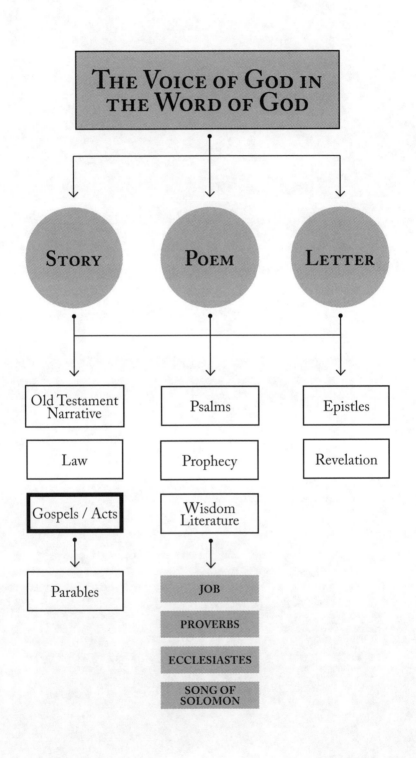

THE VOICE OF GOD IN THE WORD OF GOD

STORY   POEM   LETTER

Old Testament Narrative	Psalms	Epistles
Law	Prophecy	Revelation
Gospels / Acts	Wisdom Literature	
Parables		

JOB

PROVERBS

ECCLESIASTES

SONG OF SOLOMON

Chapter 6

RECAPTURING THE VOICE OF GOD
IN THE GOSPELS/ACTS

THE MEANING OF A BIBLICAL TEXT MAY HAVE MORE TO DO WITH THE
AUTHOR OF THE TEXT THAN THE WORDS OF THE TEXT ITSELF.[1]

Christ is present in all of Scripture, but it is dynamically true in the Gospels
when we have the spoken words of Christ before us. Think about what Jesus said
in John 14:10: "Do you not believe that I am in the Father and the Father is in me?
The words that I say to you I do not speak on my own authority, but the Father who
dwells in me does his works."

The Gospels record the words and works of Jesus. The words and works of Jesus
are the words and works of God. So when we understand Jesus' activity, we
understand God. Trying to understand the divine would be daunting if we did not
have some help. Thankfully, the words and works of Jesus are communicated to us
through the words of men. Matthew, Mark, Luke, and John serve as literary tour
guides through the mind and work of God. They are not going to tell us everything.
No time for that. However, they are going to tell us everything we need to know and
more than we can ever completely understand.[2] It's not all, but it's enough.

These four authors not only recorded the words and works of Jesus, but they
also had a thoroughgoing understanding of the Hebrew Bible, what they called "the
Law and the prophets" (Matt 4:17), "Moses and all the prophets" (Luke 24:27), or
"the Law of Moses and the prophets and the Psalms" (Luke 24:44). These were all
descriptors of our Old Testament. They knew their Bibles because it was the cen-
terpiece of their cultural heritage as Jews. Yet, they knew it for another reason. As
we will see, they knew their Bibles because they knew Jesus. Here's the fact of the
matter: the entire Old Testament actually points to Jesus. Sadly, this fact was lost on

---

1. Jesus said, "But when the Helper comes, whom I will send to you from the Father, the Spirit of truth,
who proceeds from the Father, he will bear witness about me." My thinking is that the author of the book
has a purpose, and that purpose gives shape to the interpretation of the individual pericopes that compose
the book. Concomitantly in the participation of the text, the Holy Spirit of Jesus Christ is leading us
through the words of the Word. Although this idea is not discussed in this chapter, my thinking here is
implicitly influenced by Timothy Wirada's case that John 15:26–27 "obliges us to see the Gospels as a
special kind of text." See Timothy Wirada, *Interpreting Gospel Narratives: Scenes, People, and Theology*
(Nashville: B&H, 2010), 213.

2. There is evidence that while the Gospels are unique, they follow a pattern found in early Graeco-
Roman biographies. See Mark Strauss, *Four Portraits, One Jesus: A Survey of Jesus and the Gospels*
(Grand Rapids: Zondervan: 2007).

the very people for whom Jesus came. It was also lost on the disciples themselves. Thus, in the passages cited above Jesus, in post-resurrection appearances, opens up the Bible for them to show how it is all fulfilled in him (see, for example, Luke 24). God was speaking in the Old Testament, and the words he spoke were about his Son. That mystery is finally unveiled in the Gospels.

This means the Gospels are the interpretive key for the entire Bible. The Old Testament is explained by the presence of Christ as recorded in the Gospels. Acts–Jude explains the manifest presence of Christ in the church. The book of Revelation is simply the revelation of Jesus Christ regarding his return (Rev 1:1). Revelation makes explicit what the Gospels assume. And the fulcrum that leverages the weight of salvation history is the Gospel witness. Thus, the definition of *gospel* as "good news" is simply the best way to understand the Gospel genre. So what we call the gospel message is the good news that Paul distills for us in Romans 3: that all are sinners and by implication deserve God's wrath (v. 23), that Jesus intercepts the wrath of God on our behalf by being the propitiating sacrifice (v. 25), and that God offers free salvation through faith (vv. 24–25) is only possible because of the message of the Gospels. Thus, we have before us one of the most challenging and provocative of all the biblical genres.

The Gospels, as we will see, are their own genre. They include all the elements of a biography, yet these Christological biographies are not constructed with the chronological historical structure we assume to find in modern biographies.[3] They contain parables, but the parables cannot be interpreted as stories that stand on their own, since they are often interpreted in the dialogue and setting around them. All of these elements, and more, make the Gospels unique as their own genre.

They are unique, yet at the same time they contain multiple literary genres within them. No other biblical books contain as many different genres as the Gospels/Acts. They include narrative, parable, wisdom, instruction (exhortation), and exposition. So while there may be many things that make preaching the Gospels daunting, here are two primary aspects on which we shall focus: the weight of the message and the variety of the medium. To say it more concisely, the Gospels are one grand message presented through many different vehicles.

Herein lies the challenge for the preacher. When a preacher is preaching from a Gospel, his sermon structure may change from week to week. While this seems daunting, it is the very thing that keeps the preaching fresh and invigorating. The changing genre of the Gospel texts allows us to—perhaps even demands that we—alter our sermon form. This is wonderfully liberating, and it is the challenge of the medium. And just as the medium of the text is to control and change the preacher's sermon structure, so also the message of the text changes the preacher. We preachers are being changed because the unchanging nature of the text causes us to change. To be embedded in the form of the text is to be formed by the text.

So, let's talk about the features of the Gospels/Acts for interpretation and for communication, and then some words on structure.

---

3. The idea of the Gospels being Christological biographies will be discussed in more detail later.

INTERPRETATION: HEARING THE VOICE IN THE GOSPELS

The Gospels Are True

This may seem like an odd inclusion, especially for the audience of this book, but we need the reminder for two reasons. First, if you believe these events are true—the actual recorded events of the life and times of Jesus the Messiah—you stand against much scholarship. Fortunately, this is not true of the school where I teach, but the party line in much of the academy is that the Gospels are vague representations of reality. Second, the preacher must be convinced of the historicity of the Gospels because he will be forced to reconcile the historical events recorded in the text, deal with the difficult sayings of Christ, and explain his miracles. There is a naturalist in all of us that wants a naturalistic explanation for the supernatural. But sometimes it's just not there.

Even with that said, we must be confident in what God has chosen to reveal about himself. These inspired words written about Christ are not only true, but they are enough. Although we may prefer the Gospels have a more factual bent or apologetic interest, they do have just the right take on the events they record. Our responsibility is to put ourselves under the text as obedient doers, never standing above the text as obstinate disciples.

Each Gospel Is One of a Kind

The Gospels are narratives, and they are narrative biographies. They tell the story of the man, Christ Jesus. However, these biographies are different than we might expect. For example, a modern biography would be very keen on the chronology of events. It would also notice how these events merge with the events that were going on in the world during their time: Alexander and the Plutonic wars; Lincoln and the American Civil War; Martin Luther King and civil rights. The individual and the factors that they influenced in a chronological fashion are synonymous. You would expect the same in the Gospels. And, in fact, we do have some specific historical references in the Gospels, especially in Luke 2:1, as well as the numerous accounts of Paul's interaction with government officials in Acts. However, we have surprisingly little information. In fact, instead of a historical setting, the writers are often more concerned with other aspects of the biblical setting. They are concerned with demonstrating how the life and times of Jesus Christ are a direct fulfillment of prophecy. So, instead of setting the stage with the current political scene, Matthew begins with a long Jewish genealogy. And this is not just any genealogy. It is very selective to show a relationship between King David and Christ. This raises some questions. Why include a genealogy at all? Why select a certain way to tell the genealogies and not just list all the people in them?

The answer is that Matthew is not simply concerned with external people or strict chronology because he has a certain point to make.[4] He is not relaying life and times; he is answering a specific question: Is this Jesus, Son of Mary, the Messiah? As we will discuss later, his choice of this question to answer shapes the way that he tells his narrative.

---

4. It is important to note that this arrangement was a normal way to approach biography in the time of Christ.

Perhaps it is best to describe these Gospels as Christological biographies.[5] They are biographies, yes. But they are biographies that explain who Christ is. Since the entire concept of a "Christ" figure is welded from Jewish sacred literature and concepts, it stands to reason that the Gospel writers would be concerned with telling us that this Jesus was in fact fulfilling all that was previously said about him. These are indeed Christological biographies.[6] In other words, these biographies are written to show how Christ fits as the central figure in all of salvation history. We should always ask this question of the Gospel texts: "What is this saying about the Christ?" As we will see, this question, especially in Matthew, will help us understand the text. So in this way, the Gospels are their own unique genre. They are like nothing else in all of literature. But there is another feature that makes these Gospels unique: the tension of narrative, theology, and history.

The tension. The Gospels appear to be narrative, and that they are. But as we established, they are not just any type of narrative: They are Christological narratives. They are narrative, so they are story. They are narratives that are actual accounts, so they are history. But they are narratives that communicate profound spiritual truths, so they are theology. We might tend to think that the genre of narrative is not a good medium for teaching theology. Have you heard about the novelist who loved to give tight, didactic, boring lectures? Neither have I. It seems that the very thing that would make a novelist great is his or her ability to tell a story. However, as Christological biographies, the Gospels are all three: theological, historical, and narrative. The narratives are God's chosen means to communicates theology. The seeming tension between narrative and theology may be in our minds, but this is God's chosen means to communicate.

The Gospels are four of a kind. God entrusted the transmission of the Gospels into the hands of four men. This fact produces four different Gospel accounts. The Gospel accounts do not have disparate facts; however, they do have four different ways of telling the same story.[7] There is much that can be said about this, but let's discuss three things specifically related to preaching.

Each Gospel Has a Unique Purpose

The author of each Gospel has a unique purpose. This purpose can be either explicit or implicit. Think of John's explicit purpose for why he wrote his Gospel: so that his readers might "believe that Jesus is the Christ, the Son of God; and that by believing you may have life in His name" (20:31). Everything John includes is moving the reader closer to believing that Jesus really is the Christ. Luke has a similarly explicit purpose statement. He wants to write on things in consecutive order so that his recipient, Theophilus, "may have certainty concerning the things you have been

---

5. The emphasis is on the biography and in much of the story the Christology, we can surmise, is assumed by the early Christian audience who would be reading them. This is why issues such as, for example, the pre-existent nature of Christ is explicit in John but implicit in the Synoptics. See Simon J. Gathercole, *The Pre-existent Son: Recovering the Christologies of Mathew, Mark and Luke* (Grand Rapids: Eerdmans, 2006).

6. See Andreas J. Köstenberger and Richard D. Patterson, *Invitation to Biblical Interpretation: Exploring the Hermeneutical Triad of History, Literature, and Theology* (Grand Rapids: Kregel, 2011).

7. Ibid., 374–75.

taught" (1:4). Accordingly, Luke includes more details in his story, and he does it in a way to affirm that Jesus is in fact who the disciples claimed that he was.

Mark's Gospel does not have such an explicit thesis statement, but it is no less clear that he wants the reader to understand that the kingdom has come (1:15), and that Jesus has power over all things, as seen from the progression of stories that illustrate his power. Matthew as well has an implicit, and not explicit, thesis. However, it seems clear that Matthew, through his multiple references to Old Testament prophets, wants the reader to understand that Jesus is in fact the Davidic Messiah. So as we read these texts, we ask how this section we are reading contributes to the overall theme of the book. There is meaning on that macro-structural level that influences our micro-exposition.

Each of the Gospels has, as David Jackman has stated, a melodic line.[8] That is, they have many different stories, but like a song, there is a melody that is woven through the entire Gospel. When you identify the melodic line, you will be able to hear it in the individual Gospel stories.

They Each Have a Unique Structure

When we think of structure, we often think of an outline of a Gospel. Outlines can be helpful for understanding, but not so much for preaching. Think about the following structures and how they each are building from a theme in the book. Jackman helps us understand this with his outlines that demonstrate how the writers developed the melodic line in their respective books. The following outlines are from his work.[9]

Matthew[10]

There are five major teaching blocks in Matthew, all with the theme of the kingdom. Matthew's primary theme is life in the kingdom. Look at how he shows Jesus' development of the theme of the kingdom.

Jesus the Teacher of the Kingdom

Matthew 5:1–7:29	manifesto of the kingdom
Matthew 10:1–11:1	mission of the kingdom
Matthew 13:1–53	nature of the kingdom
Matthew 18:1–19:1	lifestyle of the kingdom
Matthew 24:1–26:1	consummation of the kingdom

Of course the idea of the kingdom was the idea that the Messiah would come to rule and be the King of the kingdom. Thus, in order to accomplish this goal, Matthew uses more Old Testament quotations, references, and allusions than any other Gospel writer.

---

8. David Jackman, *Preaching and Teaching New Testament: Gospels, Letters, Acts and Revelation* (London: The Proclamation Trust, 2008) [DVD].

9. Ibid. What these structures do not consider is that there are episodic connections within the stories themselves. These connections point to the author's main theme. See Wirada, *Interpreting Gospel Narratives*, 186–93.

10. Craig L. Blomberg sees the structure of Matthew built on the five main sermons of Christ, bookended with the infancy and the resurrection. See his helpful chart in *Jesus and the Gospels: An Introduction and Survey* (Nashville: B&H Academic, 2009), 144.

The Old Testament Idea of Christ in Matthew:

Matthew 1:22–23	Matthew 8:17
Matthew 2:5–6	Matthew 11:10
Matthew 2:15	Matthew 12:17–21
Matthew 2:17–18	Matthew 13:14–15
Matthew 2:23	Matthew 17:10–13
Matthew 3:1–3	Matthew 21:4–5
Matthew 4:1–11	Matthew 27:9–10
Matthew 4:14–16	

Mark

Mark's Gospel is more condensed. Many of the stories, parables, and teachings of Matthew are found in Mark, but in a shorter, more condensed way. Mark built his book around two distinct halves.

First Half—Who Is This Jesus?

Authority.

Mark 1:17–20	over disciples
Mark 1:25–28	over evil spirits
Mark 1:29–34	over diseases
Mark 2:1–12	over sin
Mark 2:23–28	in interpreting God's law
Mark 4:35–41	over a storm / nature
Mark 5:35–43	over death

Debates.

Mark 1:27	in the synagogues
Mark 4:41	among the disciples
Mark 5:42	with the crowds

Answers.

Mark 2:7	a blasphemer
Mark 3:22	possessed
Mark 6:14–15	a resurrected prophet
Mark 6:3	a carpenter
Mark 1:24; 5:7	"the Holy One of God"

Second Half—What Sort of Christ?

Mark 8:31	
Mark 9:31	crucifixion and resurrection
Mark 10:33–34	

Climax of the Gospel.[11]

"And when the centurion, who stood there in front of Jesus, heard his cry and saw how he died, he said, 'Surely this man was the Son of God!'" (Mark 15:39).

Luke

Luke is concerned with Jesus as Savior. Thus, Luke has more information about those for whom Christ came to save, and the lost themselves, than found in any other Gospel.

Jesus the Savior

Luke 1:31, 47, 69, 71, 77
Luke 2:11, 30
Luke 8:48
Luke 7:50
Luke 8:12

In the synagogue sermon at Nazareth (Luke 4)—Jesus defines his fulfill-ment ministry in terms of salvation.

John

John's purpose is perhaps the most explicit of all the Gospel writers. In John 20:31 he writes, "But these are written that you may believe that Jesus is the Christ, the Son of God, and that by believing you may have life in his name." In order to accomplish this goal, he includes many signs that are intended to invoke faith in the Messiah. He also has a prologue that is perhaps the most expositionally dense of all the Gospels.

Structure[12]

Seven Signs.
1. Jesus changes water to wine. (John 2:1–11)
2. Jesus heals the official's son. (John 4:46–51)
3. Healing at the pool of Bethesda. (John 5:1–9)
4. Feeding of the five thousand. (John 6:1–14)
5. Walking on the water. (John 6:16–21)
6. Healing of man born blind. (John 9:1–7)
7. Raising of Lazarus. (John 11:1–46)

Seven "I Am" Sayings.
1. "I am the bread of life." (John 6:35)
2. "I am the light of the world." (John 8:12)

---

11. Blomberg sees Mark as two halves: Jesus' Ministry and Jesus' Passion. The center of the halves is 8:30–31: "And he strictly charged them to tell no one about him. And he began to teach them that the Son of Man must suffer many things and be rejected by the elders and the chief priests and the scribes and be killed, and after three days rise again." Blomberg, *Jesus*, 144.

12. Blomberg understands John this way: Intro (1) and Resurrection (20–21) are bookends. The two halves of the book are the Seven Signs and Seven Discourses 1–11 followed by the Passion 12–19. Ibid., 144.

3. "I am the gate." (John 10:9)
4. "I am the good shepherd." (John 10:11)
5. "I am the resurrection and the life." (John 11:25)
6. "I am the way and the truth and the life." (John 14:6)
7. "I am the true vine." (John 15:1)

John's Prologue.
1:1   "In the beginning was the Word, and the Word was with God, and the Word was God."
1:14a "The Word became flesh and made his dwelling among us . . ."
1:17   "For the law was given through Moses; grace and truth came through Jesus Christ."

Jesus Himself Is the Focus of All He Claims.
John 3:31–32; John 5:24
John 8:42; John 12:49
John 14:9

Jesus' Identity

John 2:1–11

This, the first of the miraculous signs, Jesus performed at Cana in Galilee. He thus revealed his glory, and his disciples put their faith in him. (John 2:11)

John 12:32–33

"'But I, when I am lifted up from the earth, will draw all men to myself.' He said this to show the kind of death he was going to die."

Two Major Sections
Chapters 1–12   Jesus' ministry
                 Revelation of the Word to the world
Chapters 13–21   Jesus' death and resurrection
                 Lifting up of the Word for the world

Acts
According to Polhill, Acts has two main divisions the first being the work of the Jerusalem church (1–12) and the second being the journey and work of Paul (13–28) with subdivisions under each. "In the Jerusalem portion chaps. 1–5 treat the early church in Jerusalem; chaps 6–12, the outreach beyond Jerusalem. In the Pauline portion 13:1–21:16 relates the three main missions of Paul; 21:27–28:31 deals with Paul's defense of his ministry."[13] What is helpful in preaching the book of Acts is its choronological flow.

---

13. John B. Polhill, *Acts,* New American Commentary (Nashville: B&H, 1992), 72.

You see the gospel moving out from the epicenter of Jerusalem to all the rest of the world, and then coming back toward Jerusalem.

From the above structures it becomes clear that while there is much material in the Gospels that is the same, each of the Gospel writers develop their material in a unique way.

The Stories Are Representative and Not Exhaustive

Because of these unique purposes, the material in the Gospels is selective. There is much more that could be told about Christ. John ended his Gospel by saying that if all the works of Jesus were transcribed in books, the world could not contain them (John 21:25). The Gospels, therefore, represent a small cross section of the words that Jesus said. Every miracle our Lord performed is not recorded. Nor is every reaction to a scribe, every moment of compassion to one in need, or every act of seeking the lost sheep. We do not have an itinerary of each day in a journal type format, nor a detailed biography. If John is trying to get us to feel the weight of his hyperbole, we can say that at best we have a small sampling.

Our reaction to this is to wonder what details were left out. But that is nonsense, the answer to which would only lead to useless speculation. It is far better to focus on what was included. However, while the author does not give us a personal journal entry that spells out his motivation behind each passage, he does give us bread crumbs. Not to follow that trail would be unwise.

The Gospels/Acts Include Multiple Genres

One of the most fascinating literary features about the Gospels is that they each contain multiple genres. This is because, as we saw earlier, while the book of Acts reads like a narrative of the church and shares much in common with the literary strategies of the Gospels, the Gospels are their own type of genre. This unique genre has been referred to as Christological biography.[14] Think about what it would encompass in order to get a big picture of the life of Christ. Imagine what it would take to describe the events of Christ's life if you had witnessed them. First you would need some purely expositional literature. This is the type of literature that explains the doctrine of the very fact that there is an incarnate God; for an example, see John 1:1–5.

Then, of course, the dominant genre would be narrative. You would need to tell the stories that comprised the life of Christ, beginning with his birth and childhood, and then going all the way to his ascension and the commissioning of the disciples. This narrative would demand sub-genres, such as dialogue with others, as well as pure narration, where you had to fill in the gaps with what was going on.

And of course you would have to include the teaching of Christ. The teaching of Christ often consists of short pithy statements, such as his words to the Pharisees when they demanded a sign from heaven (Matt 16:1–4; Mark 8:11–13), as well as longer sermons, such as the Sermon on the Mount (Matt 5–7). Among his teaching we find the genre of parables. The parables consume much of the teaching of Christ,

---

14. Sidney Greidanus, *The Modern Preacher and the Ancient Text: Interpreting and Preaching Biblical Literature* (Grand Rapids: Eerdmans, 1988).

but because of their uniqueness they are considered their own genre and will be discussed at length in another chapter.[15]

So, the Gospels are narrative, but they are also more. They are a biography, but a unique type of biography at that. In order to accomplish the goal of communicating all that Christ did and said, multiple genres had to be used. Let's discuss them briefly.

Narrative[16]

Character development. The Gospel writers will use clues to show us how a character in the story develops. We know something about the character of Zaccheaus beyond his stature. Clearly he was curious enough to climb a tree to see Jesus; he was open enough to welcome him into his home; and he was repentant enough to develop a plan to sell his possessions. However, the most prominent way we understand character development is from the dialogue.

Dialogue. From the dialogue between the characters, we learn exactly what it is that the Gospel writers want us to learn from what Jesus is teaching. We also understand a little more of how we can identify with the characters Jesus is teaching. Think about Jesus' interaction with the woman at the well in John 4. We have a sense of Jesus' way with people: he demonstrates compassion by stopping to talk (v. 4), he is willing to break down cultural barriers to reach her (vv. 7–9), he is incredibly direct (v. 18), and he ultimately presses her to true worship (vv. 21–26). The woman is incredulous that he would stop (v. 9), knows the party line of her culture (vv. 19–20), is desperately thirsty spiritually (v. 15), and ultimately responds in joy when she understands who Jesus really is (v. 39). We know all of this from the dialogue.

Most importantly, from the dialogue we understand how Jesus responds in certain situations. We learn as much from his strategy in this interaction as we do from his explicit teaching. We know how he welcomed people, challenged people, what he thought of unrighteousness, the law, and the disciples' role within civil government. So when looking at dialogue, our first question is not one of identification: "How am I like this?" Rather it is a question of understanding: "What is the Gospel writer trying to communicate about Jesus?" Once we answer the second question, we will understand how to frame the first question when we preach.

Narration. In order to move the story along, the Gospel writers, as well as Luke in Acts, will include certain amounts of narration. This is most dominant in Acts. For example, Acts 15 contains the following words: "Some men came down from Judea . . ." (v. 1), "The apostles and the elders came together to look at this matter . . ." (v. 6), and "All the people kept silent . . . after they had stopped speaking James answered . . ." (vv. 12–13). This is pure narration, and it is included to give pace and meaning to the flow of events. This is basic, but it is vitally important. The narration provides the linguistic links in the chain of events. The narration is also

---

15. See Amos Wilder, *Early Christian Rhetoric: The Language of the Gospel* (Peabody, MA: Hendricksen, 1964), 69–88.

16. Leland Ryken notes that there are several subtypes of narrative in the Gospels: Annunciations and Nativity Stories, Calling or Vocation Stories, Recognition Stories, Witness Stories, Encounter Stories, Conflict or Controversy Stories, Pronouncement Stories, Miracle Stories, Passion Stories, and Hybrid Stories. See Leland Ryken, *Words of Delight: A Literary Introduction to the Bible* (Grand Rapids: Baker, 1987), 377–82.

the place where we see most explicitly how the Gospel writers felt we should understand these events. So it is critical we understand narration. The Gospel writers were inspired by God to write these words in this way. Thus, the reason why they wrote these words in these ways—including some things and excluding others—is important for our understanding of the text. If a writer pauses to provide a lot of detail (like the crowds following Jesus in Luke 14:25 or the physicality of the healed leper in Luke 17:15), we observe that and communicate it. If a writer does not provide detail to things we would really want to know (like what happened between the triumphal entry and the temple cleansing in Luke 19:44–45), we can assume the detail is not critical to this writer's interpretation of the story and we can move along. Therefore the question is now, Why did he exclude that detail? Where else does he want the reader to focus attention? The details are important—even the omitted details. That is, move along while refusing the temptation to supply details where the inspired Gospel writer did not give any.

Subplot. In all of this, it is important to remember that the plot to every smaller story in a Gospel is a subplot that pitches to the larger plot of the book. It may not be obvious at first. This is because stories are often grouped with other stories, and those groups as a whole pitch to the larger story of the book. We will discuss this more below when we examine the individual author's intentions for the book.

Parables

The parables in the Gospels are more than fascinating. The genre of parable will be dealt with in the next chapter, as they demand a different homiletic approach.

Longer Discourse

Within the Gospels there are some passages that include some longer teachings of Christ. Consider the following:

> The Sermon on the Mount in Matthew 5–7
> The Sermon on the Plain in Luke 6:20–49
> The Eight Parables in Matthew 13
> The Parabolic Teaching of Mark 4:1–34
> The Kingdom Parables in Matthew 18
> The Five Parables on Lostness in Luke 15–16
> The Instruction and High Priestly Prayer in John 14–17
> The End Time Parables in Matthew 23–25
> The Warnings of Luke 12

Jesus is always teaching. And every narrative is used for the purpose of our instruction, edification, and exhortation. However, these are only a sampling of some passages that include longer discourses. These discourses have unique features. Let's look at two of them.

First, these discourses will often include rhetorical markers. These rhetorical markers help us understand how the discourse is bookended. Think about the Sermon on the Mount. It begins with Jesus seeing the crowds (5:1), and then after it is concluded the crowds were amazed (7:28). However we interpret the information in the Sermon, the context is important to Matthew. He wants us to think about this in terms of the needs and the response of the crowd. Similarly, like rhetorical markers, each of the discourses has a unique audience. Often the notation of the audience *is* a rhetorical marker. For example, the five parables of Luke 15 and 16 begin in 15:1 with, "Now the tax collectors and sinners were drawing near to him," and the following parables address how Jesus feels about sinners compared with the Pharisees. In Matthew 13, Jesus teaches eight parables. Four of them are for the crowd mentioned in verse 1, and four are for the disciples mentioned in verse 10. Again, the mention of the audience is a rhetorical clue as to the interpretation.

Second, the long discourses will have one central theme. This theme may be nuanced differently according to which Gospel writer is recording the events. Why this is the case will be discussed below, but for now, it is sufficient to know that the arrangement of similar material may vary from Gospel to Gospel. This should not be disconcerting, for in fact it is helpful. The individual arrangement allows us to understand more clearly what each Gospel writer was trying to accomplish in his writing. However, while there is one central theme, it may encompass several different issues. The High Priestly Prayer covers many issues, but the essence of the prayer is found in John 17:21.[17] Everything that is prayed reflects the fact that the disciples are in Christ and that Christ and the Father are one. The visible unity of the disciples pitches to the goal of John's Gospel: that all would see this unity and believe in Jesus.[18]

Let's think about these two features using the long discourse of Matthew 13. First, note the rhetorical markers. Jesus begins by teaching many things in parables (13:3). Then after he finished the parables, he departed (13:53). So from this we deduce that Matthew wants us to see 13:3–52 as one long discourse. Now note the audience. Jesus begins by speaking to the crowds, but this discourse has multiple audiences. At times you have the sense that he is speaking to the whole crowd (v. 3), at other times to the disciples directly (v. 36), and at other times to the disciples with the crowds listening in (v. 10).

Within this discourse, every parable that Jesus teaches is about the kingdom. That is clearly the ". He covers many different issues about the kingdom, including who will be in the kingdom, what to do about the enemies of the kingdom, and how to respond when we find the kingdom. So there are many issues, but the one central theme is obvious.

However, there is also another important clue as to the theme. The first parable, the parable of the Soils, is about understanding. Those who are true believers hear and understand the word. Understanding is not merely intellectual assent; rather, it is understanding that leads to action. After all, the second and third soils know enough to have an initial response. What they don't have is the type of understanding that causes them to endure and bear fruit. They don't have true understanding because they have hard hearts. Jesus explains this parable, finishes telling the rest of his parables, gets to the end, and then turns to his disciples and asks, "Do you understand?" (v. 51). Their answer is critical. If they do not understand they cannot respond and obey. They affirm that they do understand, so he tells them a parable explaining that with this understanding they should be able to teach others from their storehouse of

17. "That they may all be one, just as you, Father, are in me, and I in you, that they also may be in us, so that the world may believe that you have sent me" (John 17:21).
18. See John 13:35 and 20:31.

knowledge (v. 52). So again, all the parables in Matthew 13 are about the kingdom and call the hearer to truly listen (v. 9) and understand.

Subgenres: Genealogies

The genealogies in Luke 3:23–37 and Matthew 1:1–17 have unique purposes based on the intentions of the author. However, they both demonstrate that Jesus is the Davidic King just as had been promised by the Old Testament. The preacher has to decide how to approach these texts: Should they constitute an entire sermon or be preached with the surrounding narrative? Like always, there is an exegetical concern and a pastoral concern. If the genealogies are preached as an entire sermon, the critical thing to remember is that they are a part of the narrative. In Luke they are placed in a way that sets up Jesus' ministry. In Matthew they set up the entire book by showing that Jesus is the Davidic King. Therefore, the genealogies are important and should not be neglected. And, they should be preached in the context of the entire narrative.

The Gospels Are Heavily Intertextual

We often forget that the Gospel writers are heavily inter-textual, meaning they are dependent on the Old Testament. Therefore, to understand the meaning of a text, we must ask if there are allusions to an Old Testament text in the Gospel.

Why Did the Gospel Writers Rely So Heavily on the Old Testament?

The short answer is that Jesus led them to this. After Jesus had resurrected he pulled up alongside some disciples who were walking on the road to Emmaus. Luke records the events. After a bizarre encounter where they do not recognize him, he finally opens their eyes and "Then, beginning with Moses and with all the prophets, He explained to them the things concerning Himself in all the Scriptures" (Luke 24:27). And later, with a larger audience of disciples, "He opened their minds to understand the Scriptures" (Luke 24:45). Think of what this means. First, this means that the Gospels are the interpretive key to the entire Bible. The Gospels explain Jesus, who explains the Old Testament. Acts–Jude contain the words and works of those who followed Christ, and Revelation is the story of Christ coming back. The Gospels are the key, the hinge, the fulcrum by which hope is leveraged into reality.

Secondly, this means that the apostolic tradition—the apostles' teaching—was certainly laced with this interpretation of Scripture. Peter, who was present when Jesus taught this, in Acts 2:14–36 preached the first Christian sermon about Christ from Joel 2, Psalm 16, and Psalm 110. The first Christian sermon was an explanation of Jesus from the Old Testament! So if this was the immediate tradition, then we can assume that years later, when the Gospels were written, this teaching was firmly established in the church. It is right to assume that when the Gospel writers wrote, they wrote under the influence of the teaching of this hermeneutic. They are explaining to us the Jesus that they experienced and were using the language of the Old Testament to do so. How exciting!

Have you ever wondered why Jesus referred to John the Baptist as the greatest born among women? Think about this passage:

> Truly, I say to you, among those born of women there has arisen no one greater than John the Baptist. Yet the one who is least in the kingdom of heaven is greater than he. From the days of John the Baptist until now the kingdom of heaven has suffered violence, and the violent take it by force. For all the Prophets and the Law prophesied until John, and if you are willing to accept it, he is Elijah who is to come. He who has ears to hear, let him hear. (Matt 11:11–15)

This is a provocative statement considering all who were ever born. However, John's greatness has more to do with his chronological position than his qualification. The words and works of Moses and Elijah—all of the prophets and the law—find their fulfillment in Christ. John is the final prophet. He is the one to put a capstone on all the Old Testament prophets. He is even Elijah who will precede the Messiah. And so, he is the greatest. He is in the position to bring it all to fulfillment. The issue is not greatest by superiority, but greatest by proximity. He is the closest to Jesus! Again, the Gospels are the turning point of the entire Scripture.

The Gospels Call for Belief

The call for belief is most explicit in John 20:31, "these are written so that you may believe that Jesus is the Christ, the Son of God, and that by believing you may have life in his name." However, all of the Gospels are calling one to accept that Jesus is the Messiah. The whole tenor of the narratives is apologetic in nature. They are leading us to believe.

COMMUNICATION: RECAPTURING THE VOICE OF THE GOSPELS

Timing Is Everything

Since the Gospels are primarily narrative, the preacher will spend a great deal of time telling stories. *All that has been said in the chapter on Old Testament Narrative about using a structure of scenes instead of a structure of points applies here.* Thus, with the rarest of exceptions, the preacher should refuse the temptation to give away the point of a story before the story is told. This may seem like an odd practice since we assume that our people know the stories already. However, it's more probable the people to whom we preach don't truly know the stories, even if they think they do. So, when you are telling the story of the rich young ruler, you must tease out the story. Allow the people to feel the self-righteousness of his posture, to see the gentle way Jesus, knowing everything, sets him up to see his own heart. Jesus is not impressed with his self-righteousness, but gives him a chance to change. Jesus always gives hope for the self-righteous. At this point in the telling of the story, there should be a pause. This is a great opportunity for the rich young ruler to repent. And it is a great opportunity for us to repent of our own self-righteousness. The listeners should feel their own responsibility in the rebuke of Jesus. Then, similarly, they should feel the weight of the rich young ruler's refusal when, in stone cold rejection, he turns to his money and away from Jesus. Again, don't give away the point of the story at the beginning. Allow the text to slowly simmer to a boil.

Variety Is Essential

Narrative is the primary genre in a Gospel. But as we have seen, there are also many types of internal genres as well as many features to the genre of narrative itself. This means that we can have variety in our sermon structure. If you are preaching through Matthew, you will begin with a genealogy, move quickly to some challenging narratives—including the temptation narrative, and then on to the Sermon on the Mount. Each of these texts has a different structure, and so should your sermons.

Also, the length of the text preached may vary. There is wisdom in preaching the whole genealogy in Matthew, all 17 verses. Yet when you come to chapter 5 you could preach one beatitude per sermon. So the sermon structure will vary. This is liberating and life-giving—both to the preacher and his people—because it keeps us fresh and allows for variety in presentation.

Fill the Screen

However, one of the temptations in taking a smaller text is that we neglect to tie it to the broader themes around it. Remember, every conversation, or healing, or teaching, is a part of a narrative. That narrative is a part of a larger group of narratives, and that group of narratives comprises the entire point that the Gospel writer wants to make. If we do not understand this, we can isolate individual stories and treat them as if they are individual lessons—like Aesop's fables. However, each story is a subplot within the main plot of the larger story. That is where it draws its meaning. There is meaning both in the internal structure of a smaller text, and meaning in the external structure of the Gospel narrative.

Understanding this dynamic of the Gospels is more of a science. But knowing when to preach it is more of an art. What I mean by this is the discipline of understanding a text in its context will allow the preacher to understand the broader themes of Scripture. Knowing that each story in a narrative text points to a larger theme does not mean that we identify that theme the same way in each sermon. For example, if I am preaching through Luke, every time I see Jesus moving toward Jerusalem, this is a good opportunity to teach our people that Luke understands these events as moving Christ further down the road to his sacrifice. This, in a sense, is the ultimate "point" of every narrative. Now, when you are preaching in the travel narrative, say the parable of the Shrewd Steward in Luke 16:1–13, you may bring that point out. It certainly fits in with the story. However, you may have just addressed this fact in a previous sermon on the Prodigal Son, so it is not necessary. The principle is that we pan out every once in a while to let people see where this individual narrative fits into the larger picture. It is essential that we do this. People will not see the big picture without it. When to do this, how often, and how long, is a pastoral concern dependent on your preaching context.

Embrace the Tension

Think about the impact of the statement we just made. In each text we preach from a Gospel there is a historical element—a record of what has really happened. There is a theological element—a truth that is to be clearly grasped. There is a narrative element—a story that is to be told. Preaching a Gospel means embracing this tension.

We must be story tellers—but not just story tellers. The temptation in the Gospels is to pull up a bar stool, put our hands on our knees, and just tell the story. We weave together the provocative details of the narratives, pepper them with some contemporary parallels, and send everyone home amused but unchanged. However, we cannot do this. Yes, the Gospels are narratives, but to preach the provocative story without the theology behind it implies that they are *only* narratives. Sure, some have treated the Gospels as only theological lessons, but to react with a sermon that is only a story is to commit the same sin of imbalance. The thrust of doing narrative preaching exclusively can be a reaction that equally misrepresents the text.

We must teach theology—but the theology of the narrative. Skipping straight to teaching theology without grounding it in the theology of the narrative is another temptation. We see what Jesus is doing, and we want to explain it in light of what the Bible teaches about his activity. And this is what we must do. However, it is possible to take a beautiful narrative and re-present it as a theological lecture. If we want to teach about Jesus' power over the demonic world from Mark 5, or Jesus' understanding of lostness from Luke 15, the material to do exactly that is there. However, each of these doctrines is embedded in a story. Perhaps we think that the nature of teaching is fact driven, or "point" driven. Thus, we need to find the points that are being made. There are points of doctrine to extract, but certainly that is not what the Gospel writers had in mind. They are trying to build one big point from the story. They are trying to connect that point as a subplot to the episodes that surround the story. And they are trying to use all of it to advance the point of the book. At the end of the day, if our sermon on a narrative sounds more like a lecture than a story— perhaps we have missed something in the re-presentation of it.

We must reconstruct the history—but only in service of the story. So before us, we have a text. It is loaded historically, and it is loaded culturally. When we understand the relationship between Pilate and Herod, then we can understand the Passion Narrative more fully (Luke 23). When we understand the giving practices in the temple, the story of the widow with her one mite becomes so much more real (Mark 12:41–44). It would be difficult to understand the power of the foot-washing narrative without an understanding of this custom (John 13:5–11). So, there is meaning that can be missed if we do not understand the historical-cultural context in which the narrative is embedded. However, remember that this culture and history is serving the overall point that the writer wants to make, just as is the narrative and the theology. The temptation for some is to spend so much time in the historical reconstruction of events, or the cultural background, that we miss the point of the text. The cultural background is there, it is interesting, and sometimes it is essential to identify. However, remember that everything we say in the pulpit, we say to the exclusion of something else. While we are talking about the background of the text, we can do so to the exclusion of the text itself. We are not preaching the event, but the text. So the answer to the question of how much background material to bring in is, "Only enough to carry the story line along." Much more than that may be interesting, but not useful. And, it may even be a distraction.

Before we belabor this point too much, let's use a quick example: the nativity narrative of Luke 2:1–21. If we were inclined to reconstruct the history and culture, we might spend a lot of time on the ranching patterns of shepherds, the conditions of the inns, or the governmental arrangement of the time. All of these details are there, and all of these details are there for a reason: to help carry the story along. However, perhaps as with no other text, our curiosity about these things can cause us to miss the point of the story.

Another approach would be to ignore the culture and just deal with the story. A sermon such as this would speculate deeply about verse 19 and what exactly Mary treasured in her heart, the irony of a king in a stable, the fear of the shepherds, and the climactic scene when they see the baby Jesus. The narrative is as rich as any, but there are some major theological clues that need to be mined out.

Why is it that Jesus was born in Bethlehem? Why is it that the angels said what they did? What relationship do the angels' words have to other angelic songs of praise such as Revelation 4–5? How could God incarnate himself as a man? These are huge theological questions. They are questions that are, at least partially, answered in the narrative. However, the narrative itself must not be neglected. Presentation is important. And so is re-presentation. Therefore, we answer these questions in the flow of the story, while rejecting the temptation to force a lifeless didactic outline on a beautiful narrative.

Remember the Main Character

There is the ever-present desire to identify with the characters of the story.[19] We feel the joy of justice when the Pharisees are rebuked; we feel the joy of forgiveness when sinners are forgiven; and we at least sympathize with a formerly spotted leper who now has spotless skin. These characters draw us into the story, and they should. Every preacher instinctively knows the power of this. We begin to describe a character only to see the listeners' heads come up. They want to identify with what is going on in the story. Knowing that these are Christological biographies helps us know what to do with the characters when we preach. Each of the characters is telling us something about the main character—Jesus. This is their function in every narrative. Identification with the characters is possible, but over-identification is also possible.[20]

In Mark 2 Jesus heals a paralytic who is lowered through a roof. It is simply an amazing narrative. It has everything—suspense, action, and verbal slams on the religious sect. There is so much to preach here. However, the temptation exists to preach this text as strategies for getting people to Christ—the friends were persistent, they were insistent, and they loved. There is a temptation to preach from the perspective of the healed man—he thought he needed to walk, but he really needed his sins forgiven. And of course from the Pharisees, who are so self-righteous they do not realize that Jesus can forgive sins. However, this text has a central character in Christ. Beasley-Murray notes,

> Observe, however, the moral of the narrative. Its center of
> interest is not the healing as such, but the saying, "The Son of
> Man has power on earth to forgive sins." Contrary to the notions

---

19. See Timothy Wirada, "Are Gospel Writers Interested in Individual Characters?" in *Interpreting Gospel Narratives: Scenes, People, and Theology* (Nashville: B&H, 2010).
20. Sidney Greidanus, *The Modern Preacher*.

of any crass observers present, the greater act of power is not the healing of paralysis but the miracle of forgiveness.[21]

All of this and more are things with which we can identify. However, what protects us from seeing this simply from man's perspective is the practice of panning out from this story to see what is around it. We see that the same title for Jesus in Mark 2:10 is used in 2:28 when he says the "Son of Man" is Lord over the Sabbath. Clearly this title has implications for Christ's power over all things—in this case, sin and the law. If we pan out further we see in the Gospels that this was Jesus' favorite reference for himself. But this reference is not just Jesus' humble way of identifying with humanity. If we pan out to the level of the canon we see that this title must be an allusion to Daniel 7:13–14, where the "Son of Man" is given all power and authority over everything!

So, yes, there is human interest here. However, it is in service of the real story of the real character, Jesus Christ, the Messiah who has all power. So when our people sing the closing song and gravitate back to their real worlds, of course we want them to have in their grasp that Jesus understands and identifies with them. But we must go beyond that. My brother can identify with my sins, but he can't do anything about them. Our people need to understand that Jesus, the Son of Man, not only identifies with them, but he has all power to eradicate the eternal effects of their sin by forgiving them! That's a Jesus worth serving. So, brothers, preach the characters, but preach them in service of the main character, Jesus, the all-powerful Messiah.[22]

Mind the Gaps, But Don't Mine the Gaps

Since these are Christological biographies, they communicate amazing things. However, in order to do this they must leave some things out. The types of things that they leave out are also important. Why don't we know more about the birth of Christ? Why is the Passion Week difficult to reconcile among the Gospels? Why is there more than one Great Commission? Well, all of these things speak to the authors' purposes. Our temptation, of course, is to fill in the gaps. "In many cases readers will supply missing information easily, hardly noticing they are doing so."[23] If the text does not tell us how someone feels or what time something happened, we do not have to speculate. There are gaps in the Gospels, but these are gaps that do not need to be mined and filled in with imagination.

However, the gaps are there for a reason. So while we do not mine the gaps, we do mind them, meaning that the absence of information is just as telling as its presence. So we can acknowledge that the gaps are there and let them lead us to the larger purposes of the author.

Preach the Text in Front of You

The Gospels are unique in that the first three contain much duplicate material. For this reason the Gospels of Matthew, Mark, and Luke are often called the Synoptic

---

21. George R. Beasley-Murray, *Preaching the Gospels from the Gospels* (Peabody, MA: Hendrickson, 1996), 18.

22. "Reduced to its essence, exegesis is simply a matter of carefully listening to what the apostles have said about Jesus." Wirada, "Are Gospel Writers Interested in Individual Characters?," 201.

23. Ibid., 38.

Gospels. They seem to share a common view. One would think that if you really wanted to explain what was going on in a text, you would find the answer by a composite of all the Gospel accounts. But this approach assumes we are preaching a story or an event. We are not. We are not preaching a story; we are preaching a text. My responsibility is to say what the text says, the way the text says it. Therefore, I am not asking the question of the text, "What happened?" More specifically I am asking the question, "What does this writer want me to understand about what happened?" The difference is critical.

So preach the text in front of you. You are not under a tertiary responsibility to bring in what another Synoptic said about the event. However, there are times when you compare texts.

Compare and Contrast the Gospel Text

This may seem contradictory to what was said above, but there is a reason to compare Synoptic Gospels. The first reason is that when we compare Synoptic Gospels we can understand exactly what makes the one we are preaching unique. In other words, we do not compare so that we can preach a composite of the events; we compare because it helps us understand what is unique about the certain text we are preaching. For example, in the Sermon on the Mount in Matthew 5:3, Jesus begins with, "Blessed are the poor in spirit . . ." We would interpret this to mean that those who understand their sin, those who are broken over it, are blessed with the initial requirement to enter the kingdom. However, in the Sermon on the Plain in Luke 6:20, Luke has Jesus saying, "Blessed are the poor . . ." The implication of the statement is that those who are actually financially poor are blessed. Now, upon reading Jesus' words, we may be concerned as to which is correct.

What was actually said? We need to understand that the two are easily reconciled. The poor in spirit are broken and realize their problems keep them from what they want. This leads to mourning and meekness. If someone is poor financially, it causes the same problems. Their financial brokenness is a metaphor for spiritual brokenness. But again, this is not the issue. The question is, Why did Luke use those words? Part of the answer may be found in the fact that Luke has a keen eye for the marginalized. There is more about women and Gentiles in Luke than in any other Gospel. It would make perfect sense for Luke to say this.

The point is simply that when we interpret individual events, we should look first to the purposes of the author, before looking to reconcile the event with the other Gospel accounts.

Be Honest with What's Not There

If we approach a situation that the author has chosen not to resolve, then we are not under obligation to resolve it. We do not know how Jesus walked on water. We do not know how he turned the water into wine or multiplied the fish and loaves. If he wanted to communicate that to us, he could have. The temptation in these moments is to make something up, to try to scratch the itch of curiosity. But remember, our goal in preaching is to teach people how to read Scripture. When we grasp for a resolution that is not there, we teach our people to do the same.

Be Confident and Cautious

When we preach, we must preach with the conviction that the Word we are preaching is true. We must also never assume that all our people share the same conviction. Our tone, spirit, and attitude toward the text will teach people their hermeneutic.

We Must Call Others to Respond

When preaching a Gospel, a gospel appeal is always appropriate. In fact, I'm of the conviction that the gospel should be in every sermon. That is a discussion for another time. However, it would be easy to argue that a sermon from the Gospels should appeal to the gospel. This can be done implicitly or it can be done explicitly. But at some point in the sermon, we must call others to respond to Christ in faith with brokenness and repentance.

We Must Depend on the Old Testament

Since the Gospels are dependent on the Old Testament, our strategy is simple: we want to go to their source, understand it, and then show it in the sermon. If Matthew wants us to understand Jesus as the One who will shepherd God's people, Israel (Matt 2:6), as a quotation from Micah 5:2, and if he wants to carry that theme throughout his Gospel (see Matt 9:36; 18:12–14; 26:31), then surely this is an Old Testament theme that is important for understanding Matthew's message. Matthew understood that the Messiah, Jesus Christ, was fulfilling all the prophecies predicted of him, for he is acting exactly like the true Shepherd of Israel. Therefore, to communicate the meaning of these texts we should point our people to these realities and help them understand how the first-century Jew would have thought about this. God inspired the text, which means this is how God wants us to think about God. The Gospel writers' dependence on the Old Testament is important.

STRUCTURING A SERMON FROM THE GOSPELS

1. Identify the Genre

As noted above, there are multiple structures in the Gospels. So, the first thing to do is identify the genre. Once this is done, the structure will become clear. Narrative and expositional types of structure are covered in their respective chapters. The example, therefore, will focus on a subgenre in the Gospels, the discourses or sermons.

Narrative Structure. If it is narrative, then identify the scenes and use the scene structure as the structure for the sermon. This will not always be clean. Often you will have three or four scenes, or two simple scenes followed by commentary. Parables have a clear narrative structure, but they will be discussed in the next chapter.

One of the unique features of Acts is the "We" Narratives. While there has been debate about this, the implication is that Luke is traveling with Paul. This heightens the drama and is something that can be brought out when preaching. This is a first hand account.[24]

---

24. Polhill, *Acts*, 24.

Expositional. There are a limited number of passages where there is direct discussion of a topic. If so, the same deductive structure used for an epistle will be good here.

Discourse. There are plenty of sermons in the Gospels. Sermons are also found in the book of Acts where 19 sermons or formal addresses are found.[25] As a preaching strategy, structure your sermon in the same way as the speaker structured his sermon. Structurally, this should be a natural progression just as the original speaker intended. The question arises about the intended audience. Namely, should you re-preach the sermon as it was originally preached, or preach a sermon about someone preaching a sermon? The answer of course is both. We need to re-present the sermon as it was presented to the original audience. However, in order for this to be recast for contemporary times, it is important to recognize how the original audience would have understood the message.[26]

There is a tremendous amount to be learned from these sermons. Note that the apostles practiced a homiletic that used Scripture to interpret the events they were experiencing.[27] As you preach this, you point this out to people. As they are hearing what the apostles are saying to them, they are also getting a sense of the same strategy. You are teaching them the apostolic hermeneutic. The Scripture is not becoming the Word of God to them; the Scripture is the Word of God. The apostles are operating under the assumption that God has in fact spoken.[28] So, we are trying to re-present the sermon to a new audience, while taking the occasion to point to the motives and ambitions of the original preacher.

In the example below, the sermon is structured around the three main divisions of Peter's sermon. The structure seems clear. I also tried to identify the main idea of the sermon and bring it to the surface so that the listener can see it. As to the tone, it is important to make the listeners feel like they are watching this sermon be preached to others. It is good to stop and say, "Watch what Peter is doing here." What this does is draw the listener in like a third party observer to what is going on. Then, you can make it clear that this is a message intended for them.

2. Watch for the Hybrid

Since the Gospels have so many genres, it is expected that a given text will have more than one genre represented. In fact, many texts are a combination of genres. In Matthew 13, Jesus teaches using eight parables, Matthew interjects some prophecy, Jesus annotates his own parables, and all of this is in a narrative framework. So where are we to begin? The answer is to decide first, using the exegetical and pastoral criteria noted in chapter two, the length of text you want to choose. This really makes the decision about structure for you since, once the passage is broken down into smaller units, you are really only preaching one genre.

---

25. James Montgomery Boice, *Acts: An Expositional Commentary* (Grand Rapids: Baker, 1997), 10.

26. For a discussion of the intended audience of the Gospels, see Richard Baukham, ed., *The Gospels for All Christians: Rethinking the Gospel Audiences* (Grand Rapids: Eerdmans, 1998).

27. The example below demonstrates how the apostles used the text as well. The quotations demonstrate the guilt of the Jewish audience because the Christ was clearly portrayed in the Prophets. They are without excuse. See John Phillips, *Exploring Acts*, vol. 1: *Acts 1–12* (Chicago: Moody, 1989), 49.

28. See Peter Adam, *Speaking God's Word: A Practical Theology of Preaching* (Downer's Grove: InterVarsity, 1996), 15–25.

However, there are times when a narrative will have a parable (see Luke 13:1–20). If this is the case, then preach the whole narrative (or discourse) and use the parable as the illustration. There are other times when Jesus will comment on a parable. If so, then tell the parable and use the commentary as Jesus did. In other words, allow the text to dictate the structure even if it is a hybrid text. Remember, we can have as many different structures as there are texts, which means there can be multiple genres represented in the texts.

Sample Sermon

Reverse Engineering, Acts 2:14–41

PREACHING STRATEGY

The text is answering the question, "How do we explain these events we are seeing?"

So the strategy with the sermon is to observe how Peter is interpreting these events—then at the end, we see how they are applied to us.

Introduction

I rarely saw my father get angry, but two of the times I saw him get angry had to do with a lawnmower. My five-year-old brother removed the gas cap from the lawn mower, found the grass clippings nearby, and shoved the grass clippings in the gas tank. Not good.

My father upgraded one year to the top-of-the-line lawnmower. And my brother saw this engineering marvel in the garage and just could not help himself; he was dying to know how this thing worked.

My father came home to find all the parts of the lawn mower laid out on the garage floor. Actually, this was brilliant. If you want to know how something works you have to know how it's made. If you want to know how something is put together, you take it apart. It's called reverse engineering. You understand assembly from disassembly.

This morning we are going to reverse engineer . . . a sermon. Not any sermon, but the first Christian sermon ever preached.

We are going to figure out what makes this sermon work by disassembling it and looking at its component parts. It's found in Acts 2. Take your Bibles and turn to Acts 2:14.

Transition: What are the components of a Christian sermon? The main idea of the sermon is found in verse 36: Jesus is Lord and Christ. But let's look at the way Peter gets to that idea.

CONTEXT

BODY

1. Biblical Explanation: Peter explains what they are seeing using Scripture (Acts 2:14–21)

> Peter said, the disciples are not drunk. Actually, the Spirit com-
> ing is something that was predicted by the prophet Joel.[29] Peter
> takes the audience to Scripture to explain what happened. So he
> gives an explanation as to what happened. Now he moves from
> explanation to confrontation.

> This entire sermon is dependent on three key OT texts, starting with Joel.
> Observing this is critical and a wonderful opportunity to demonstrate how
> dependent the apostles were on the OT.

2. Confrontation: His confrontation is simple: you killed Jesus (Acts 2:22–36)

> This is an interesting appeal. We will often say to people, "God
> has a wonderful plan for your life." He has a story that he wants
> to write for your life. Peter said, "God has a story and in the story
> you are the villain." However, your sin does not abort or thwart the
> plan of God. How does God respond? What is God's plan? He
> gives two responses supported by two Scriptures:

1.) You killed Jesus, but God raised him (vv. 24–32)

Jesus quotes another Scripture to support his claim.

For David says concerning him, "I saw the Lord, always before
me, for he is at my right hand that I may not be shaken; therefore my heart was glad, and my tongue rejoiced; my flesh also will
dwell in hope. For you will not abandon my soul to Hades, or let
your Holy One see corruption."

Not only did God raise him from the dead, he exalted him.
Look at verse 33.

2.) You killed Jesus, but God exalted him (vv. 33–36)

Being therefore exalted at the right hand of God, and having
received from the Father the promise of the Holy Spirit, he has
poured out this that you yourselves are seeing and hearing.

---

29. "Peter referred to this text first because it was the clearest and most obvious Old Testament prophecy of the outpouring of the Holy Spirit." Boice, *Acts*, 48.

In other words, even though you killed Jesus, God raised him up.

> This is a good place to confront the listeners with their need for Christ. However, I am waiting for full application until the main idea is given. See note below.

3. Expectation: Repent and Be Baptized (Acts 2:38–41)

And Peter said to them, "Repent and be baptized every one of you in the name of Jesus Christ for the forgiveness of your sins, and you will receive the gift of the Holy Spirit."

Conclusion

So there it is. We have the sermon disassembled lying there in front of us: explanation (here is what the Bible says about this), confrontation (here is where you are indicted in this), followed by God's expectation (repent and be baptized).

Those are the component parts lying there like the parts of that lawn mower. By the way, you know why my dad was so upset about the lawn-mower? It wasn't that my brother took it apart; rather, it was because he did not know how to put it back together.

So, let's put this sermon back together. Peter's sermon was about God's plan, so to put this sermon back together we are reconstructing God's plan. And this sermon is about us. We just read verse 39.

> What Peter did was confrontational. So, mirroring that strategy, we turn the tables on the listener. We were objectively looking into the scene; now we are confronted with God's Word and his subsequent expectation. The choice was made not to weave that into the sermon (which would not be a bad option) but to save it to the end. Now that the main idea is clear, we have to deal with God's expectation for us!

Explanation

You see there is an explanation to everything in your life. Acts 17 says the reason God created you when he did and how he did is so that you could seek him.

Confrontation

God is angry at you because of your sin. He will unleash that anger. However, Jesus Christ stood in the way of the wrath of God. On the cross he absorbed the wrath of God for you.

If you will throw yourself at his mercy, you can be saved from God's wrath.

Expectation

God's expectation is that you turn from your sin, choose another direction, and be baptized.

God is not just inviting. He is expecting. There is only one right response, and that is to come.

REFLECTION

1. How important is the author's overarching purpose to understanding the meaning of an individual unit of text?
2. What types of genre are in the Gospels?
3. Is good story telling enough when preaching a Gospel?
4. Why is it important to preach the text and not the event?
5. Is it necessary to compare the synoptic Gospels? Is it helpful?

RESOURCES

Beasley-Murray, George R. *Preaching the Gospel from the Gospels.* Peabody, MA: Hendrickson, 1996.

Blomberg, Craig L. *Jesus and the Gospels: An Introduction and Survey.* Nashville: B&H Academic: 2009.

Boice, James Montgomery. *Acts: An Expositional Commentary.* Grand Rapids: Baker, 1997.

Jackman, David. *Preaching and Teaching New Testament: Gospels, Letters, Acts and Revelation.* DVD. London: The Proclamation Trust, 2008.

Wirada, Timothy. *Interpreting Gospel Narratives: Scenes, People, and Theology.* Nashville: B&H Academic, 2010.

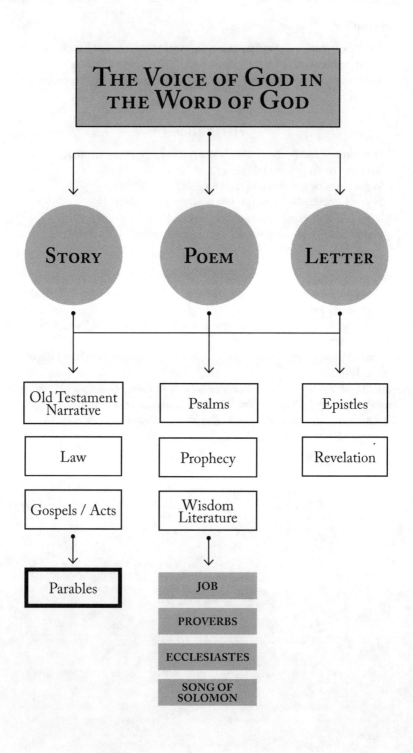

THE VOICE OF GOD IN THE WORD OF GOD

STORY

POEM

LETTER

Old Testament Narrative	Psalms	Epistles
Law	Prophecy	Revelation
Gospels / Acts	Wisdom Literature	
Parables		

JOB

PROVERBS

ECCLESIASTES

SONG OF SOLOMON

Chapter 7

RECAPTURING THE VOICE OF
GOD IN THE PARABLES

TRUE PARABLES

WHAT MAKES PARABLES SO FASCINATING IS THAT THEY ARE TRUE. They never *happened*, but the theology behind them is true. Thus, you have true theology in a fictional story. The events of the parables are not true. There was not a prodigal son, a shrewd steward, or a woman before an unjust judge per se. Jesus is not recalling history, he is telling a story. And this fact makes the parables *more* provocative. Think of it. If these stories were actual events, they could be told by Mark, or Peter, or John. They would be *just* true stories. But these are not just true stories; these are stories that Christ invented. The parables of Jesus come from the very imagination of God.

Parables have been defined as "a short narrative that demands a response from the hearer."[1] Some are shorter than others and border on a simple metaphor. Therefore, our simple working definition will be "narrative metaphors,"[2] namely stories that are analogous to spiritual truth; they are truth gleaned from the very mind of God. This means that every detail and nuance, every character development and plot first existed in the imagination of God. Thus the parables are so much more important than if they were just events. So we approach them with an appropriate sense of wonder and awe. With this in mind let's move to the features of the parables and their corresponding strategies.

INTERPRETATION: HEARING THE VOICE OF GOD IN THE PARABLES

The parables are narrative, but contain multiple structures.

If, indeed, there is meaning on the structural level, what is the structure of a parable? The immediate answer is that parables are a unique form of *narrative*. They are inductive stories that develop toward a main point. However, even within

---

1. Andreas J. Köstenberger and Richard D. Patterson, *Invitation to Biblical Interpretation: Exploring the Hermeneutical Triad of History, Literature, and Theology* (Grand Rapids: Kregel, 2011), 426–27. See the helpful chart on the continuum between "Short Simile or Metaphor" and "Long Allegory."

2. This helpful definition is from Jason Lee, "Lectures on Parables" (D.Min. Seminar on Narrative Literature. Southwestern Baptist Theological Seminary, July 7, 2009).

parables the narrative form varies. Some parables are fully developed stories with plot twists and character development. Other parables are just two verses. So these narratives have varied structure. Since we are arguing that the structure of the text should be the structure of the sermon, then perhaps the best way to categorize these narratives is not based on their content, but on their structure. There are some parables that have a *full narrative structure*; i.e., they have a setting, a plot, character development, and make an explicit point. The other main group of parables has a *short narrative structure*. By this we mean that they are shorter in length, but, more importantly, they accomplish their function without fully developed characters and scenes; many details are not supplied. Thus, these shorter parables are leaner, precise, and more direct—sometimes doing all their work in one or two verses. These are one and two verse parables. The last group is double parables. Double parables are two short parables told sequentially, that mirror each other in their structure and purpose. They are not completely identical, but close.

PARABLES BY NARRATIVE STRUCTURE

Full Narrative Structure
1. The Prodigal Son (Luke 15:11–32)
2. The Ten Virgins (Matt 25:1–13)
3. The Wheat and the Tares (Matt 12:24–30, 36–43)
4. The Rich Man and Lazarus (Luke 16:19–31)
5. The Talents (Matt 25:14–30; cf. Luke 19:12–27)
6. The Laborers in the Vineyard (Matt 20:1–16)
7. The Sower (Mark 4:3–9, 13–20)
8. The Good Samaritan (Luke 10:25–37)
9. The Great Supper (Luke 14:15–24; cf. Matt 22:1–14)
10. The Unforgiving Servant (Matt 18:23–35)
11. The Unjust Steward (Luke 16:1–13)
12. The Wicked Tenants (Matt 21:33–41; Mark 12:1–12)
13. The Pharisee and the Tax Collector (Luke 18:9–14)
14. The Two Builders (Matt 7:24–27; Luke 6:47–49)
15. The Unprofitable Servant (Luke 17:7–10)
16. The Rich Fool (Luke 12:16–21)
17. The Unjust Judge (Luke 18:1–8)

Short Narrative Structure
18. The Two Debtors (Luke 7:41–43)
19. The Two Sons (Matt 21:28–32)
20. The Faithful and Unfaithful Servants (Matt 24:45–51; Luke 12:42–48)
21. The Dragnet (Matt 13:47–50)
22. The Children in the Marketplace (Matt 11:16–19; Luke 7:31–35)
23. The Seed Growing Secretly (Mark 4:26–29)
24. The Barren Fig Tree (Luke 13:6–9)
25. The Friend at Midnight (Luke 11:5–8)
26. The Householder and the Thief (Matt 24:43–44; Luke 12:39–40)

Double Parables
27. The Lost Sheep and Lost Coin (Luke 15:4–10; cf. Matt 18:12–14)
28. The Hidden Treasure and Pearl of Great Price (Matt 13:44–46)
29. The Tower Builder and the Warring King (Luke 14:28–33)
30. The Mustard Seed and Leaven (Matt 13:31–35; Luke 13:18–21)

This is not a common way to categorize parables. A more common way would be to do so by theme,[3] or by theological topic.[4] Craig Blomberg's insightful proposal is that all parables have as many points as they do main characters; therefore, he organizes the parables by the number of main themes they contain.[5] These proposals are helpful, and the divisions are logical. However, what we are after is a sermon structure. We are trying to see how the shape of the sermon is determined by the shape of the text. We are not asking how parables may be organized, but rather what about their structure influences the way they should be preached? Therefore, the organization above is not thematic or theological, but structural.

The Parables Do Not Give Away Their Meaning at the Beginning
Parables are inductive. You don't know the point of a story until the story ends.[6] Therefore, our listeners should not know the point of the sermon until somewhere toward the end of the sermon. Parables are inductive, which means that their meaning is derived from the last part of the parable, from the last scene. These are not lectures where Christ is trying to work out several points of a proposition. Rather, they are stories that move the listener from an apparently normal story to a surprise ending.

The sermon strategy here is obvious. Don't give away the point at the beginning. Especially in the long parables, allow the meaning to be teased out over the course of the parable and then present itself at the end. This was Jesus' strategy, and we will do well to follow it.

Parables Move around Scenes, Not "Points"
Think for a minute about the word "point." It assumes that there is a truth to which we are pointing. This is not unlike navigating unfamiliar terrain as a tour guide—we point to things along the way. A preacher who is not committed to preaching a text of Scripture will predetermine points then match those points to a text. The preacher who is somewhat dependent on the text will point to truths in the text, but may not

---

3. An example of a topical/thematic organization can be found in many different works. Examples of topical arrangements are Arland Hultgren, *The Parables of Jesus: A Commentary* (Grand Rapids: Eerdmans, 2000); or Kline Snodgrass, *Stories with Intent: A Comprehensive Guide to the Parables of Jesus* (Grand Rapids: Eerdmans, 2008).

4. David Wenham's wonderful book on the parables organizes them around their relationship to the kingdom and its revolutionary nature. David Wenham, *The Parables of Jesus* (Downers Grove: InterVarsity, 1989).

5. Craig Blomberg, *Interpreting the Parables* (Downers Grove: InterVarsity, 1990).

6. It is true that an author may set up a story that hints at the main idea of the story. For example, the parable of the Pharisee and the Tax Collector begins with, "He also told this parable to some who trusted in themselves that they were righteous and treated others with contempt" (Luke 18:9). Still the point that Jesus is making is not explicitly clear until the end of the story. This is an example of giving the topic without the main idea (i.e., the subject without the complement), which you do not really know until the end of the story.

follow the flow of the text. The preacher who is completely lashed to the Scriptures wants only to make the point(s) that the text is making. He will point to nothing else.

Like Old Testament Narratives, the parables can yield many preaching points broadly speaking, but I am convinced that there is a truth that is dominant in a story; i.e., the reason that story is being told. Of course, we can point to many truths. They are truths, after all, so why not point to them? I believe the reason is that there are clues in each text that lead us to believe that some truths trump others. There is a hierarchy.[7] There may be more than a singular truth in a parable. Though many observations could be made, there is a truth that seems to dominate. To say it another way, *there is a purpose in the parable to which all the other observations seem to point*. This is the central idea that we want to identify. The clue to finding that truth is—you guessed it—in the structure.

Therefore, we need to think like a scriptwriter telling stories, not a preacher making points. A film develops its story line around scenes. There are multiple scenes in a two-hour movie, but there are a few very significant scenes around which the story turns. Jesus is telling these stories in a very few minutes, so he is just highlighting the major scenes in the story. Much of the detail is left out or is assumed, but that material is not necessary to carry the story along. What *is* necessary are scenes that move the story in a certain trajectory. So, it is critical to identify the scenes in the parables.

The Setting Is Important, but Brief

The set up for the parables is unique. Jesus is telling short stories, so reams of context are self-defeating. He just lets listeners assume things. However, this does not mean that the setting, if one is given, is not important. Pay careful attention to the setting as it helps us understand what about Jesus' approach the biblical writer thought was significant.

The Parables Have a Specific Audience

Think of the three parables of Luke 15. They were addressed to the scribes and Pharisees (Luke 15:1–2). Then Jesus turns to his disciples to tell another parable (16:1); however, the scribes and Pharisees were listening in (16:14), so he addressed a final parable to them (16:19). This inclusion by Luke is important to the interpretation of the parables. The first three parables are directed to the Pharisees; the fourth parable is directed to the disciples; and the final one is again addressed to the Pharisees. In each case, the intended audience shades the meaning.

In developing a sermon strategy, it is imperative to understand the audience of the parable and allow that information to influence how it is told. It will help the listener understand the strategy of Christ.

---

7. In the history of interpretation there have been many different approaches to parables. Jochaim Jermias famously suggested a one-point approach. More recently Blomberg has argued that there are as many points to a parable as there are main characters. There may be multiple ideas in a parable; however, it seems that these stories are bullets that may graze several ideas, but have one targeted audience. In other words, even in parables with multiple ideas, they are not all equal. There is a dominant idea. For a helpful recent history of interpretation and discussion of the state of the academic conversation, see Blomberg, *Interpreting the Parables*, 13–165.

The Parables Have a Specific Purpose

The parables have a two-fold effect. To those who have ears to hear, they help them understand what the kingdom is like. For those who do not have ears to hear, they expose their unbelief. The parables are much about believing, and specifically understanding the way of the kingdom (Matt 13:10–16; Mark 4:10–12; Luke 8:9–15). The interpretation of the parable keeps this dual purpose of Christ in mind: calling believers to understand and exposing unbelief.

The Telling of Parables Is Telling a Story about Someone Telling a Story

After all this talk of narratives, let me say that these are not just stories. The Gospel writer is actually telling a story of Jesus telling a story. Since God used the Gospel writers to record these stories, we are not surprised that they have embedded clues that point to their meaning in the material surrounding the parable. Think of our metaphor of a camera panning out. When we pan out we find that the placement of a parable in its surrounding literary context provides clues to its meaning. Thus we are asking both "Why did Jesus say this?" and, "Why did the Gospel writer place it here in his narrative?" or, "How does this parable shed light on the overall theme of the book?" The placement of the parable leads us to learn more about the main theme that the author wants us to know about Jesus. The parables then are told by Jesus, and they teach us about Jesus.

Parables do not always function allegorically.[8] Much of the theology that Christ is trying to communicate is developed through the individual characters. Unlike OT Narratives, all of the characters are completely fabricated by a Master Storyteller. So one must look carefully at the character to see exactly why Christ painted it the way he did. In this way parables function as allegory—the characters have one to one correlation with some one else or some other truth. An example would be the Prodigal Son where the father represents Christ, the younger brother the sinners, and the older brother the Pharisees (Luke 15:11–32).

However, it is interesting that Jesus only unpacked two parables in this way: the parable of the Soils and the parable of the Wheat and Weeds (Matt 13:18–30, 36–43; Mark 4:1–20). So how should we interpret parables? Should we always look to the parable for a correlation to every character or simply look to one main idea? I believe that we can fairly relate the characters as analogous to something else; however, our principle aim is to determine how these characters contribute to the main theme Jesus is trying to communicate in the telling of the parable. So, we must be careful of over-identification with characters and one-to-one correlation when interpreting the other parables. The point of a parable is not in immediate correlation with certain events or people; rather, it is in the application of a single idea derived from the whole. To say it another way, identify the allegory, then move beyond the one-to-one correlation that Jesus wants to press.[9]

---

8. This statement is debated. My point is that preaching a parable in which every detail is pressed for meaning leads the preacher to interpret details as significant that may simply be contributing to a dominant idea.

9. See Leland Ryken's helpful discussion on allegory and parables in *Words of Delight*, 407–9. See also Köstenberger and Patterson, *Invitation to Biblical Interpretation*, 426–28.

However, it stands to reason that at least the main characters in the story are analogous for someone or some people.[10] It would be best to identify who the character is, who the character represents, and the modern day equivalent. Think of the Prodigal Son:

The Prodigal Son (Luke 15:11–32)

Character	Representing	Analogous to
Prodigal	Tax collectors and sinners	The unrighteous who need to repent
Older brother	Pharisees	The self-righteous who need to repent
Father	Jesus	Jesus

In the above chart each character represents a specific person. However, this is not always the case. *Remember, the thrust of the parable is to support the driving idea or the dominant theme.* The function of the characters is to build toward that theme. In some parables there will be direct correlation, but in others there is not. So, when preaching, emphasize the driving theme and do not feel pressure to resolve the reason for the existence of each character. For example, in the parable of the Shrewd Steward, while it is clear who the debtors and the manager represent, it is not equally as clear who the business owner represents. There does not seem to be a clean one-to-one correlation. It is best not to force this, but allow this supporting character to do just that—support what else is going on in the story.

Example: Luke 16:1–9

Character	Representing	Analogous to
Business owner	?	?
Master's debtors	Unbelieving	Lost who are trusting in money
Manager	Those following Christ	Christian who must steward his resources for evangelism

In this parable we are not preaching the individual characters as if they are points; we are finding the thrust of the parable and simply preaching that dominant theme.

The Parables Are Culturally Distant

It is a little obvious to say that the stories themselves are embedded in a culture far removed from the modern audience. It matters little if the exegesis is scintillating and the content is theologically tight if the preacher does not draw immediate parallels from his culture to the contemporary culture. If our people do not understand the workings of first-century shepherds, landowners, and wedding feasts, the parable will be lost on them. Jesus used images that were familiar to his audience and needed no explanation. He just assumed they understood and off he went. A great

---

10. In the history of interpretation there is a tradition of allegorical interpretation. Although this is a strained hermeneutic, there is still much to be learned from some in this tradition such as the wonderful *Exposition of the Parables in the Bible* by Benjamin Keach (Grand Rapids: Kregel, 1974). See also the vital work on parables by William Arnot, *The Parables of Our Lord* (London: Bibliobazzar, 2007).

theological truth was expounded using an everyday story. The problem is that time and space have removed the cultural impact of these stories. It is critical that we understand this cultural background.[11]

Yet, there is an inherent temptation here. We could so fall in love with the cultural background, the fascination of it all, that we miss the theological point Christ is attempting to communicate, a point that is imbedded in the text of Scripture, not so much the details of the story. A sermon that focuses on cultural background rather than the biblical context becomes a lesson in first-century culture that falls squarely in the category of interesting but unhelpful. Preach the text, not the event.

To avoid this danger, some have rejected the cultural context altogether and opted to recast the story in a contemporary light exclusively. This extreme also seems problematic since it assumes that the preacher knows the context of the parable well enough that he can actually recast it. The culture of the parable is so removed from us that it demands to be unpacked. Yet, the parable needs to be unpacked with contemporary parallels. Both cultural nuance and contemporary setting are necessary and, if done well, should result in a sermon that translates the meaning, and the impact, of the parable into a relatable situation. We will discuss this below.

Parables May Have a Surprise in Them

The hero of one parable is a hated Samaritan. A father welcomes back a son who wanted him dead. A landowner praises a steward who stole from him. A day worker is paid the same wage for working all day as someone who only worked for a few hours. When a surprise element is strong, the only way to get the rhetorical impact of these stories is to understand the background that made these stories shocking in their own right. David Wenham argues that these surprises are all about the surprising effect of the kingdom and its radical counter to the established religion.[12]

The surprise is a rhetorical device that is a clue for meaning, and therefore for preaching. As much as possible, we want to show the listener the scenes of the story, surprise them with a twist in the story, and allow them to have resolution at the end of the story. In other words, we are trying to recapture the rhetorical effect that Christ was intending when he told these stories. Take a moment to scan the sermon at the end of the chapter (pp. 118–20) before reading the next section.

COMMUNICATION: RECAPTURING THE VOICE IN THE PARABLES

Translate the Parable for the Modern Audience

The meaning of the parables is culturally nuanced. How can we understand the problems of sowing among rocks and thorns without an understanding of earthly soil problems? So many issues need to be understood when preaching parables, including the way first century workers are paid, the way inheritance was distributed,[13] the relationships between fathers and their sons,[14] or the value the Pharisees placed

---

11. See for example Kenneth Bailey's helpful works, such as *Poet and Peasant and Through Peasant Eyes* (Grand Rapids: Eerdmans, 1983).

12. Wenham, *The Parables of Jesus.*

13. Darrell Bock, *Luke 9:51–24:53* BECNT (Grand Rapids: Baker, 1996), 1309.

14. See Kenneth Bailey, *Finding the Lost: Cultural Keys to Luke 15* (Saint Louis: Concordia, 1992), 114.

on money. These cultural clues help us understand how a first-century listener would have understood the parable. But how do you deal with these issues with a limited amount of time? The strategy mentioned above is to translate the parable into a contemporary setting. This can be done several ways. Perhaps the least desirable is to make the translation the whole sermon. After all, we are not telling stories; we are teaching people how to read the Scripture. Sometimes the best approach is to take one issue or one scene in the story and bring it into contemporary vernacular. We do this intuitively. We should also do it intentionally. In the example below a translation is given at the end of the first scene where a contemporary retelling of the son's disobedience is translated into a contemporary context. The reason this is inserted here is because the story is so familiar, we lose sight of the extent of the son's rebellion against the father. It is stronger than mere disrespect. It is a rejection of his identity as a son.

This assumes of course that we know the cultural context. There are several resources to help here and much good material is given in the exegetical commentaries. Consult the appendix for more sources.[15]

One word of caution: Do not get so absorbed in the modern translation that the theology is glossed. If we capture the audience but never get to the point, then what are we doing? We are not Garrison Keeler, Paul Harvey, or any number of other storytellers—we are preachers. We are attempting to mine this parable for its Author-intended theological meaning, excavate that posit of truth, and show it to people. Don't miss the point while telling the story. The story is a means not an end, not the end in itself.[16]

Identify Christ's Strategy

Look for the strategy Christ uses in telling the story. Again, the biblical author gives us clues. Every detail of the story is important because it was put there for a purpose. This is not an admonition for hyper-allegorization of a parable. The way Jesus told parables was conditioned by the context in which he was teaching. Every detail is not to be mined for contemporary application; however, they serve are clues regarding the approach of Christ in telling the story.

So, when preaching the parable, the sermon strategy is to identify Christ's strategy in the telling of the story. Consider the following examples:

Luke 15:1. Luke begins with a discussion of the Pharisees' suspicion of Christ's table fellowship with sinners. So he tells them three stories, all revolving around

---

15. Outside of good exegetical commentary, another good source of cultural information are the works of Kenneth Bailey. Kenneth Bailey, *Poet and Peasant and Through Peasant Eyes: A Literary-Cultural Approach to the Parables in Luke*, combined ed. (Grand Rapids: Eerdmans, 1983). See also his other works: *Finding the Lost*; *Jacob and the Prodigal: How Jesus Retold Israel's Story* (Downers Grove: InterVarsity, 2003); *The Cross and the Prodigal: Luke 15 Through the Eyes of Middle Eastern Peasants* (Downers Grove: InterVarsity, 2005); *Jesus Through Middle Eastern Eyes* (Downers Grove: InterVarsity, 2008).

16. Those with a compositional hermeneutic might feel uncomfortable with the suggestion that there is meaning in the cultural clues. While I am sympathetic with this hermeneutic, and do believe that some parables have a strong canonical referent, the goal in preaching seems to me not only to represent information, but to, as faithfully as possible, represent the effect on the modern listener that it had on the original listener. In fact, in this process the canonical referents can be illustrated more strongly.

a desperate search for what was lost. You could preach these stories wonderfully, but if you fail to identify the explicit allusions to the shepherd, the woman, and the Father as metaphors for Jesus, then the point of the stories is lost. These are good stand-alone stories, but that misses the point. They are more accurately understood, and therefore more powerful, when placed in the proper context.

Matthew 13:1–23. Matthew begins his retelling of eight parables of Christ with "that same day . . ." This chronological marker goes all the way back to when the day first begins at the beginning of chapter 12, a chapter filled with antagonism by the Pharisees. The Pharisees did not believe—they were the hard soil that would not receive the Word. This context seems to have a great deal of bearing on the interpretation of the parable. Also, in verse one Matthew mentions that a very large crowd is gathering as Jesus tells the story of the parable of the Soils. Could it be that Christ is admonishing the crowd that everyone there will not get the truth?

Matthew 20:1–16. The explanation of the parable of the Landowner is wrapped up in the context, namely in the story of the Rich Young Ruler.

Luke 10:29, 36. The context of the parable is a lawyer testing Jesus about the greatest commandment, and then attempting to justify himself by asking Jesus to identify his neighbor. Jesus responds with the parable of the Good Samaritan, but then changes the lawyer's question by asking his own in return. Which question was the parable designed to answer? Your assessment will dramatically change how you preach the parable.

Preach the Double Parables Carefully

When approaching a double parable, look for two things: (1) What is similar about the two parables? (2) What is different? The long parable brings you along for the meaning. Not double parables. These are quick shots that are effective because of their rapid pace. The double parable works like a one-two punch.

Perhaps the best known of these is found in Luke 15, the parable of the Lost Sheep and the Lost Coin. Really this is a triple parable because of the lost son that is in the same chapter. Let's look at this as an example, asking the two questions.

What is similar? Notice that these three parables all have a similar structure. Something is lost, something is found, and then there is rejoicing. The similarity of the three parables could be diagrammed like this:

The Lost Sheep	The Lost Coin	The Lost Son*
The shepherd loses (v. 4).	The woman loses (v. 8).	The father loses (v. 12).
The shepherd searches (v. 4).	The woman searches (v. 8).	The father searches (v. 20).
The shepherd finds (v. 5).	The woman finds (v. 9).	The father finds (v. 20).
The shepherd rejoices with friends (v. 6).	The woman rejoices with friends (v. 9).	The father rejoices with friends (v. 24).

* For a comparison of the semantic relationship between, and the chiastic structure of, these three parables, see Kenneth E. Bailey, *Poet and Peasant and Through Peasant's Eyes* (Grand Rapids: Eerdman's, 1976), 144, 156.

So, clearly Jesus is trying to teach a lesson about something that is lost then found, followed by rejoicing. We preachers have a tendency to make this observation based on the parallel of these three stories. However, there is something curious about this chart.

What is different? There are three stories, all with the same structure—almost. The above chart only works if you cut off the last scene of the last parable found in verses 25–32. The last scene shows the older brother's rejection of the younger brother and the father going to seek after the older brother, which is the principal theme Christ is driving home. He is exposing the difference between how he views lost people (like the father) versus how the Pharisees view lost people (like the older brother). So it could be more accurately diagramed like this:

The Lost Sheep	The Lost Coin	The Lost Son
The shepherd loses (v. 4).	The woman loses (v. 8).	The father loses (v. 12).
The shepherd searches (v. 4).	The woman searches (v. 8).	The father searches (v. 20).
The shepherd finds (v. 5).	The woman finds (v. 9).	The father finds (v. 20).
The shepherd rejoices with friends (v. 6).	The woman rejoices with friends (v. 9).	The father rejoices with friends (v. 24).
		A father loses a son (vv. 25–30).
		A father searches (vv. 26–32).

Look at the curious ending to the last story. It ends with no rejoicing. No resolution. The older brother is just outside of the house. This is curious, but it actually complements the structure of the previous parables. In the first two parables Jesus is telling the story of something that was lost and then found. A sheep was lost, found, and then rejoicing followed. A coin was lost, found, and then rejoicing followed. A son was lost, then found, followed by rejoicing, and a son was lost. The last story ends in mystery. Was the older brother restored? The structure is telling us something interesting—something that is a clue to the meaning.

It seems that the story of the Prodigal Son is more about the older brother and less about the younger brother. After all, if Jesus wanted to tell a story about something being lost and found, he could have stopped with the story of the Lost Sheep. That is what he did in Matthew 18:12–14. However, he continues with the story of the Lost Coin as well. He is driving home the point of "lostness" by telling a provocative double parable. Again, if this was his point he could have stopped there, but he presses in further to tell the story of the Lost Son. If he wanted to only press the idea of what was lost, he would have stopped the story after the second scene, but he does not. He adds a surprise ending. He tells them about an older brother who is so self righteous that he cannot welcome home the younger brother. This is a clue that points to the meaning of this parable.

Let's pan out and look at the chapter context. Luke 15:1 begins, "Now the tax collectors and sinners were all drawing near to hear him. And the Pharisees and the scribes grumbled, saying, 'This man receives sinners and eats with them.' So he told them this parable."

This parable was not told in a vacuum void of context. The context was the religious establishment criticizing Jesus for befriending sinners. Jesus responds by launching into the double parables of the Lost Sheep and Coin. Jesus' response pits their view of lostness against his view of lostness. They reject lost sinners. Jesus not only accepts lost sinners, he seeks them. What a provocative picture of the grace of Christ.

After the telling of the double parable, they should have understood the message clearly. What they reject, he seeks. However, if that were not clear enough, he twists the knife by telling the story of the Prodigal Son. In this third story, there is not only something lost and something found, there is also the rejection of what was lost and then found by the older brother. Now the story of the prodigal comes into focus. The story is about being lost; it is about seeking; it is about rejoicing; but what distinguishes this parable from the others is this last scene. The self-righteous older brother really stands out as curious in light of the surrounding context. The parable is about Jesus (like the father) seeking the lost (younger brother) and seeking those who do not seek the lost (older brother). The last scene serves as both an invitation and a warning to those whose hatred of sinners keeps them outside the house.

Now all we have done is look at the internal structure and the external structure, but we have arrived at something interesting. It seems the point of the story of the Prodigal Son is found in the last scene: *it is a warning about being self righteous.* The driving point that Christ is trying to make comes from both the internal structure, the frame, and the external structure, how it is framed in the chapter. Both structures point to the idea of self-righteousness as the driving theme.

STRUCTURING A SERMON FROM A PARABLE

1. Look for the Narrative Structure

The most obvious strategy is to look for the narrative structure. There should be some clues to the structure including a setting, characters, a plot, and—most importantly—a scene structure. Remember, the purpose is not to lay out a dramatic story for the sake of it; the point is to tell an abbreviated, blunted story so that the message can come across. The example from Luke 15 is used below because it has a clean scene structure.

2. Shape the Sermon in a Creative Way around the Unique Structure of the Parable

If each parable has a unique structure, the question we should ask is "How can our sermon reflect that structure?" The most obvious structure to work with is a full narrative structure. It is here that one can take into account all of the other things that have been said about the narrative structure in sermon development.[17] We follow the flow of the narrative and allow the sermon to rise and fall with the flow of the text. This is clear enough. However, what about all the variations that are in parables? Some parables are much shorter, so developing them as full narratives would

---

17. See the strategy for preaching narrative in chapter 4.

involve a lot of conjecture. What follows are five potential sermon structures for preaching parables.

1. Developed narrative. In the developed narrative, the entire sermon moves around the scenes of the story. Like preaching an Old Testament Narrative, the preacher will give the setting, and then each scene will develop until the end of the parable. Since this really is the way Christ explained his stories, this should be the default shape for most of the parables of extended length. This is better for full narratives with apparently applicable scenes such as the Prodigal Son, the Good Samaritan, the Shrewd Steward, the Rich Man and Lazarus, etc.

As with an Old Testament Narrative, the sermon mirrors the story in that it is told inductively, meaning it works to the main idea and not from the main idea. As in all stories, the point is not given until the end.

2. Translation first. In this model, the story may still be told inductively. However, instead of starting with the setting of the story or a traditional introduction, the sermon actually begins with a translation—that is, a retelling of the story that recasts the parable in a contemporary light. Start the sermon with this modern translation as a hook to get them into the story. This approach is good for sermons where the parable may be short and its function is an illustration of a larger teaching. This can also be a good approach for parables when the scenes of the story do not seem to be immediately translatable.

For example, in the story of the Prodigal Son the brief setting is important to the development of the story in its context. The audience will of course already understand something of a father/son relationship. However, think about the parable of the Unrighteous Steward (Luke 16:1–8). In this parable a steward is called to give account of his management. The cultural context indicates that the steward works for a landowner who serves as a tenant for several people/families who own plots of land. Bridging this story into a contemporary cultural context up front will more easily draw the listener into the story. In other words, there is a cultural barrier to be overcome initially that could be bridged by placing the contemporary translation up front.

3. Translation last/during. In this model the parable is told, then the translation is given, or the translation is given as a running commentary throughout the sermon. If the entire parable is translated up front, the remainder of the sermon is the application or the points of the parable. This can be done by giving all but the last part of the parable. Even if giving it all up front, we want to tease out the meaning so that the main idea is given at the end.

4. Outline form. In the outline form the preacher develops points from the parable and delivers them deductively, as working from a main idea. As a rule, this form is not recommended. I do include it here because it is an option that theoretically could be used on some parables.

For example, the Parable of the Soils (Matt 13:1–23) has a full narrative structure. However, Jesus' explanation of the parable tells us exactly what this parable is about. So a preacher could ask the question, "How do people in the kingdom respond to Jesus?" Then provide the following points:

1. Some have hard hearts.
2. Some have shallow hearts.
3. Some have thorny, distracted hearts.
4. Some have fertile hearts where the Word thrives and bears fruit.

This outline makes sense because Jesus took the time to interpret the parable. Here the first part of the text could be read first, and perhaps the explanation given by Christ could be read as each scene develops. The same method could be applied to the parable that follows the parable of the Soils, the Wheat and the Weeds (Matt 13:24–30, 36–43).

However, even in this example it is important to note that Jesus is not trying to give us a strategy on how to deal with peoples' responses to the gospel. That is an application, and a necessary one. However, this is not about our strategy as much as it is his success. The more immediate point he wants to make is the growth of the kingdom despite obstacles. Even though it will be rejected by hardness, by shallowness, by distractedness, it will ultimately produce over the top, exponential fruit in those hearts ready for it. So, this is a caution against choosing a theme of points simply because we want to use an outline. That could tempt us to take an angle to the text that does not reflect what is going on in the text as a whole.

5. *Parable-in-context.* In a parable-in-context, the parable is preached as a part of a larger whole. The preacher will preach the larger passage in context, and use the parable as a supporting illustration, much like Christ did. The danger here is to gloss over important details by assuming the listener, and the preacher, knows what it means at first pass.

Consider for example Luke 14:25–33. The pericope is a discussion of the cost of discipleship. Jesus gives the main idea in the very last verse, "So therefore any one of you who does not renounce all that he has cannot be my disciple." Then he concludes with a brief parable about the salt of the earth. Many applications can be made from this parable. However, in its context it is a warning—if you reject the King of the kingdom and do not carry out the function of influence, there is no second chance. Thus, the ideal approach is to preach this parable as it was used by Christ—as a warning to those who will not be disciples.

I am assuming that the preacher will not preach the parable out of context. For example, the kingdom parables of the Hidden Treasure and the Pearl of Great Price (Matt 13:44–45) are perhaps best preached as one sermon. This is because they both make a point coming from the context of Matthew 13 and the details of the kingdom. If they are removed from this context, they could be made to mean any number of different things.

3. Decide Where to Explain the Main Idea

In most cases, the main idea will come at the end. In the example below, the full main idea becomes clear in the third scene, so that's where it's placed in the sermon.

But again, once it is given it will need to be unpacked—so leave room for the explanation after it is given.

4. Leave Room for Jesus' Commentary

Sometimes Jesus will add commentary to the parable, and we must privilege his interpretation and insight in our retelling of the parable.

The text will feel like a narrative followed by commentary. In the sermon, we can mirror this approach. We teach the full narrative. Then at the end, we add the commentary of Christ. Bring the story to resolution, then add the commentary of Christ at the end.

5. When Preaching a Shorter Story, Preach the Entire Teaching of Christ

There are some very short parables. As noted earlier, in those instances, structure the sermon around the whole pericope and then use the parable as supplementary material.

Sample Sermon: The Prodigal Son

Luke 15:11–32

> **PREACHING STRATEGY**
>
> It seems that the questions the text is raising are, How does Jesus approach sinners and how should I approach sinners?

Introduction

The F-16 went down in enemy territory. The pilot was in a hostile country being chased by mercenaries and had no hope of escape. He was lost, and there was nothing he could do to find himself. Jesus is going to tell the story of something that, if it is lost, it can never find its own way home again.

> **INTRODUCTION**
>
> This introduction is not a complete story. It has an abrupt ending. I am only trying to plant in the hearers' minds the idea of lostness. The reason is that, leading up to the Prodigal Son parable, Jesus tells two other stories about lostness. I want them to feel the weight of being lost in an attempt to recapture the rhetorical effect that Christ was using.

Setting: v. 11

Jesus is being criticized for eating with tax collectors and sinners. So he decides to tell them a story about how he feels about lostness. He tells them three stories. The story of a lost sheep, a lost coin, and a lost son.

Scene One: The Prodigal Departs (vv. 12–20a)

The story of the prodigal's rebellion. Translation is given here.

> The contemporary translation is inserted here. People think they know the story, but generally they cannot conceive of the depth of this son's rebellion. So it is helpful to try to describe his rebellion in a contemporary parallel.

Scene Two: The Father Seeks the Returning Prodigal (vv. 20b–24)

The story of the prodigal being restored by a father who is willing to break every social convention to get to his son demonstrates that the story is not about the sin of the son but the love of the father. Jesus, like this father, seeks sinners.

> The idea of Jesus seeking sinners seems to be the only point. In truth it is a set-up for the next scene. However, it is so critical that it needs some development. Much needs to be made of the overwhelming love of the father toward the son.

Scene Three: The Older Brother Protests (vv. 25–32)

The story of the older brother's inability to love what the Father loves. Still, the father goes out of the house to seek him. Notice how the father went out of the house to seek the younger brother and in the end goes out of the house to seek the older brother. This leads us to the point of the story:

Main Idea: Jesus seeks the unrighteous, and Jesus seeks the self-righteous.

> The main idea is only clear here. So after the main idea, time is given to unpack it. This is the most natural place for application since we do not know what to apply until this point.

Conclusion

When the Air Force found the location of their pilot, how did they react? They could ignore him. They could say he is getting what he deserves by being shot down. They could blame him and reject him. However, do you imagine that is what they did? No, they sought him. In fact they deployed several aircraft, dozens of Marines, and spent millions of dollars. All this because one pilot was down and he would not be saved unless he was sought. Jesus seeks sinners. And if we are not seeking sinner, then we are self-righteous, and Jesus is seeking us as well.

So, how does the story end? Do the brothers reconcile? We don't know. As the curtain closes on the story, the younger brother is inside and the older brother is outside. And the father is seeking both of them. This is the one parable Jesus tells without an ending. It's his way of turning the issue back to his audience and asking, "Who are you? Are the unrighteous in need of repentance, or are you the self-righteous in need of repentance?"[18]

REFLECTION

1. How are parables different than regular narratives?
2. What do you do with smaller parables?
3. What did we mean by the modern translation of the parable?
4. Is Jesus trying to reveal truth or conceal truth by telling parables?
5. What two questions do you ask about double parables?

RECOMMENDED RESOURCES

Arnot, William. *Parables of Our Lord*. Grand Rapids: Kregel, 1981.

Bailey, Kenneth. *Poet and Peasant and Through Peasant Eyes: A Literary-Cultural Approach to the Parables in Luke*. Grand Rapids, Eerdmans, 1976.

Blomberg, Craig. *Interpreting the Parables*. Downers Grove: InterVarsity, 1990.

Kistomsaker, Simon. *The Parables: Understanding the Stories Jesus Told*. Grand Rapids: Baker, 1980.

Snodgrass, Klyne. *Stories with Intent: A Comprehensive Guide to the Parables of Jesus*. Grand Rapids: Eerdmans, 2008.

Wenham, David. *The Parables of Jesus*. Jesus Library. Downers Grove: InterVarsity, 1989.

---

18. Bailey, *Finding the Lost*, 188–90.

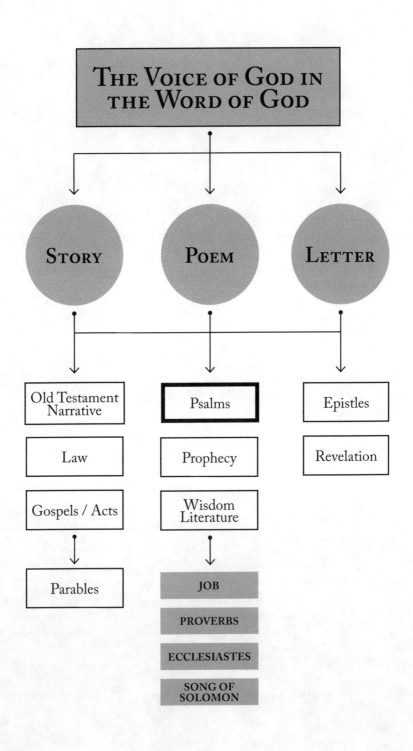

THE VOICE OF GOD IN THE WORD OF GOD

STORY

POEM

LETTER

Old Testament Narrative

Law

Gospels / Acts

Parables

Psalms

Prophecy

Wisdom Literature

JOB

PROVERBS

ECCLESIASTES

SONG OF SOLOMON

Epistles

Revelation

Chapter 8

RECAPTURING THE VOICE OF GOD IN PSALMS

THE MOST ACCESSIBLE TRUTHS ARE POETIC.

In our spiritual journey we receive scriptural truth from books and sermons, and they set our course on a different trajectory. These moments argue for keeping a spiritual journal in which we write things down so as not to forget them. After all, we want to access them at another point in life.

Yet, some of the most powerful truths are ones we don't have to write down. No need to dig them out of a journal. The reason for their heightened accessibility is that someone took the painstaking energy to set them to music—to *set* them. Once sung, they are firmly set in our minds. So if our hearts want to praise God, we don't reach for a book; we go to the hymns and songs that provide us with a ready source of comfort, grace, assistance, encouragement, and exhortation. The truths set to music are no less powerful; they are just more easily accessible.

Perhaps this is why much of the Old Testament is given as poetry. The focus of this chapter is preaching the Psalms; however, what is said about Hebrew poetry in the Psalms will apply to the rest of the poetry in the Old Testament. The books of Psalms and Lamentations contain the most poetry, but the books of Job, Ecclesiastes, Song of Solomon, Isaiah, Jeremiah, Amos, and Hosea also contain large amounts of poetry. The genre is so powerful that it is given a major portion in Scripture. Therefore, if we understand how songs function in general, we understand how psalms work in particular.

OF SONGS

Think about how songs work.

When I hear a song, I appreciate that song if I can identify with it. In the psalms we read of fear, triumph, loathing, regret, pain, and ecstasy. The psalms are intensely personal. When you read Psalms, it is as if you are singing next to some-one who is not too self-aware. We are rearing back and praising God, no matter who is watching.

As a result the psalms do not take the time to tie up all the loose theological ends. They are micro-expressions of deep inexhaustible truths. Those of us in vocational ministry are often very discriminating about the lyrics of hymns and worship songs. Pastors are so especially because they are responsible for what a congregation knows about the Word. Since the "stickiest," most accessible way we understand the Word is through music, we are responsible to make sure that what our congregations sing is theologically and biblically accurate. Therefore, the accessibility of truth is only helpful if it is precise. Yet the psalms do not always satisfy our desire to have everything that tight. They are not intended to tell us everything there is to know about God in a way that would please the most ardent theologian. This is what makes us nervous about the psalms. We hear David cry for vengeance on his enemies (Ps 35:3) and we want to say, "Yes, but what about forgiveness?" We hear him suggest that the arm of the wicked will be broken (Ps 37:17) and the sword with which they kill others will enter their own hearts (Ps 37:15), and we wonder about God's offer of salvation for all people. In fact, about half of all the psalms could be classified as complaints.[1] But these psalms are true. Again, in psalms such as these, the psalmist is singing at the top of his lungs with no regard to wrap all this up in tight theological categories.

This is the way the psalms work. They do not fit our molds of understanding God, and they do not fit in neat homiletical forms (praise God). They are as messy and difficult as the human condition. And yet, they are the perfectly inspired Word of God. They are as true as John 3:16.

The preacher who wants to communicate them effectively will need to preach them as they are. Don't mess them up by reading NT theology into them before they are understood on their own. While we do preach from a theological construct, we should take the time to take the listener to the theology. Let them walk through the front door first; then show them the foundation. Let the listeners experience the psalm: let them feel God's anger at his enemies, experience David's confusion and anxiety, and let them hear the songs that Israel would sing to recount God's faithfulness. Let the listeners engage all of this, and engage it poetically. Let them feel the weight of what is being said. Then, and only then, frame it in Christian theology. The goal is to zoom into the text before panning out to the attendant theology. If we preach the new covenant before the old, we've missed something chronologically. Why would we need the Psalms themselves?

It is a little ironic that given our choices we preachers so naturally gravitate to the Epistles.[2] I understand the urge. They are clean, neat, and seem to lay out in structural ways that are natural for preaching. And, often they do not have the lumbering baggage of human emotion. But for the same reason, they are not as accessible. The goal, then, is to preach songs within a canonical context, with all of its attendant biblical and systematic theology, but first allow the poetry to breathe. When we preach the song in the context of the whole Bible, we have given people the rare gift of accessible truth, an internal journal. Christian truth is accessible with songs. Scripture is more accessible through Psalms. Make the connections and people are given a rare gift. This is especially the case since, as we will see, the Psalms ultimately are about Christ.

---

1. David G. Firth, "Preaching Praise Poetry," *Reclaiming the Old Testament for Christian Preaching*, ed. Grenville J. R. Kissling, Paul J. Turner, and Laurence A. Kent (Downers Grove: InterVarsity Academic, 2010), 86.

2. For discussion regarding the errant notion believed by some preachers that the Psalms are for singing only, and not for preaching, see J. Clinton McCann Jr. and James C. Howell, *Preaching the Psalms* (Nashville: Abingdon, 2001), 16.

CHRIST, THE SKILLFUL SHEPHERD

Psalm 78 is a remarkable psalm for many reasons. It is remarkable because it tells the story of Israel, unfolding progressively through her history. It begins with a cry to listen to all "our fathers have told us . . . the glorious deeds of the Lord and his might" (vv. 1–4). Verse two is quite remarkable: "I will open my mouth in a parable; I will utter dark sayings of old." The idea seems to be mysterious, "dark" sayings. Yet, these sayings are no longer hidden because he is now revealing them. He tells the story of Israel from the call of Jacob, the deliverance in Egypt, the occupation of the land, and the reign of David. David's leadership is described thus: "With an upright heart he shepherded them and guided them with a skillful hand" (v. 72). So the truth that is revealed of old is that through all the staunch rebellion God kept his covenant to Israel, even bringing them a warrior king like David to lead his people. But that is only the first part of the story.

The rest of the story is found in Matthew 13 where there is a shift in Jesus' ministry and parables become his primary form of teaching (Matt 13:1–3, 10). When his disciples ask him why he is using parables, he explains that the mystery of the kingdom will still be dark to some, but they are blessed because they see it (vv. 10–17). He then goes on to teach eight parables. Right in the middle of the eight parables Matthew, the narrator, inserts this:

> All these things Jesus said to the crowds in parables; indeed, he said nothing to them without a parable. This was to fulfill what was spoken by the prophet: "I will open my mouth in parables; I will utter what has been hidden from the foundation of the world." (vv. 34–35)[3]

This is, of course, a quotation from Psalm 78. So, now we see what is really going on. Psalm 78 is about David, but it is more about the Good Shepherd than it is the shepherd boy. David's place in Israel's history showed him to be the best human king. But, as they say, a man at his best is a man at best. David demonstrated the weakness of a fallen human king. Israel would not have a real King until the Messiah came to shepherd his people Israel. So the great story of old (Ps 78:2) was the story of Jesus. Jesus is the One who leads with an upright heart. Jesus is the One who guides us with a skillful hand. And it is Jesus who is the One whom God chose to shepherd his people.

Plain and simple, these are songs about Christ, whether there is an explicit Messianic connection or not. This makes Colossians 3:16 an even more fascinating text. Paul writes, "Let the word of Christ dwell in you richly as you teach and admonish one another with all wisdom, and as you sing psalms, hymns, and spiritual songs with gratitude in your hearts to God." Mark Futato has observed that the categories that Paul uses (psalms, hymns, and spiritual songs) are all categories that are

---

3. David Wenham suggests a chiastic structure pointing to vv. 34–35 as the focus of the text. If the chiasm is there, it further reinforces the idea that Matthew's arrangement of the parables was itself to show that Jesus was the Christ. See David Wenham, *The Parables of Jesus*, Jesus Library (Downers Grove: InterVarsity, 1989).

used for psalms in the Septuagint. Thus the use of the psalms is the medium through which we express gratitude to God and demonstrate the indwelling Christ.[4]

THE END GAME

The oddity of preaching Psalms is the mixing of genres. We are preaching songs. It seems more natural to preach sermons and to sing songs. This is part of the challenge. How do we speak a song? Remember, this is all God's Word and the psalms, like the rest of Scripture, lead to salvation. In other words, while these were originally intended to be sung, God has designed that we preach them.[5] It's God's desire that we preach songs. Now that we know our mission, the question is, How do you preach a song?

It is good to pause here and remember the end game. We are after the meaning of the text. We are not after imitation but re-animation. In other words, what about the structure of this poem influences the meaning of the text? The use of repetition and parallelism can greatly influence the direction a song takes. If a song is effective, the meter, rhythm, and lyrics all emphasize the content that the artist wants to communicate. We are seeking the meaning that is highlighted by the structure of the poems. So, any discouragement you feel about wrapping your mind around ancient poetry should be tempered by the fact that we are using the same approach here as with any text: we are taking the structure of the text and showing how it supports the driving theme of the text.

These Are Songs, But They Are More Than Songs

Of all the poems to exist, biblical psalms represent the poems that are inspired and infallible. They affirm the covenant of Abraham, tell the story of Israel, and ultimately point to Christ. These are the songs that best describe my faith as a Christian. And, of course, the biblical story will end with a song. Revelation 4 and 5 describe a scene in heaven when God the Father and Jesus Christ, the Lamb of God, are praised forever with a new song, a song that everyone on earth will sing. God is the One who writes the songs the whole world will one day sing.

So, let's talk about the interpretation and communication of Psalms.

INTERPRETATION: HEARING THE VOICE IN THE PSALMS

Psalms Are Poetry

Interpreting Hebrew poetry can be an intimidating task. It is intimidating for two reasons. First, we do not understand how the individual verses "work." In other words, what exactly is it that makes them poetic? Second, often we do not see movement in the psalm. Where exactly is this song going? If we are reading a classic

4. Mark Futato notes the debate regarding whether *logos tou Christou* is a subjective genitive, "this is the word Christ spoke," or an objective genitive, "this is the Word about Christ." He concludes that this can be taken as a pregnant expression, taken to mean both. See Mark D. Futato, *Interpreting the Psalms: An Exegetical Handbook*, Handbooks for Old Testament Exegesis (Grand Rapids: Kregel, 2007), 174.

5. Psalms is part of "all Scripture" that is to be preached (2 Tim 3:14–16). More significantly, in the first Christian sermon Peter included both Psalm 16 and Psalm 110 (Acts 2:14–41). One can assume that Peter's choice of text, and understanding of that text, was influenced by Christ who personally taught Peter and the disciples how the Psalms pointed to him (Luke 24:47).

poem, such as Poe's "The Raven," we do not have either of these problems. The first stanza of Poe's classic reads,

> Once upon a midnight dreary, while I pondered, weak and weary,
> Over many a quaint and curious volume of forgotten lore—
> While I nodded, nearly napping, suddenly there came a tapping,
> As of someone gently rapping, rapping at my chamber door.
> "'Tis some visitor," I muttered, "tapping at my chamber door—
> Only this and nothing more."[6]

Notice what is familiar to us. The rhyming (dreary/weary; napping/tapping; door/more) makes this sound like a poem. In fact, the words rhythmically flow together, even when they don't rhyme. This, of course, is an intentional rhythm created by Poe. We also see movement here. The poem begins with him pondering; then the tapping begins. And this poem tells a story giving it progression. Poe is characteristically abstract. Yet, even in the abstract form we can feel poetic style and movement. Hebrew poetry is different.

Hebrew poetry works by parallelism: rhythmic features that relate the concept of the line to the previous line. What rhyme is to English poetry, parallelism is to Hebrew poetry. So, in Hebrew poetry the emphasis is not that words have a similar sound, but a similar meaning. The lines after the first line either explain, expand upon, or show a contrast to the previous line. So, the dominant force in Hebrew poetry is parallelism, not rhyme.

Think of the first stanza of Martin Luther's song, "A Mighty Fortress Is Our God."

> A mighty fortress is our God,
> A bulwark never failing,
> A helper he among the flood,
> Of mortal ills prevailing.[7]

Notice it has the familiar qualities of rhythm. Each line is balanced in wording. Notice also the rhyming (failing/prevailing). The song also has a wonderful logical progression to it. A progression that perhaps is influenced by a psalm. Luther based his song on Psalm 46:

> God is our refuge and strength,
> A very present help in trouble. (v. 1)
> Be still, and know that I am God.
> I will be exalted among the nations,
> I will be exalted in the earth!
> The Lord of hosts is with us;
> The God of Jacob is our fortress. (vv. 10–11)

---

6. Edgar Allen Poe, "The Raven," accessed February 10, 2014, http://www.poetryfoundation.org/poem/178713.

7. Martin Luther, "A Mighty Fortress Is Our God," in *Great Hymns of the Faith*, ed. John Peterson (Grand Rapids: Zondervan, 1968), 36.

Note the parallelism. In verse 1 the second line helps us understand the first: How is God our refuge and strength? He is a very present help in trouble. In verse 10 we are given the reason that we should be still and know that he is God: he will be exalted above all the earth. There is no rhyme in this psalm. However, there is a parallel structure where successive lines give previous lines meaning. Therefore, a defining quality of a Hebrew poem is its use of parallelism. So, as you read the Psalms, look for parallelism. This is what makes it poetic. Let's look at the nature of parallelism and one other dominant literary feature of Psalms, imagery.[8]

Parallelism

This is the defining feature of Hebrew poetry in the Psalms and in other poetic books in Scripture. Think of it this way: the poet offers an idea, then offers commentary on that idea. The first line says something; the second line comments on it. This may seem like a strange literary device, but if you grasp this device, you have grasped the principle literary device of the Psalms. This is where meaning is embedded.

David Jackman notes that parallelism works on three levels.[9] The author will either reinforce the idea, explain the idea, or contrast the idea. Within these three levels there is movement. Let's look at some examples of each:

Reinforce
Your word is a lamp to my feet
And a light to my path.
(Ps 119:105)

These two lines say essentially the same thing, the latter reinforcing the former.

Explain
The LORD is the strength of his people;
He is a saving refuge among the anointed.
(Ps 28:8)

How is the Lord the strength of his people? More specifically, he is a saving refuge. The psalmist did not say anything new, but repeated the idea with further explanation.

Contrast
The wicked lie in wait to destroy me,
But I consider your testimonies.
(Ps 119:95)

The first line presents a proposition, and the second line has meaning when contrasted to the first.

---

8. Köstenberger and Patterson note concreteness and tenseness, in addition to these two, that are four main features of Hebrew poetry. See Andreas J. Köstenberger and Richard D. Patterson, *Invitation to Biblical Interpretation: Exploring the Hermeneutical Triad of History, Literature, and Theology* (Grand Rapids: Kregel, 2011), 271–73.

9. David Jackman and Robin Sydserff, *Preaching and Teaching Old Testament: Narrative, Prophecy, Poetry, Wisdom* (London: The Proclamation Trust, 2008).

While the psalms may be intimidating to preach, if you can grasp the essence of this parallelism, then you have a handle on the genre. Another way to say this is that all the psalms have movement.

Movement

Futato notes that there is more going on with parallelism than mere repetition; there is also movement.[10] In other words, when reading the parallelism, see if there is a slight difference from the first part of the line to the second. The difference is an intentional shift in meaning. So, now the second part of the line is not to be understood simply as a commentary on the first. It is not that the second part of the line[11] is serving the first, but the first part of the line is serving the second in that it lays a foundation upon which the second line will build. Think of Psalm 25:16–17.

> Line 1   Turn to me and be gracious to me,
>   For I am lonely and afflicted.
>
> Line 2   The troubles of my heart are enlarged;
>   Bring me out of my distress.

Why should God be gracious? Because the author is afflicted. Why should God bring him out of his distress? Because the troubles of his heart are enlarged. In these cases the second part of the line did not repeat what was going on in the first part, but moved it to give it fuller meaning.

Here is another example from Psalm 27:5–6:

> For he will hide me in the shelter in the day of trouble;
> He will conceal me under the cover of his tent;
> He will lift me high upon a rock.
>
> And now my head shall be lifted up
> Above my enemies around me,
> And I will offer in this tent sacrifices with shouts of joy;
> I will sing and make melody to the LORD.

In the first part of the first line in verse 5, the psalmist is confident of shelter. In the second part of the line the specific type of shelter is clarified. From the second part of the line in verse 5 we know exactly how his head will be lifted up. We know that the shouts of joy will be composed of songs. Therefore, this is not redundancy; it is movement.

At the conclusion of this section it is important to note that the parallelism serves as a means to reinforce a truth in a beautiful way. Sometimes, when I am wearing my hyper-exegetical glasses, I find myself trying to extract the faintest meaning from a word whose placement in the verse, while rich with meaning, often serves to reaffirm another truth, not to layer it with more meaning. As Leland Ryken observes,

---

10. Futato, *Interpreting the Psalms*, 37–41.

11. A line is the "basic unit of Hebrew poetry. A line is not to be confined with a sentence in English, because many lines contain more than one complete sentence." Ibid., 27–29. See below for how to understand lines of Hebrew poetry in preaching.

"There is no need to press biblical poetry at once in a utilitarian direction. It is beautiful and delightful in itself."[12]

Now, open your Bible to any psalm and see if you can find parallelism. Did you see it? Now, let's look at the second dominant feature of the Psalms.

Imagery

The imagery of the Psalms is not difficult to see. Think of the opening lines of the Psalter. The blessed man is described in chapter one when he writes,

> He is like a tree
> Planted by streams of water
> That yields its fruit in its season,
> And its leaf does not wither.
> The wicked are not so,
> but are like the chaff that
> wind drives away.

The poet gives us images,[13] and yet, these are not abstractions. That is why they communicate so effectively and are so easily remembered.

Think for a moment about how a poem works. The intent of these poems is not to exhaust a theological idea. Rather, psalms function to poetically express ideas about particular things. This could be anything. However, the point is that they are small pictures of larger ideas. The small idea they are dealing with may be a feeling or an event. The preacher, therefore, will need to figure out how to move from the specific to the general. In other words, how does this event, this moment in time, speak to the character of God and his work in the world? One way to do this is to carefully incorporate illustration.

The relationship between imagery of the Psalms and sermon illustration is important. The images of the text bring illustrations to mind. The classic example of this is the most famous line in the book, Psalm 23:1, "The LORD is my shepherd . . ." The most intuitive thing for a preacher to do is to turn this metaphor into a full-blown illustration demonstrating all the ways God is like a shepherd. An illustration can convey that God cares for his sheep, protects his sheep, and provides shelter for his sheep. God even, like a good shepherd, corrects his errant sheep and brings them back into the fold. As you are reading this you can probably think of a dozen ways to illustrate this using an agricultural metaphor. And this is as it should be—imagery is the stimulus for imaginative illustrations. However, let me wave a caution flag.

The temptation is to preach the illustration of the imagery and not the truth that it is illustrating. This type of preaching looks like this:

"Here is the truth about God in the text . . ."
   "Here is the image the text provides . . ."
      "Here is an illustration of that image . . ."
         "Here is how God is like my illustration . . ."

12. Leland Ryken, *Words of Delight: A Literary Introduction to the Bible* (Grand Rapids: Baker, 1987), 184.
13. Köstenberger and Patterson, *Invitation to Biblical Interpretation*, 273.

In this errant last step the illustration took a subtle, but costly turn. There was so much energy given to the illustration that it became the focus and not the imagery of the text. The illustration should point the listener back to the text, not away from it.

Imagine you are preaching Psalm 23. You find the most wonderful illustration about sheep. Then you spend the rest of the sermon preaching the application of the illustration. However, that strays from the point of the text. The point of the Lord being the Shepherd is provision: "The LORD is my shepherd, I shall not want." Discipline is a provision, but you can see how the imagery could feed an illustration that strays from the point of the text.

An illustration should affirm the image of the text. It expands the imagery so that the truth of the imagery is clearer.

"Here is the truth of the text . . . "
    "Here is the image of the text . . . "
        "Here is an illustration of the image . . . "
            "Here is the truth affirmed by the illustration . . . "

The point is to allow the illustration to come full circle—to affirm the truth of the imagery, not to stray away from it. To use the previous example, one could preach Psalm 23, use a brief illustration that supports the imagery of shepherding, but then return to the text. The warning is against an illustration that appears larger than the text rather than serving the text.

Affective

Poems do not operate at a purely intellectual level. The words a poet uses, and the way that they move, are intended to produce an emotional effect on the listener. This is known as the affective dimension of the poetry.[14] Let's return to the beloved Psalm 23. The psalmist does not want, is led, is restored, does not fear, is comforted, and is followed by goodness and mercy. The tenor and movement of the psalm are all emotionally connected.

In preaching we want to first engage the mind. However, the psalmist does not go from the mind to the will, but from the mind to the heart and then to the will. The trajectory is instructive for preaching.[15] A sermon on Psalm 23 should teach the truth of God's provision, illustrate how this is true even with an emotional connection, and then call the listener to "follow all the days of his life." It would be hard to argue, considering the nature of the psalms, that preaching should never appeal to emotion.

Psalms Have a Unique Structure

The psalms fall into several categories: hymns, laments (corporate and individual), songs of thanksgiving, and spiritual songs.[16] Psalms is divided into five books with each book ending with doxology.

        Book 1: Psalms 1–41
        Book 2: Psalms 42–72
        Book 3: Psalms 73–89

14. Jackman and Sydserff, *Preaching and Teaching Old Testament* [DVD].
15. Ibid.
16. Claus Westermann, *Praise and Lament in the Psalms* (Atlanta: John Knox, 1981), 16.

Book 4: Psalms 90–106
Book 5: Psalms 107–50

Most of the psalms are authored by David, many by the sons of Korah, and others by Asaph.[17] However, the macro-structure of the Psalter does not bear as much influence on the meaning of the individual texts as it would, say, in a narrative genre like the Gospels. However, this is not to suggest that there are not intratextual relationships. However, the real challenge of preaching the Psalms is the micro structure of the individual psalm.[18] Relying on the work of Futato, let's look at the smallest unit of communication and move out to the largest using Psalm 1 as an example.[19]

The smallest unit of Hebrew poetry used in the Psalms is a *line*. Look at the very first line in Psalms:

> Blessed is the man who walks not in the counsel of the wicked,
> nor stands in the way of sinners,
> nor sits in the seat of the scoffers. (Ps 1:1)

Essentially a line is "one complete parallelistic expression of thought."[20] While lines often form verses in our English Bibles, a line is not to be confused with a verse as sometimes a line may extend outside of the boundaries of a verse. However, when we talk of parallelism, we are discussing the parallelism that is found within an individual line.

Lines are grouped together to form a strophe. "A strophe is a group of lines focused on a common theme."[21] The strophe, as a grouping of lines, is the basic unit of thought in Hebrew poetry. A strophe is to poetry what a paragraph is to prose. Most English Bibles set the strophes apart by separating them with a blank line between each one. So, perhaps you are already thinking that in the same way an epistle is broken into paragraphs or pericopes, a psalm is broken into strophes. If so, that is a helpful way to think of it.

Let's stay with our example of Psalm 1. Read through Psalm 1 and see if you can get a sense of the divisions of the text. As you can tell, they are divided by sense or meaning. The first two verses describe the way of the blessed man. The second two verses contrast the end of the blessed man with the end of the wicked. And the last two verses describe the fate of the wicked man. So, the psalm itself has movement. That movement is built upon consecutive strophes.

Strophes can be grouped to form stanzas. More common in longer psalms, a stanza is built when strophes are grouped according to a particular theme. So when reading a longer psalm, you may find that individual strophes are thematically arranged.

---

17. David A. Dorsey, *The Literary Structure of the Old Testament: A Commentary on Genesis–Malachi* (Grand Rapids: Baker, 1999).

18. There is significant discussion on the macro structure of the Psalms. However, the focus of this work is the structure of individual preaching units, while we acknowledge that the meaning of the individual units may be influenced by their place in the cannon. See for example Hermann Gunkle, *Introduction to Psalms: The Genres of the Religious Lyric of Israel* (Macon: Mercer University Press, 1998).

19. Futato, *Interpreting the Psalms*.

20. Ibid., 28.

21. Ibid.

This macro view of the psalm will help you better understand its structure. Notice Psalm 20. There are two strophes in verses 1–3 and verses 4–5. However, the prayers contained therein are all tied together semantically with the word "may" in the English Bible.

The Psalms Demonstrate Redemptive Praise

The psalmists have no fear in expressing complaint. However, they are equally exuberant in their praise toward God. It seems odd on one level that the two should be so vibrant in one book. Yet, this is because there is a relationship between exuberant praise and difficult times.

Walter Brueggemann suggests that the psalms progress in a specific pattern. They begin in a life situation, present a problem, and then end with a climax about the character and nature of a God who would redeem and save.[22] Bruegemann calls this orientation, disorientation, and new orientation.

Think of how this moves in the most famous Shepherd Psalm, Psalm 23.

Orientation
The LORD is my shepherd; I shall not want.
He makes me lie down in green pastures.
He leads me beside quiet waters.
He restores my soul.
He leads me in paths of righteousness for his name's sake.

Disorientation
Even though I walk through the valley of the shadow of death,
I will fear no evil, for you are with me;
Your rod and thy staff, they comfort me.

New Orientation
You prepare a table before me in the presence of my enemies;
You anoint my head with oil; my cup overflows.
Surely goodness and mercy shall follow me all the days of my life,
and I shall dwell in the house of the LORD forever.

Surely this song resonates with the NT believer so deeply because this is the whole of our experience. We expect life will run at a certain pace and in a certain way, but it doesn't. Things change. We get disoriented. This is when we throw our cares on Christ. It is not that he restores us back to the way things were before. No, he is too kind to do that. Rather, he allows us to function in the light of this new reality. He allows us to see things in a way that we could not have seen before. We have a new orientation to life; all of this is the blessing of disorientation. This is the ebb and flow of our Christian life. And, it is the ebb and flow of the Psalms.

---

22. Walter Brueggemann, *The Message of the Psalms: A Theological Commentary*, Augsburg Old Testament Studies (Minneapolis: Augsburg, 1984), 21.

The Psalms Are Personal, and They Are Actually about God[23]

As noted, about half the psalms are complaints. Many psalms express personal lament, frustration, thanksgiving, or joy. They are intensely personal. At first blush the modern preacher may be encouraged that there is such a variety of tones in Scripture. What comfort to know that this is actually a part of the perfect Word of God. This seems to make God so accessible. At the same time, such variety presents a challenge. The psalms do not seem like God's words to us; they appear as man's words to God. This is someone's prayer; it's as if we are flipping through the pages of a journal. How are we to preach another man's thoughts? How do you preach a prayer? Time taken to translate the text will yield the fact that someone complained. How are we to deal with this? Yet, the psalms are instructive even when they are not instructing. In this way they function more like a testimony and less like a lecture.

When David cries, "Hear my prayer, O LORD; give ear to my pleas for mercy! In your faithfulness answer me, in your righteousness! Enter not into judgment with your servant, for no one living is righteous before you" (Ps 143:1–2), he is actually petitioning God to hear his prayer. David never tells us what he wants us to know about God; he just prays. However, remember that ultimately David is not the only author. It was by the hand of God that these prayers are included in Scripture; there-fore, their inclusion is not by the hand of David as much as they are by God. The question we can fairly ask then is, "What does God want me to learn about himself through this psalm?" Second, "What does God want me to know about how I should approach him?" Through this psalm we learn that God is in fact merciful. We also learn a great deal about approaching God. When we approach God we acknowl-edge that he can do whatever he wishes. And we also learn from this prayer that we can ask anything from him. More precisely, since God can do anything, we can ask anything. Even though some psalms are complaints and cries for help, they are ultimately about the character of God. Why would these petitions even be offered to him if he was not able and willing to deliver and save? Let's look again at Psalm 143.

> A plea that recognizes God's character (vv. 1–2)
> A testimony of suffering (vv. 3–6)
> Specific requests (vv. 7–11)
> Hope of deliverance (v. 12)

Even though the psalms are filled with complaints, the complaints are hopeful. We should not confuse complaining with whining. Whining is born of self-loathing. The type of complaint in the Psalms is an assessment of one's situation that is focused on God's ability to deliver the psalmist out of the situation. Why? Because God is just that great. It is because God is righteous that in his righteousness he can bring the soul out of trouble (v. 12). He can protect us from enemies (141:9). He can vindicate us (35:23). He can answer (4:1). So, in this sense the complaints are expressions of praise for they are directed to the only One who has the capacity to change the situation. In this way, complaint becomes praise.

---

23. By personal I mean relational and not individual. Of course the psalms had a unique corporate function in the nation and history of Israel.

The Psalms Are Foundational to the New Testament

Psalms is the most oft-quoted Old Testament book in the New Testament. Jesus begins his ministry with the Sermon on the Mount, and the Sermon on the Mount with the Beatitudes. Compare the third beatitude with Psalm 37.

> "Blessed are the meek, for they shall inherit the earth."
> (Matt 5:5)

> "But the meek shall inherit the land."
> (Ps 37:11)

The most frequently quoted psalm in the New Testament is Psalm 110, a psalm that is foundational to the book of Hebrews. It is quoted in Matthew 22:44; Acts 2:34–35, and Hebrews 1:13. It is alluded to in Matthew 26:64; Mark 14:62; 16:19; Luke 22:69; Romans 8:34; 1 Corinthians 15:25; Ephesians 1:20; Colossians 3:1; and Hebrews 1:3; 8:1; and 10:12.[24] Moreover, the dramatic battle scene that ends the entire Bible (Revelation 19) is a fulfillment of Psalm 2. Throughout the New Testament there are references to the Psalms. The most explicit ones are of course the messianic psalms such as Psalm 2, Psalm 22, and Psalm 110. This is not to mention the shepherding motif that runs throughout the Psalms (Psalms 23; 28:9; 49:14; 78:71–72; 80:1) and its connection to Christ (John 10:1–18; Matt 13:34–35).

COMMUNICATION: RECAPTURING THE VOICE IN THE PSALMS

Preach the Psalm, Not the Story

While this was discussed in chapter two, it bears repeating here. We are preaching the text, not what is behind the text. The story behind the psalm may be fascinating and shed light on its meaning. However, if the author wanted to retell the story alone he could have. But he didn't. He wrote a song.

Psalm 78 is the retelling of the history of Israel from the exodus to the time of David. It is a wonderful retelling, and preaching it would demand some context. However, the purpose is clear enough. The psalmist affirms in verses 5–8 that God gave his law so that,

> A future generation—children yet to be born—might know . . .
> so that they might put their confidence in God
> and not forget God's works, but keep his commands.
> Then they would not be like their fathers,
> a stubborn and rebellious generation,
> a generation whose heart was not loyal
> and whose spirit was not faithful to God.

The back story to the psalm goes just there: in the back. The back story serves to gives us clues to application in the sermon.[25] However, if it seeps to the foreground

---

24. William Hendriksen and Simon Kristemaker, *Exposition of Thessalonians, the Pastorals, and Hebrews* (Grand Rapids: Baker, 1995).

25. "Appropriate alignment with the implicit demands of the textual world constitutes valid application of the text. In other words, this world is the texts' direction for application in the future," Abraham

and stays there during the sermon, then we will have preached the meaning that is behind the text to the exclusion of the meaning that is in front of the text. For example, Psalm 142 is the prayer of David when hiding from Saul in the cave. There is a temptation to preach the narrative of 1 Samuel 22:1–2. However, what is behind the text serves to lead us to what is in front of the text—its application to our lives. So, preach the meaning of the text. When bringing up the context of a psalm, do not let that context dominate the story.

Point to God and Man

When preaching Psalm 78, or a similar psalm, we begin with painting the words of the prayer. These are prayers from man to God, and we approach them as such. However, these are inspired prayers. Recall our two questions to ask about each psalm, "What does this teach me about God?" and "What does this teach me about how to approach him?" What we learn about God could serve as an outline, but be careful. The psalms are not "four things we need to know about God." They are not outlines. They are poetic prayers. In the example we just examined, David shifts from recognizing God's character (vv. 1–2), to a testimony of suffering (vv. 3–6), to a specific prayer of deliverance (vv. 7–11), to a final declaration of hope that God will deliver (v. 12). People can be encouraged that they can approach God in this way. The psalms do not provide a license to whine; they are instead a promise of hope. They give voice to our questions about justice. We wonder why God does not attend to us more. Why not direct that question to the only One who can do anything about it? You will honor him with the magnitude of your request, asking big questions for a bigger God.

So, what is this psalm about? God or David? The psalm is an honest and hopeful prayer for deliverance based on God's character. Both will need attention in this psalm.[26]

Show Them the Glory

The glory of the Psalms is Christ. This is because the trajectory we just mentioned is the trajectory of Christ. Christ was oriented in heaven, was willingly disoriented on this earth, and then experienced a new orientation when raised, ascended, and glorified. His glory was manifested in the trajectory. And so is ours. In order to show us this glory, God tells us the story of the children of Israel who were oriented toward God in the promised land as the blessed family of Jacob. They were disoriented in Egypt and the wilderness, and then reoriented in the promised land. However, just like our lives, they were disoriented again, and would find ultimate hope in the reorientation found in Christ their Messiah. And so do we.

So, when preaching the Psalms we are preaching a trajectory of the gospel. Show them how God uses this pattern in our own Christian experience. Then encourage them with the words that the God who loves them wants to reorient them to an entirely new life. Then show them that this way of living is a way of daily imitating

Kuruvilla, *Privilege the Text! A Theological Hermeneutic for Preaching* (Chicago: Moody, 2013), 42.

26. Mark Futato encourages the exegete to ask "Covenant Questions" about the psalm. The idea is that each psalm is born out of relationship with God and others. Therefore, to help communicate the psalm, it is fair to ask, "(1) What does this text teach me to believe? (2) What does this text teach me to do? (3) What does this text teach me to feel?" Futato, *Interpreting the Psalms*, 206.

the gospel. The death to life paradigm is like breathing for a Christian. We are constantly, in big and small ways, being disoriented and reoriented. This is the pattern of the gospel transposed over life. And it is glory.

Show and Tell

The strategy here has more to do with interpretation than communication. When trying to discern the meaning of a text, note the parallelism. When you preach, show the listener how the parallelism reinforces, explains, or contrasts the ideas. When preaching through a series of psalms, show them how this one feature will open up the psalms for them.

Also, show them the affective element of the psalm. They will understand from the meaning that the psalm has an emotional design, but showing it to them in the text actually reinforces this in profound ways. We then teach the listener that the Holy Spirit has inspired these affective designs; they are from God. This produces the wonderful effect of both affirming the emotions they may struggle with, and teaching them how Scripture anticipates what we feel.

Follow the Text

Futato suggests two approaches to sermon structure from the Psalms: analytical and topical.[27] Let's discuss these two approaches using Futato's designations.

Analytical. In the analytical approach the preacher is taking the units of thought as they come in the text; he uses what we would understand as a text-driven sermon in so much as the shape of the text is determining the shape of the sermon. The natural strophe divisions in the text become the divisions of the sermon. The process then becomes similar to what it would be in the exegesis of a New Testament epistle. You find the textual divisions, translate them, then find the meaning. However, this presents a practical problem when we approach some longer poetic texts.

Topical. When preaching a larger text such as Psalm 119 or Psalm 105, it may be wise to preach it as a topical arrangement. The word "topical" may be a little misleading. We are still preaching the text, not just a topic. Commonly, a topical sermon refers to the practice of selecting multiple Scriptures to deal with a topic. This is not the case in this arrangement; rather, we have chosen the text first. We have studied the text thoroughly, understand its structure, and then let the main idea emerge. Once the main idea has emerged, we then select from the text the ideas that best represent a means to communicate that major idea. So, the outline of the text is not completely arbitrary. We are trying to pick the texts that best represent what is being communicated. The purpose of the sermon is to say what the text is saying about its topic, not to exhaust the topic. This is not unlike preaching from the book of Proverbs. The sermons themselves are representative samples since many chapters in Proverbs are not written chronologically.

---

27. Futato, *Interpreting the Psalms*, 197–204.

Make the Connection

When we find a psalm to which the New Testament refers, be sure and point out the connection. This serves the secondary purpose of giving people a sense of the wholeness of the Bible. This is a treasure beyond comparison. Imagine a junior-high student who comes to faith in Christ and sits under your teaching for six years until he graduates from high school. Do we want to send him off to college armed with a collection of stories? Or do we want to send him out "canonized"? That is, with an appreciation for how the Bible teaches us the Bible. God is so loving that he gives us a guide to understand his Word within his Word. It is as awesome in its mercy as its mystery. We must show people the connections.

The principle goal, however, is communicating the meaning of the text. If God has given us a complete canon, then the translation of one particular verse has meaning in light of the whole of Scripture. The translation tells what it says, and the interpretation tells us what it means. And the interpretation is always done in light of the canon.

So, when preaching Psalm 110, it is imperative to take it to the New Testament. The New Testament gives the Psalms their complete meaning.

Connect to Christ

Of course, the Messianic Psalms naturally connect to Christ. But what about the other texts? Whether every text is Christological is a matter of debate. However, what is not debated is that the Psalms reflect a passionate love for God from a covenant people. The songs represent the hardship, failure, and hope of a people who are waiting on God. And we are such a people. They were waiting for a Messiah to come; we are waiting for a Messiah to return. They were living in hope of deliverance and so are we. So, as the psalms surface issues related to grief, sorrow, joy, suffering, and vengeance, preach those texts informed by Christian theology. Take the psalms to their New Testament parallels. Then, preach the corollary doctrine. In other words, explain the psalm and then preach how it fits into New Testament doctrine. As we noted, the order is important. We are not preaching the doctrine. We are explaining where a psalm fits into New Testament theology.

STRUCTURING A SERMON FROM A PSALM

Length of Text

In chapter 2 we briefly discussed choosing the length of a text. The Psalms illustrate how this is a genre-specific decision. The length is a pastoral concern and an exegetical concern. There might be a rationale for preaching all of longer psalms such as Psalm 78 or Psalm 118 in one sermon. There is an organic flow that makes it appealing. However, there are things that will not be able to be covered. So, what may be more practical is a length of text that allows you to deal with all the strophes in the text. We chose Psalm 24 for the sample below. It has three major strophes. It can be handled well in the length of time of a normal sermon.

Identifying the right length of text may take a little more reading and thinking. Reading is always critical, but perhaps more so with the psalms. The psalms, as poetry, say something, and they mean something. The poems are not vague, but they are filled with images and nuances. Therefore, we are reading to get to the meaning since the first pass may not get the full meaning. This is why Ryken observes that a good reader of poetry is not afraid to stare at the poem.[28] It will not yield its meaning without meditation, and there is no meditation without reading.

Divide the Text in the Strophe Structure

While the verse structure of the Scripture is a late convention, the strophe structure of Hebrew poems is less arbitrary. This is an advantage to the preacher. Think of Futato's two different types of structure for a sermon on a Psalm, analytical and topical.[29]

Analytical. This should be the default structure since the preacher is trying to let the structure of the text be the structure of the sermon. Identify the strophe in the text and then build the ***exegetical work out of the individual strophe. The strophes provide natural textual divisions, and therefore the sermon structure***.

Topical. There are other psalms that simply cover one topic. The meaning of the psalm may be recaptured by simply walking through the psalm, or one can develop divisions that organize it around certain topics. Either approach is acceptable. The main point is that the sermon structure is to capture the sense of the psalm.

The best example of this is Psalm 119. At 176 verses, this is the longest chapter in the Bible. The theme of the psalm is delighting in the Word of God. Yet, a verse-by-verse, line-by-line exposition would lead to a year-long study on one chapter. So an analytical approach might not be helpful. Also, the poem is an acrostic arranged by the letters in the Hebrew alphabet. So, it is clear that the author, by his chosen structure, has not arranged the psalm thematically. But, due to the length of the psalm, a thematic arrangement might be the best way to approach the preaching of the psalm. A series through this chapter could include the major themes such as the authority of Scripture, our love for Scripture, and Scripture's prescriptive insight into our lives. When the sermon is preached, the texts selected may be from different parts of the chapter. This is still an exposition since it is uncovering the deposit of truth that is in the text. It is violating the poetic order so one may capture the sense of the whole.

Tend to the Tone

While it is important to convey the tone of all the literary genres of the Bible, it is especially true with Psalms. The structure itself will lend a tone. In Psalm 23, it is the progression of provision. In Psalm 24, the tone moves from narrow introspection to the full-blown glorification of the King of Glory. When outlining this sermon, I want to reflect that in my word choices.

This is why in the sample below I chose not to use "points," but "moves." This is a poem, not a lecture. While the listener will not see my preaching notes, the difference will come through in the way I communicate. The sermon will not feel like a list, and I will never say, for example, "now notice the next point." I refrain from saying such things because there is a rising tension in these texts that I fear will be lost if treated like a lecture.

---

28. Ryken, *Words of Delight*, 215.
29. Futato, *Interpreting the Psalms*, 197–203.

My goal is that the listener perceive the structure of the text, more than the structure of my outline. The sermon's infrastructure is a vehicle used to communicate the text's structure.

A Word about Introductions and Conclusions

The gospel is all throughout Scripture. Therefore, the sermon should end with the hope and anticipation of Christ. Recall that many of the psalms are on a trajectory of orientation, disorientation, and reorientation, and they deal with the realities of life in an honest and genuine way. Such raw honesty gives the listener the permission, and the mandate, to be honest as well. A sermon's introduction not only sets the topic, but also the tone for the rest of the sermon. Introductions that, through illustration or personal story, allow the church attenders to be honest with their condition are effective.

Likewise, conclusions that take things to the gospel are the most effective. This is not to say the conclusion to the sermon should end predictably. It shouldn't. This is inconsistent with the tenor of the psalms. They are not predictable and clean. So this is why ending the sermon with a tie to the gospel is a natural fit. You don't need the gospel because things end neatly. You need the gospel because they don't. The gospel does not return life to normal. The gospel creates a new reality that transcends the old. That is the end.

Sermon Sample: Psalm 24

PREACHING STRATEGY
It seems the text is asking the question, "Who can stand before God?"

Introduction

The New Testament teaches that heaven is a place of unlimited joy, unlimited happiness, and unlimited pleasure, but only for a limited group of people. Jesus had many who followed him in the crowd, but a small number of true disciples (Matt 5:1), and even one of the disciples did not make it. Jesus also constantly warned that there would be fake among the real. So that leads us to the question, "Who exactly is it that will go to heaven?" You might think, *That's easy; those people who pray a prayer go to heaven.* But that's not what our text says. So, who is it that goes to heaven?

The introduction gives the subject without the complement. The goal of this introduction is to simply raise the question, "Who goes to heaven?" Most listeners feel like they know the answer—which is what makes this psalm compelling.

Move One: God Rules over the Earth (Ps 24:1–2)

The question of who goes to heaven is even more profound in light of verses 1–2, which tell us that God owns everything by virtue of creation. All of creation is his. He is so mighty that he built this earth.

Then, based on God's authority, we are asked a question, "Who can ascend to the hill of the LORD?" Before the temple was built, they would go up to high places to worship since the altars were on hills. So, more precisely, the question is, "Since all the earth is God's, who can ascend there?!" Who can go into the presence of God and worship? We would say in a modern context, "Who can be saved?" The answer is twofold.

> These opening verses are important context to the pending question.

Move Two

1. Those who go to heaven must have perfect purity (v. 4a).
They have clean hands and they have a pure heart.

2. Those who go to heaven must have perfect integrity (v. 4b).
They do not give their soul over to what is false.

3. Those who go to heaven are justified and seek the face of God (vv. 5–6).
They are blessed, vindicated, and seek the face of God.

So that's it: the people who go to heaven must have perfect purity and perfect integrity.

> Evangelicals raised to believe in the doctrine of grace alone may balk at this statement. And that's the point. The worst thing that could be done at this point is to let them off the hook too soon. Let them feel the weight of God's expectations. It is here that they are developing a thirst for grace—a grace that will not taste sweet unless they taste the bitterness of their inability to meet God's demands.

Move Three

But the problem is that none of us are pure. No one finds God accessible. Fortunately, the psalmist is not through. Look at verses 7–10. The gates of the city are personified. They are not big enough to accommodate the King who is coming back from battle in victory. This is perhaps a picture of the ark of the covenant coming back into the city.

However, we no longer have the ark because the presence of God is within us in the person of the Holy Spirit. When Jesus died on the cross, the veil that separated the ark from the outside world was torn, giving us free access to God. It was Christ who died to give us access to the Father.

In the same way, we know that when we stand before God we will not have perfect purity or perfect integrity. If that were the case heaven would never be populated. So Christ gives us his perfect purity and his perfect integrity. Christ removes the debt and places in my account a credit of grace that can never be exhausted. This is what it means to go into heaven with perfect purity and perfect integrity. When the King comes into his heavenly city one day, I will be with him, a part of his victory parade.

> Here is the natural connection to Christ.

Conclusion

Imagine that you are thousands of dollars in debt. You go to the bank to plead your case and the banker pulls up your account and slides it across the desk to you. As you stare at the page you notice two things. You have no debt in your account, and there is more money in your account than you could ever spend. This will never happen in life, but this is exactly what Christ has done for us. The King of Glory has removed all the penalty of sin, and credited our accounts with an amount of grace that can never be exhausted.

QUESTIONS FOR DISCUSSION

1. What is the most distinguishing feature of Hebrew poetry?
2. In what three ways does this feature work?
3. What are the three basic units of Hebrew poetry?
4. What are two potential ways of structuring sermons from Psalms?
5. What criteria will help you decide the best approach of the two?

RECOMMENDED READING

Bateman, Herb, and Brett Sandy. *Interpreting the Psalms for Preaching and Teaching*. Atlanta: Chalice. 2010.

Brueggemann, Walter. *The Message of the Psalms: A Theological Commentary*. Augsburg Old Testament Studies. Augsburg, 1984.

Dorsey, David A. *The Literary Structure of the Old Testament: A Commentary on Genesis–Malachi*. Grand Rapids: Baker, 1999.

Firth, David G. *Preaching Praise Poetry*. Reclaiming the Old Testament for Christian Preaching. Downers Grove: InterVarsity Academic, 2010.

Futato, Mark D. *Interpreting the Psalms: An Exegetical Handbook*. Handbooks for Old Testament Exegesis. Grand Rapids: Kregel, 2007.

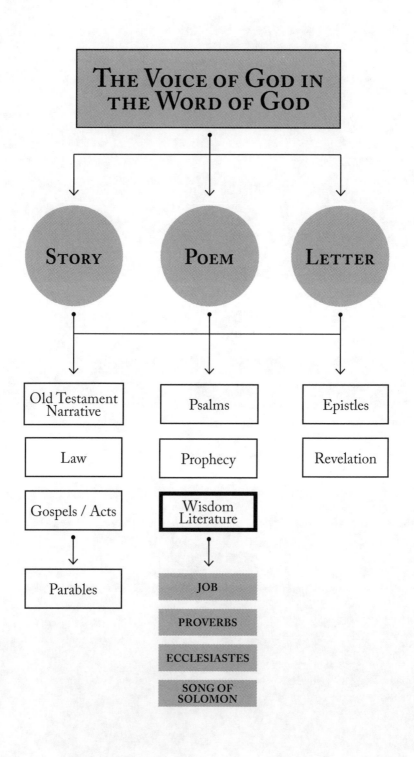

THE VOICE OF GOD IN THE WORD OF GOD

STORY

POEM

LETTER

| Old Testament Narrative | Psalms | Epistles |

| Law | Prophecy | Revelation |

| Gospels / Acts | Wisdom Literature |

| Parables |

JOB

PROVERBS

ECCLESIASTES

SONG OF SOLOMON

Chapter 9

RECAPTURING THE VOICE OF GOD
IN THE WISDOM LITERATURE

IN HIS CLASSIC ALLEGORY, *THE PILGRIM'S PROGRESS*, JOHN BUNYAN WRITES OF THE ADVENTURES OF TWO TRAVELING COMPANIONS, CHRISTIAN AND HOPEFUL. They were warned along the way not to give in to the words of the Flatterer, but they did not listen. Flatterer spread a net for their feet and they were caught. The Shining One comes to deliver them from the net. Before he sends them on their way, Bunyan sees one more scene in his dream. He writes,

> Then I saw in my dream, that he commanded them to lie down; which when they did, he chastised them sore, to teach them the good way wherein they should walk; and as he chastised them he said, "As many as I love, I rebuke and chasten; be zealous therefore, and repent." This done, he bids them go on their way, and take good heed to the other directions of the Shepherd. So they thanked him for all kindness, and went softly along the right way, singing:

> "Come hither, you that walk along the way;
> See how the pilgrims fare, that go astray!
> They catched are in an entangling net,
> 'Cause they good counsel lightly did forget:
> 'Tis true, they rescued were, but yet you see
> They're scourged to boot: Let this your caution be."[1]

This passage may strike us as strange. It seems odd that the Shining One would actually whip the travelers, and stranger still that the travelers would take it, and really insane that they would thank him and go on their way singing. But this is not the song of masochistic lunatics. Rather, it is the song of people who understand the precious value of wisdom: wisdom is the garland around our heads that should identify us (Prov 1:9); wisdom should be our most intimate friend (Prov 7:4); and wisdom should be bound to our hearts always (Prov 6:21). And therefore the travelers

---

1. John Bunyan, *The Pilgrim's Progress* (Springdale, PA: Whitaker House, 1981), 161–62.

can be thankful for these wounds that gave them so much grace and protected them from harm.[2]

The Wisdom literature of Scripture refers to Proverbs, Ecclesiastes, Job, and Song of Solomon. Since each book is unique, we will deal with each one separately. However, the feature that makes them all Wisdom literature is their proverbial way of leading us along on our journey. Unlike the direct commands of the Old Testament and the imperatives built on the theology of the New Testament, the Wisdom literature serves as a traveler's guide to life.

Unlike in most travelers' guides, much more is at stake here. A travel guide to a foreign city will give you suggestions and a list of "must see" sights. But they really are not must see. If you refuse to see the Pantheon when in Rome, you still live and breathe and carry on with life. However, if you ignore wisdom, then on some level you actually lose your life. You might even cry out,

> How I hated discipline,
> and my heart despised reproof!
> I did not listen to the voice of my teachers
> or incline my ear to my instructors.
> I am at the brink of utter ruin in the assembled congregation. (Prov 5:12–14)

After all, following the advice is the difference between wisdom and folly:

> The fear of the LORD is the beginning of knowledge;
> fools despise wisdom and instruction. (Prov 1:7)

And the risk/reward is huge.

> For the simple are killed by their turning away,
> and the complacency of fools destroys them;
> but whoever listens to me will dwell secure
> and will be at ease, without dread of disaster. (Prov 1:32–33)

So, Wisdom literature is a travel guide, but like all travel guides, it is only effective if it is actually used to navigate. Wisdom literature is not a set of suggestions. It represents the base line of wisdom. A life of joy or regret is the outcome for following or ignoring the wisdom contained therein.

Most everything we experience in daily life—work, family, and marriage relationships—is addressed in these books. However, there might be a tendency in some to think that since these books are practical they are not as theologically rich as others. Nothing could be further from the truth. When preaching through Proverbs one will have to deal with the personification of wisdom in chapter 8. In Ecclesiastes there is the thorny pessimism of all of life. This is not to mention the whole problem of theodicy in the book of Job. In the Wisdom literature we see the winsome charm of a traveler giving advice to other travelers, but we also have the questions of theology behind the wisdom. To preach the practical wisdom without the theology behind it is an approach that misrepresents the text and, in the end,

---

2. Derek Kidner, *The Wisdom of Proverbs, Job, and Ecclesiastes* (Downers Grove: InterVarsity, 1985), 11.

helps no one. Preaching Wisdom literature is both theology and practice; it is doing both diagnostics and prognostics.

So let's talk about the features of these three books respectively, and consider a template demonstrating how to preach them.

INTERPRETATION: HEARING THE VOICE IN JOB

The Structure Is a Story

The book of Job has a narrative feel to it. However, the narrative is eclipsed with long passages of poetry that are admonitions, condemnations, pleas for mercy, and conversations between Job and his friends and later between Job and God. Derek Kidner suggests the following outline:

Outline of Job

1. Prose Prologue (chaps. 1 and 2): the cynic's taunt

    Satan suggests that the religion of so prosperous a man as Job is sheer self-interest. He is given leave to test Job to the limit.

2. Poetic Dialogue (3:1–42:6): the sufferer's outrage, the moralists' bias, and the LORD's high wisdom.

    1) Job's lament (chap. 3).
    2) Three rounds of speeches by Job's comforters, punctuated by Job's protests (chaps. 4–27) and followed by a poem on man's search for wisdom (chap. 28) and by Job's apologia (chaps. 29–31).
    3) Elihu's interruption (chaps. 32–37).
    4) The Lord enlarges Job's horizon (chaps. 38–41).
    5) Job bows to his divine Lord's will (42:1–6).

3. Prose Epilogue (42:7–end): Job is vindicated and restored.[3]

The first two chapters of the book open with a narrative. Satan is coming before the throne of God to test Job's faithfulness to God. In these first few chapters we are given remarkable insight into the entire book. We have the setting of the narrative, the plot, and all the characters—along with Job's telling confession, "Naked I came from my mother's womb, and naked shall I return. The LORD gave, and the LORD has taken away; blessed be the name of the LORD" (Job 1:21). A good reading of Job's character is also provided: "In all this Job did not sin or charge God with wrong" (Job 2:2).

The bulk of the book contains the poetic dialogues between Job and his supposed friends. The book closes with a short narrative concerning Job's vindication and restoration.

Job Is Narrative Poetry

One of the unique features of Job is that the bulk of the book is poetry. The poetry follows the patterns that were discussed in the previous chapter on Psalms. It is the pattern of Hebrew parallelism. In particular, a form of parallelism known as

---

3. Ibid., 56–57.

synthetic parallelism is often used. The second or third part of a line will modify in some way the first part of the line. Look, for example, at the first line of poetry from chapter 3.

> Let the day perish on which I was born,
>   And the night that said,
>   "A man is conceived."
>
> Let that day be darkness!
>   May God above not seek it,
>   Nor light shine upon it. (vv. 3–4)

Notice that the lines that follow do not simply repeat what was said in the first part of the line, but they add to and reinforce the meaning by description.

Notice also that the lines are organized into strophes. Look again at Job's lament in Job 3. It is built around three strophes, all lamenting the day of his birth (vv. 3–10; 11–19; 20–26). There are some interesting features to this structure. First, notice that the web of reflection spirals outward. It begins with Job himself lamenting his birth (v. 3) then moves out in the third strophe to ask why light is given to any that God has "hedged in." So his contemplation has movement from "me" to "them."

Notice also the light/darkness metaphor that is woven throughout:

> Strophe One: vv. 3–7—Let the day be darkness; v. 9—Let the stars be dark.
> Strophe Two: v. 16—Why did I ever see the light?
> Strophe Three: v. 20—Why do the miserable ever see the light?

So, the light/dark metaphor is a way for Job to move the story from cursing to contemplation; from "Why me?" to "Why them?"

INTERPRETATION: HEARING THE VOICE IN PROVERBS

The joy of preaching Proverbs is that it gives a pastor the opportunity to preach across a wide spectrum of topics. However, its joy is also its challenge. The preacher must be able to engage the topic while using enough variety in the presentation to be faithful to the text. Let's begin with a discussion on the structure of Proverbs.

The Structure of Proverbs Is Topical and Collective

The book of Proverbs has an interesting structure. Look at this structure provided by Kidner.

1–9	A fatherly approach: exhortations for the young.
10:1–22:16	A plain man's approach: Solomon's collection of sentence-sayings.
22:17–24:22	Life's regularities, oddities, dangers and delights, noted, compared and evaluated.
24:23–34	More fatherly teachings: two groups of wise men's exhortations.

25–29	More sentence-sayings: gleaning from Solomon, compiled by Hezekiah's men.
30	An observer's approach: musings on the hidden Creator and on the idiosyncrasies of his creatures.
31	A womanly approach: a mother's home-truths (vv. 1–9); a wife's example (vv. 10–31).[4]

There is a discernible break after chapter 9. Chapters 1–9 are sequential and generally cover the topic of wisdom and why we should gain wisdom. Chapter 10 begins with a transition statement, "The proverbs of Solomon" (10:1). This overt marker shifts the attention away from the opening remarks of chapters 1–9 to a section of collected sayings. We should be aware that the sermon structure we might have been using for the first nine chapters will need to be modified. Chapters 1–9 and 31 are written with a more specific topical arrangement. The rest of the book is a collection of sayings covering an entire range of topics. There are some topical collections interspersed throughout, but the main of the book is arranged as a collection of sayings. It stands to reason that it would be difficult to preach the entire book in the same way.

The Book Is Age Specific

The book of Proverbs is the one book that is written to the young. This does not mean that others cannot benefit from the book in the same way that, married or single, we can all benefit from the teachings of the Song of Solomon or Paul's wisdom in marriage from 1 Corinthians 7. However, remembering the original audience is important. The young tend to be foolish (Prov 22:15); thus, correction is necessary. However, foolishness is not age specific. We all need wisdom.

The Proverbs Are Terse and Reductionist

The proverbs are "truth stripped to the essentials."[5] Therefore, when one reads a proverb, they are reading the truest and simplest word on a matter. They are reading a pithy statement on one subject. This terseness provides the information in as succinct a manner as possible.[6] The advantage to this is that the proverbs are easy to recall. That is their function. They are portable teachings whose structure serves as grappling hooks to our memories.

However, this wonderful feature has a potential liability. A reader could treat a proverbial observation as the last word on something. The most oft cited example of this is Proverbs 22:6, "Train up a child in the way he should go; even when he is old he will not depart from it." The difference between a proverb and a promise is that the proverbs make an observation that is generally true. However, this is not a promise that one effort always produces one outcome. This proverb is true, but the nature of a proverb is that it is a general or gnomic truth about how to live successfully in God's world. To qualify this with how we parent, and include a discussion on the free will of the child, would loosen the grappling hooks, and the proverb

---

4. Ibid., 18.

5. John A. Kitchen, *Proverbs*, Mentor Commentary (Inverness, Scotland: Mentor, 2006), 29.

6. Andreas J. Köstenberger and Richard D. Patterson, *Invitation to Biblical Interpretation: Exploring the Hermeneutical Triad of History, Literature, and Theology* (Grand Rapids: Kregel, 2011), 271.

would lose its effect. Its stickiness demands its simplicity, but its simplicity demands it be reductionist.

The Proverbs Reflect the Mosaic Covenant

The proverbs were penned under the shadow of the Mosaic covenant. Blessings were promised for keeping God's law (Deut 28:1–14). Thus, the proverbs include a father's wisdom to his son regarding much about material prosperity. However, in the new covenant the material blessings will be realized in the day to come when Christ consummates his kingdom. In the new covenant, therefore, earthly material things become of less value as we seek the kingdom that is to come (Matt 6:19–24). All of the promises of the Proverbs are true, yet the blessings will look different under the new covenant.

INTERPRETATION: HEARING THE VOICE IN ECCLESIASTES

The End of the Matter

The book of Ecclesiastes finds its center in the futility of life: "All is vanity" (1:2). While this is seemingly pessimistic, it is hardly a declaration of hopelessness. The book should not be viewed as a rant on the meaninglessness of life given by a worn out has been. Rather, the book should be viewed as a field guide who is going before us, mapping out territories, and providing insight for our traverse.

After all, life is filled with seemingly wonderful pursuits that, at the end of the day, provide little more than emptiness. That being said, wouldn't we want to know that? While the book is not as age specific as the book of Proverbs, it does contain a special admonition to consider God "in the days of your youth" (12:1). The warning makes sense considering the context of the book, which deals with most things that young people would be consumed with, namely the acquisition of pleasure and material possessions.

Topical Progression

The book does not have a general sense of chronology to it, but is rather a collection of sayings and thoughts. Kidner organizes the book like this:

A. Truths about God
  1. Creator
  2. Disposer
  3. Unsearchable
  4. Judge of all
  5. To be reverenced and obeyed

B. Truths about life
  1. Pointers to despair:
    a. The ceaseless round
    b. The fruitless search
    c. The elusive pattern
    d. The unmanageable: misrule, mischance, death

    2. Mitigations:
      a. Simple joys
      b. Common sense
      c. Enterprise
    3. The point of rest:

    God, whose service is man's raison d'etre,
      whose judgment leaves nothing without meaning.[7]

Although there is a topical arrangement, unlike Proverbs, the book does have a progression to it. It begins with a general assessment that all of life is vanity, then expands on the meaning of that terse phrase. After all the options have been exhausted, the author returns to reassess his original statement. Unwavering from the vanity of life, he concludes with this:

> The end of the matter; all has been heard. Fear God and keep his commandments, for this is the whole duty of man. For God will bring every deed into judgment, with every secret thing, whether good or evil. (Eccl 12:13–14)

The Poetry Is Magnificent

The poetry of Ecclesiastes is simply magnificent. It is filled with the terseness that is typical of Hebrew poetry.[8] At the same time, some of the images are beautiful. In fact, consider how many passages from Ecclesiastes have fallen into common idioms. Take these for example:

> For everything there is a season, and a time for every matter under heaven. (Eccl 3:1)
> All go to one place. All are from dust, and to dust all return. (3:20)
> Dead flies make the perfumer's ointment give off a stench. (10:1)

As many times as people have heard "dust to dust" or "the fly in the ointment," they may not have realized that they were quoting Solomon. There are also other wonderfully poetic passages, such as the description of the ailing body in 12:1–8 or the challenge to "cast your bread upon the waters" in 11:1–10.

Work

With the theme of meaninglessness woven in the book, the reader may miss an interesting theme in Ecclesiastes: taking pleasure in work. It is strong in the text and wildly applicable. Toil has its problems. Toil can be vanity (2:10, 11). All the toil is left to another (2:18–23). Toil can be motivated by envy (4:4). Yet the preacher writes that pleasure should be taken in toil:

---

7. Kidner, *The Wisdom of Proverbs, Job, and Ecclesiastes*, 94.
8. Köstenberger and Patterson, *Invitation to Biblical Interpretation*, 271.

> There is nothing better for a person than that he should eat and drink and find enjoyment in his toil. This also, I saw, is from the hand of God. (2:24; cf. 3:13, 22; 5:18)

The real pleasure that is taken in toil is toil itself. "My heart found pleasure in all my toil, and this was my reward for my toil" (2:10).

INTERPRETATION: HEARING THE VOICE IN THE SONG OF SOLOMON

The Song of Solomon has a varied history of interpretation. Though historically it has been treated as allegorical literature, today it is more accepted to preach it literally. The allegorical approach would read the book as a representative example for other theological realties, while the literal approach would see this as a narrative that depicts true love. Both of these things are true.

The Book Is Symbolic

There are many different interpretive approaches to the Song of Solomon. Bullock identifies four.[9] The allegorical approach treats the aspect of the love story as representative of a deeper theological meaning. In this way, the figures in the love story were vehicles for understanding specific doctrines.

The typological method generally renders Solomon as a type of Christ coming for his bride. While not viewing the book as an allegory in itself, still the ultimate purpose of the book is to point us to a future reality not necessarily germane to the intent of the human author. The mythological method, hardly helpful for preaching, would see the events in the book as representative of an ancient cult. Finally, the literal method views the book as a celebration of love between a man and a woman. This is where most modern commentators land.[10]

The truth is that the Song of Solomon is about Christ. The reason it is about Christ is not because there is an author intended hidden agenda; rather, it is about Christ for the reason that it is about marriage. Marital love exists to demonstrate the love that Christ has for his church and the responsive love that the church gives to Christ (Eph 5:18–33). The wedding ceremony is the picture of ultimate love when what has been promised is fulfilled in Christ (Rev 19:1–10).

To say that the Song of Solomon is purely allegorical is to rob it of its rich application for the church. To say that it is only literal is to miss the glory of Christ in marriage. So we preach it as literal, but note the symbolism that is there.

The Book Has a Narrative Flow[11]

The structure of the Song of Solomon is fascinating. Some find that preaching the Song of Solomon is fascinating for the reason that each of the preaching units

---

9. C. Hassell Bullock, *An Introduction to the Old Testament Poetic Books* (Chicago: Moody, 1988), 245–54.

10. "They stress that the canon would have been incomplete without a work dignifying human love, for that, too, is a part of God's creation. The Song of Solomon demonstrates a godly approach to sexual and marital concerns," in Paige Patterson, *Song of Solomon*, Everyman's Bible Commentary (Chicago: Moody, 1986), 21.

11. For helpful commentary on available books/articles on the Song of Solomon, including works on the structure of the book, see James T. Dennison, "What Should I Read on the Song of Solomon?," *Kerux:*

can stand-alone with multiple practical applications. The book progresses from the setting, courtship, wedding, to marriage, and ends with conclusion.[12]

Another way to see the book is through its chiastic structure.[13] However, for the preacher the most relevant thing about the structure, as discussed below, is that it is narrative and progressive. Therefore a sermon on the Song of Solomon will have narrative structure; a sermon series through the Song of Solomon will communicate the macro structure of the book, hinting at its narrative flow. Ginsburg divides the book into five narrative sections:[14] (1) 1:1–2:7; (2) 2:8–3:5; (3) 3:6–5:1; (4) 5:2–8:4; (5) 8:5–14.

The Wisdom Literature Is about Christ

When Jesus was responding to the scribes and Pharisees who wanted a sign, he replied that "The Queen of the South will rise up at the judgment with this generation and condemn it, for she came from the ends of the earth to hear the wisdom of Solomon, and behold, something greater than Solomon is here" (Matt 12:42).[15] The wisdom of Solomon compelled the wealthy queen to travel the distance to meet him and learn at his feet, and yet the presence of Christ, One much greater than Solomon, is here. After all, Christ is the "wisdom of God" (1 Cor 1:24).[16] So any wisdom in the Wisdom literature is a precursor to the true wisdom that is only found in Christ. He is wisdom.

COMMUNICATION: RECAPTURING THE VOICE IN WISDOM LITERATURE
PREACHING JOB

Strategy

Preach the Narrative. One way to mine out the narrative structure is to preach the whole book in one sermon. This is a good approach for any of the books of the Bible.[17] However, the value of this approach in Job is that, while the entire book is a story, the synopsis of the book can be communicated concisely, covering just three chapters (1–2; 42:7–end). The drama has a setting (throne room) and characters (God, Satan, Job, friends/family), with some wonderful character development as seen in the dialogue. It also has a classic narrative structure with a setting, problem, resolution of the problem, and a new situation.

Whether you preach it as one sermon or not, be sure and mine out the narrative feel of the sermon by allowing the rising tension of the story to develop. The challenge with the theology of the story is tough enough; so, allow the narrative flow to bring your listeners in. The flow of the narrative will be your friend when you try to explain the problem of evil. Also, remember that stories are inductive. This is a

---

A Journal of Biblical Theological Preaching 8, no. 2 (September 1993): 35–41.

12. Patterson, *Song of Solomon*, 28–29.

13. Dennison, *What Should I Read?*, 38–39.

14. Christian D. Ginsburg, *The Song of Songs and Coheleth* (New York: KTAV, 1857), 7–11, as quoted in C. Hassell Bullock, *An Introduction to the Old Testament Poetic Books* (Chicago: Moody, 1998), 220.

15. See D. A. Carson, *Matthew*, Expositors Bible Commentary (Grand Rapids: Zondervan, 1984), 297.

16. This is true regardless if one uses 1 Cor 1:24 to make a Christological connection to Proverbs 8.

17. Mark Dever, *The Message of the New Testament: Promises Kept* (Wheaton: Crossway, 2005) and *The Message of the Old Testament: Promises Made* (Wheaton: Crossway, 2006).

distinguishing feature of stories, and is true of the book of Job. The story rises and falls, and there is no resolution until the closing verses of the last chapter. So, as in all narrative, allow the story to tease out until the end with the final restoration of all of Job's fortunes (42:10).

Preach the Strophe. The most logical way to approach preaching the text is to look to the strophes in the text. In the above example a sermon built on the strophes of the chapter will begin with identifying the strophes of the chapter. The strophes are generally set off by a double space separation in most English translations. The divisions of the strophes eventually become the divisions of the sermon. Exegetical work can then be done within these divisions. It is always possible that a thematic approach may cause you to collapse two strophes into one, or divide a strophe. Such an approach still allows the text to inform the sermon, even if it is less imitation and more reanimation. "So the poetic form informs, but it does not necessarily give you a sermon outline."[18]

Consider Variety. Preaching the book of Job is a challenge if one does not tend to the macro structure of the book. The poetic section of Job is the bulk of the book, chapters 3–42. On the surface it appears as if this is a quagmire of poetry into which it is dangerous to tread. One option would be to break this up by identifying the key themes that recur in the book and then building a sermon series around these themes. All the themes of justice, righteousness, vindication, and innocence revolve around the idea of God and suffering. It would be possible to preach verse-by-verse through the whole book. However, this would be a challenge given its length and repetitive nature. It would also be possible to extract the major responses to suffering from Job's counselors. Doing so would involve extracting the core of the responses and organizing them into individual sermons in a series. However, be sure to remember both the immediate and canonical contexts of these responses.

So, exegetically we must consider the variety of options when it comes to preaching the poetic section of Job. And pastorally we must choose that which best fits our congregations.

PREACHING PROVERBS

Vary the Structure When Preaching Through the Book

The sermon flow in the first nine chapters could be preached verse-by-verse, chapter-by-chapter. It is possible for the preacher to take larger sections throughout these chapters. However, what about chapter 10 and after? Chapter 10 deals with a wise son, illicit profit, the provision of God, industrious work, God's blessings, wisdom, integrity, and foolish behavior. And that is just in the first 10 verses. Rather than trying to preach verse-by-verse, we need to preach verse *with* verse. While those of us who like to walk through books of the Bible might feel consternation in doing anything but walking through the text from beginning to end, we must remember that the reason we walk through the text verse-by-verse is to capture the

---

18. Douglas Sean O'Donnell, *The Beginning and End of Wisdom: Preaching Christ from the First and Last Chapters of Proverbs, Ecclesiastes, and Job* (Wheaton: Crossway, 2011), 149.

meaning of the individual words in their macro structure. However, for this section of the Proverbs, there is not an explicit macro structure that gives the text meaning.

Therefore we are better served asking ourselves, "What does Proverbs teach on money?" "What does Proverbs teach on relationships?" Think of it this way. Growing up, my father rarely sat me down for individual lectures on subjects. However, I could tell you my dad's primary teachings on money by giving you the collected wisdom I gained from riding in the car, going on vacation, and times spent at dinner. To understand what he said about money, I would need to collect his sayings from across the years. This is exactly what Solomon has done with his thoughts. The book of Proverbs is the longest lunch box note ever written, collecting just about everything that a father would want to say to a son. And the collected wisdom on certain topics will yield a series to preach.

So in sum, a sermon from chapters 1–9 or chapter 31 may involve taking the paragraph units (strophes) as they come chronologically in the text. In chapters 10–30, it may be wise to preach sermons that collect what the Proverbs say on a particular theme, while using a representative verse.

The representative verse strategy comes with this caution: be sure to be fair in your representation. In other words, if we are to preach on anger, as in the example below, we are saying to our people, "Here is everything that Proverbs has to say about anger." We are collecting the data, reducing it, and summarizing it. The challenge to this kind of preaching is capturing everything the book says on an issue and including it in one sermon. This is why it is best to begin with a representative text as a "home base" for the sermon, branching out from there. Choose a representative sample that says the most about the topic, and then use the rest of the texts as argumentation for this one. This assumes that there is a dominant representative text. If this is not the case, and more texts are to be included, be careful not to have listeners turn to too many texts during the sermon.

Preach Them in Light of the Whole

When preaching the proverbs, we must preach them in light of the whole of Scripture. If, for example, we are preaching Proverbs 22:6, we should pan out and discuss Deuteronomy 6 and the perpetual nature with which we are to teach our children. If our parents do not hear this, they may think training up a child only involves abstaining from certain vices and involvement in church things. We must also pan out further to the discussion of the parent-child relationship in Ephesians 6:1–4 and its foundation in the Spirit-filled home (5:18).

Think of proverbs as representative sound bites. There is a rich theology to the book of Proverbs, but the individual units are representative of other truths in the Scripture. So preach them informed by a biblical theology of each theme.

Preach to the Young

While we are not generally age specific in our preaching, this is an opportunity to preach to the young. It would not be wise to mention this in every sermon, as others might become disengaged. However, it would be good to mention this up front. It might even be wise to pull aside or visit the students for a separate meeting at the beginning of the series, introduce them to what they will be hearing, and challenge them to lean in during the series and listen closely.

Preaching Ecclesiastes

Preach the Flow

When preaching through the book, it is advantageous to preach the flow of the progression. Therefore, preaching the entire book in one sermon is advantageous since it gives the listener the ability to back up and see things in the overall flow of Scripture. When preaching a series through Ecclesiastes, the challenge will be to tease out the implications of the vanity of life, yet give hope without giving the full matter away.

Show the Poetry

When preaching through Ecclesiastes, be sure and show the poetry as you preach. It is so beautiful. Don't feel pressured to reduce the wonderful lines of verse to simple propositions. Also, remember that you will interpret them as you read them. So when you come to a poem in the book, be sure to read it in such a way that the meaning of the poem is highlighted. This may scare the less dramatic among us. However, we are not suggesting dramatic reading, but oral interpretation. Oral interpretation allows the meaning of the words to give emphasis to how a word is spoken.

In essence we read them slowly and allow the people to understand their meaning by placing emphasis on the words, pausing in the right places, and adjusting the pace of the voice. These oral clues actually transfer meaning. We are not performing. We are removing the natural barriers that keep people from seeing the beauty of the text. Preaching is about removing all distractions so that people can see and understand the text. The distraction in this case may be my inhibitions about allowing poetry to simply be poetry.

Work Study

Study the work passages and show the people the value of work. It is the pleasure of God to allow us to take pleasure in our work. This is shocking to the modern ethos that resents work or sees it only as a means of getting more. No doubt the idea of enjoying work is tucked away in a business model somewhere. It is reasonable that those who enjoy their work are the top performers, but that is irrelevant. It is in the ancient wisdom of God that we find the admonition to enjoy our work for all of our lives. So, with all the information about the vanity of work, cling to the rich teaching of the pleasure of work and show it to the people.

Preaching Song of Solomon

Preach the Symbolism

A wonderful approach to the book is to preach it literally first. Meaning, show how this book values marriage, corrects us when we err, and raises the standard for what romantic love really is. After this application is given, use the New Testament to point to how these things affirm the gospel by their demonstration.

Use the Narrative Structure

When preaching the individual units of the Song of Solomon, there are clear divisions in the strophe that are helpful for preaching. Remember the scene structure here. When you preach the individual stories within the macro story, be sure and point back to the larger themes within the book. There is more on that in the structure section of this chapter.

PREACH CHRIST FROM WISDOM LITERATURE

There are many ways to get to Christ from the Wisdom literature. Knowing Christ is the "fear of the Lord." The fear of the Lord is the beginning of wisdom (Prov 1:7); it is wisdom itself (Job 28:8); and it is the end of the matter (Eccl 12:14). So when preaching, the principle way to show the connection to Christ is to understand that being a Christian in the New Testament is tantamount to having the fear of the Lord in the Wisdom literature. The working out of the practical wisdom is simply what people who fear the Lord do.

Christ was a preacher of Wisdom literature. His Sermon on the Mount begins with an introduction that has the feel of Wisdom literature (Matt 5:1–11). The person who will be in the kingdom is "blessed." He follows the counterintuitive, countercultural wisdom of God and is blessed as a result. So when preaching, you can use several approaches to explain the Wisdom literature:

Covenant approach. How does this text fulfill or reflect the covenant? "This wisdom is given to Solomon who was the working out of a promise to his father David that his throne would never end. This was ultimately fulfilled in Christ."

Fulfillment approach. How does this text show us what only Christ can do perfectly? "The Proverbs call us to control our anger; we can't control our anger perfectly. Only Christ has done this, so we need his righteousness applied to us."

New Testament connection. Does this wisdom text have a corollary with a New Testament text? Douglas O'Donnell shows how this could happen with a direct quotation, a linguistic connection, or a thematic connection.[19]

Quotation. Is this text quoted in the NT? This is rare since only eight passages of Wisdom literature are quoted in the New Testament. For example,

"But to the humble he gives favor." (Prov 3:34)

"God opposes the proud but gives grace to the humble." (James 4:6)

Linguistic connection. Identify a linguistic connection in the English Bible between the Wisdom literature and a New Testament teaching.

"My son, if your heart is wise, my heart too will be glad." (Prov 23:15)

"This is my beloved Son, with whom I am well pleased." (Matt 3:17)

Thematic connection. Identify a theme taught in the Wisdom literature that has echoes or overtones in the New Testament.

"Wisdom has built her house." (Prov 9:1–6)

"Everyone then who hears these words of mine and does them will be like a wise man who built his house on the rock" (Matt 7:24). Jesus ends the Sermon on the Mount with the short parable of the wise and foolish builder; the wise builder built his house on Jesus' teaching.

---

19. For helpful charts on each of these approaches, see O'Donnell, *The Beginning and End of Wisdom*, 121–22, 129, 131–32.

One caveat remains, especially with regards to the fulfillment approach. The facts that Christ has come to give us his righteousness and that he alone was perfectly righteous do not exempt us from the ethical commands. In fact, in Christ they are even stronger since all Scripture can lead us to Christ (2 Tim 3:14–17).[20]

Structuring a Sermon from Wisdom Literature

In a sense, the category of "Wisdom Literature" is a synthetic category since the books themselves are all very different. The Proverbs are Wisdom literature, but they do not have the narrative feel of the Song of Solomon or Job. Ecclesiastes has a narrative flow to it, but it has long passages of instruction and wisdom. Therefore, it's not accurate to suggest one structure for Wisdom literature. Based on the above discussion, here are some structural options for the different books in the category of Wisdom Literature.

Determine the Shape of a Proverb

Analytical. Like the Psalms, in some texts you will identify the strophe and then build the exegetical work out of the individual strophe. As mentioned earlier, this will primarily be effective in the first 10 chapters of Proverbs. However, there are exceptions sprinkled throughout the book and times when this would be an ineffective strategy.

Topical. When preaching Proverbs, it is not uncommon to group texts. If so, your representative sample of a text may not have divisions. For the example below, "Proverbs on Anger," I read all the passages in the book that addressed anger. They identified the problem with anger (it reveals a dangerous vulnerability) and offered a solution. The outline then became clear:

1. What do the Proverbs say about anger? Anger demonstrates unhealthy vulnerability.
2. What is the answer for uncontrolled anger? The remedy for uncontrolled anger is true wisdom.

The purpose of the outline is not artificial ornamentation. The purpose of the outline is to facilitate what the text is doing. And the texts on anger in Proverbs raise two questions: Why is anger bad? and What is the solution?

Job

When preaching Job you can use the narrative structure to preach the entire book as one sermon. Though classified as Wisdom literature, Job is Old Testament Narrative, with long prophetic discourses. Sermons on Job should therefore follow the rules of preaching Old Testament Narrative with its scene structure, and they should follow the rules of preaching prophecy. The longer discourses in Job are in a poetic structure and can be organized sermonically like the strophes of Psalms.

Another good structural option for Job is to preach the longer discourses one chapter at a time. Some discourses span two chapters (e.g., chaps. 29–30). Structuring according to strophes is helpful for the longer discourses.

---

20. Ibid., 210.

Ecclesiastes

Like Job, Ecclesiastes can be preached effectively in one sermon. You have the cultural background of Solomon's wisdom and wealth and how this plays out like an unfolding singular narrative. However, when preaching Ecclesiastes in one sermon it may not be the scene structure that is the best, but rather an arrangement that lists all the lessons he has learned with unrestricted wealth and pleasure.

Like Proverbs, Ecclesiastes is a good book to preach topically since many topics are scattered throughout the book. For example, the theme of work in Ecclesiastes is dominant. We are given six passages in Ecclesiastes on labor and toil, and they can be categorized into four categories.

1. We are rewarded with joy in work (1:10; 2:24; 5:13–20).
2. It is vanity in that it is left to someone else (2:18).
3. It is a gift of God (3:12–13).
4. So work hard. It is fruitless (9:10).

As you can see, this list is organically connected. If you look at work in Ecclesiastes there is a progression here that could be stated, "We are to take joy in our work in this moment because eventually it will be left to someone else, and it is God's gift in this moment. So work hard."

This could make a good structure for a sermon in and of itself. The biggest advantage of this approach is that it demands that the preacher read the book carefully and meditate on its content.

Song of Solomon

Song of Solomon has a history of interpretation that is interesting to say the least. Most today reject the hyper-allegorical interpretation and opt instead for a more literal approach. However, structurally the flow is going to feel like narrative moving from scene to scene. The key will be a structure that always hints at the next narrative. So, for Song of Solomon consider a scene-by-scene narrative approach with sermons that pitch to the overall narrative of the book.

Sample Sermon

Proverbs on Anger (Prov 14:16–17)

PREACHING STRATEGY

The sermon tries to answer the question, "What does Proverbs say about anger?"

Introduction

This first part of the introduction does not address anger. However, it is helpful in setting up the rationale for taking this approach to the topic of anger in Proverbs.

Imagine you are an explorer on a journey who comes upon a displaced tribe in a jungle. You do not meet everyone; rather, the most important person comes out to meet you as a representative of the tribe. This morning, we are not going to look at every verse on anger in Proverbs, but in this representative verse we will get a sense of the whole.

Anger itself is sometimes justified. Jesus demonstrated anger (John 2:13–22). Yet, at the end of the day the anger was in service of other people and not coming from a defensive posture. All the while he was the ultimate example of looking out for the needs of others (Phil 2:1–11). However, the kind of anger that Proverbs is dealing with is different. This is anger that demonstrates a love for self above a love for others. In fact, Proverbs lists several results of this anger. Let's look at some of the proverbs asking what is the danger in anger (emphases are mine).

1. What Is the Danger of Anger?

1. A wise man fears the LORD and shuns evil, but a fool is hotheaded and reckless. A quick-tempered man does foolish things, and a crafty man is hated (14:16–17).

2. A patient man has great understanding, but a *quick-tempered man displays folly* (14:29).

3. A gentle answer turns away wrath, but a *harsh word stirs up anger* (15:1).

4. A *hot-tempered man stirs up dissension*, but a patient man calms a quarrel. (15:18).

5. *Starting a quarrel is like breaching a dam*; so drop the matter before a dispute breaks out (17:14).

6. A hot-tempered man *must pay the penalty*; if you rescue him, you will have to do it again (19:19).

7. Like a city whose walls are broken down is a man who lacks self-control. (25:28).

8. *An angry man stirs up dissension, and a hot-tempered one commits many sins* (29:22).

There are two word pictures that help us get a handle on the whole idea in the book.

A breached dam (17:14)

A city without walls (25:28)

The danger of anger is that it makes us vulnerable.

TRANSITION: So, what is the remedy?

2. What Is the Remedy for Displaced Anger?

Anger is contrasted to prudence, wisdom, patience, understanding, knowledge, gentleness, and honor (cf. 12:16; and 14:16–17, 29). "A wise man fears the LORD and shuns evil, but a fool is hotheaded and reckless. A quick-tempered man does foolish things, and a crafty man is hated"

(14:16–17). "A patient man has great understanding, but a *quick-tempered man displays folly*" (14:29).

So it is clear that the opposite of false anger is not patience or graciousness. The opposite of anger is wisdom. So the remedy for misplaced anger is true wisdom.

> *Note that this is the main idea. This "point" began with a question that is now being answered. It is important homiletically to put this together by re-asking the question and then answering it. It may seem basic, but the repetition aids clarity.*

Application

Wisdom is acting like you've seen the end of the movie, when you're only in Act 1.

We pray, "God give me more patience. We should be praying, God, give

> *Note that the application follows the stating of the main idea. So the flow is question raised, question answered (main point), application.*

me more wisdom."

Conclusion

Have you ever wondered why God blessed Joseph?

Why did God bless Joseph? Because God was angry with me. You see, he allowed Joseph to suffer so that Jesus could come to the earth fulfilling the promise given to Abraham.

Jesus lived a perfect life, then at the end of his life, he stretched out his arms and died. And in that moment God was looking down at Jesus and seeing my sin, and he raised his hand to punish me. But Jesus stood in the way, upon himself taking all of the anger of God that was aimed toward me. And there he took the perfect justice of God.

So this is why God saved Joseph . . . because he was angry with me.

And Jesus is still here. Not physically, but his Spirit is here. The Holy Spirit of Jesus Christ is in the place, and he is in you.

And Galatians 5 tells us that when the Holy Spirit is in you, there is love, joy, peace, patience, kindness, goodness, faithfulness, gentleness, and . . . self-control.

The Holy Spirit of God works through the Word of God.

Isn't Jesus wonderful? The reason God saved Joseph is because God was angry with me. And he sustained his promise to Abraham so that I could be saved from sin, and be saved from the inability to control my anger.

And through his Holy Spirit he gives me the supernatural power to do what I cannot do naturally.

But Joseph didn't know all that. No, he had to live like he knew the big picture when he only had the small picture.

> *Using the life of Joseph was intentionally chosen to illustrate the right response to circumstances and to present the gospel.*

REFLECTION

1. Is there a structure to Proverbs?
2. What does it mean that Proverbs are terse?
3. What does Ecclesiastes have to say about work?
4. Is the Song of Solomon to be interpreted/preached literally or symbolically?

RECOMMENDED RESOURCES

Kidner, Derek. *The Wisdom of Proverbs, Job, and Ecclesiastes.* Downers Grove: InterVarsity, 1985.

Kitchen, John A. *Proverbs.* Mentor Commentary. Inverness, Scotland: Mentor, 2006.

Köstenberger, Andreas J., and Richard D. Patterson. *Invitation to Biblical Interpretation: Exploring the Hermeneutical Triad of History, Literature, and Theology.* Grand Rapids: Kregel, 2011.

Longman, Tremper. *How to Read Proverbs.* Downers Grove: InterVarsity, 2003.

O'Donnell, Douglas Sean. *The Beginning and End of Wisdom: Preaching Christ from the First and Last Chapters of Proverbs, Ecclesiastes, and Job.* Wheaton: Crossway, 2011.

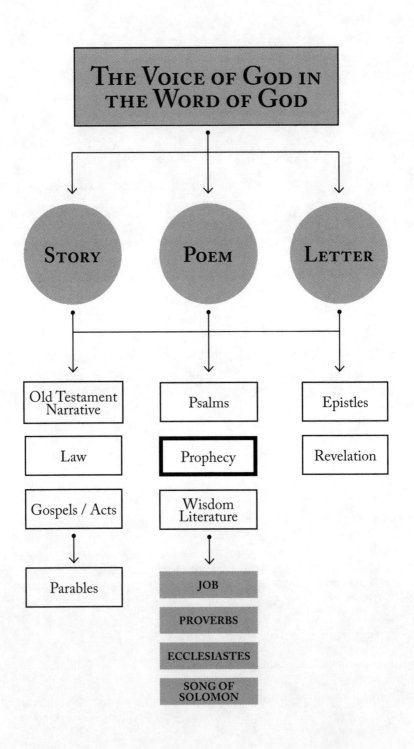

THE VOICE OF GOD IN THE WORD OF GOD

STORY

POEM

LETTER

Old Testament Narrative	Psalms	Epistles
Law	Prophecy	Revelation
Gospels / Acts	Wisdom Literature	
Parables		

JOB

PROVERBS

ECCLESIASTES

SONG OF SOLOMON

Chapter 10

RECAPTURING THE VOICE OF GOD IN PROPHECY

INTRODUCTION

THE PROPHETS WERE "THE PROPHETIC AUTHORS OF THE BIBLICAL PROPHETIC BOOKS WHOSE MESSAGE IS GROUNDED IN THE BOOK OF MOSES AND WHOSE VISION LOOKS FORWARD TO THE 'NEW COVENANT' GOSPEL OF FAITH."[1] John Sailhamer's definition of the prophets is a helpful place to begin our discussion.

First, look at the covenantal connection. The prophets were reflecting the spirit and the words of the Mosaic covenant. The prophets called Israel back to faithfulness to the covenant. However, they also anticipated the new covenant. This relates to the prophetic, predictive passages about the Messiah. Yet in a broader sense it relates to the sanctification that will be a product of the new covenant. A call for Israel to be faithful to the old covenant becomes a call to be faithful to Christ in the new covenant. It is Christ who saves us and sustains us by his sanctifying grace. In this way, the Prophets are material ripe for Christian preaching. They affirm the trajectory of God's covenant relationship and lead us to Christ in the new covenant.

Let's look closer at how the prophets lead us to Christ.[2]

Christ as Prophet

When Christ began his ministry, the people perceived that he was a prophet. They first thought John the Baptist was a prophet. Mark 11:32 says, "They all held that John really was a prophet." John the apostle writes, "When the people saw the sign that he had done, they said, 'This is indeed the Prophet who is to come into the world!'" (John 6:14). "When they heard these words, some of the people said, 'This really is the Prophet'" (John 7:40). Stephen interprets Deuteronomy 18:15–22 for us in Acts 7:37 when he says, "This is the Moses who said to the Israelites, 'God will raise up for you a prophet like me from your brothers.'" And remember when Jesus queried his disciples, asking who the people thought he was? They replied, "Some say John the Baptist, others say Elijah, and others Jeremiah or one of the prophets" (Matt 16:14). This raises important questions: Why did people think that Jesus was

---

1. John Sailhamer, "Preaching from the Prophets," in *Preaching the Old Testament*, ed. Scott Gibson (Grand Rapids: Baker, 2006), 122.

2. For a biblical theology that puts the Prophets in perspective, see Desmond Alexander, *From Eden to the New Jerusalem* (Grand Rapids: Kregel, 2008).

a prophet? What was it about him that made people make this association? The main reason must have been his teaching.

The prophets basically had three messages.[3] The first message was repentance. The people were called to repent for their sins because they had violated God's law and were in jeopardy of losing the promised land. And this is Jesus' primary message as well. There is a coming kingdom. We want to be in that kingdom. However, entrance into the kingdom is predicated on repentance. His first message is, "Repent, for the kingdom of heaven is at hand" (Matt 4:17).

The second message of the prophets was judgment. This again is the message of Christ. Christ came proclaiming that the kingdom was here now, and that the judgment of the kingdom was coming. To some the kingdom would bring life, but to others judgment. We see this all through the ministry of Christ. Think of the prophetic sounding woes toward the unrepentant cities (Matt 11:20). The most explicit expression of the kingdom come and the kingdom coming is found in the parable of the Wheat and the Weeds (Matt 13:24–30, 36–43). All those who are true wheat are gathered into the barn and saved. All those who are weeds are cast out and burned. The prophetic message of judgment could not be more explicit.

The final message of the prophets is one of hope. The very fact that there was a judgment implied that redemption was possible. And certainly Christ had a message of hope. He came with healing, bringing a message of justice, "and in his name the Gentiles will hope" (Matt 12:15–21).

So, all the key components were there. Jesus was a radical, miracle-working preacher, whose message sounded exactly like the message of the prophets. It is no wonder that people considered him a prophet. Since we know that all of Scripture speaks of Christ, we could say this another way. It is not that Christ sounded like a prophet, but all the prophets sounded like Christ. Jesus was not echoing the message of the prophets. The prophets were anticipating Christ. Let's discuss how to interpret and communicate the message of the Prophets, and issues related to structure.

INTERPRETATION: LISTENING TO THE VOICE OF GOD IN THE LITERARY FEATURES OF PROPHECY

The Prophets Have Unique Historical Settings

The settings for many of the Prophets are strange. They deal with nations that no longer exist, making traversing the cultural bridge difficult. And, this is another reason we hesitate to preach them. After all, who wants to preach something where half the message is unpacking cultural issues, and the other half is judgment! However, there is a way to do this that is both compelling and helpful.

The Prophets Use Certain Literary Devices

The Prophets are written mainly as poetry. It may seem strange that a tough prophetic message would be delivered in verse. However, think about how provocative this is. The message itself is tough, hard to deal with. But the use of poetry delivers

---

3. This distillation is in many places, but most succinctly in J. Scott Duvall and J. Daniel Hays, *Grasping God's Word: A Hands-on Approach to Reading, Interpreting, and Applying the Bible* (Grand Rapids: Zondervan, 2001), 252.

the message in high definition. The form brings attention to the content of the message. Hebrew poetry is unique from what we understand as poetry. Recall that the primary distinctive of Hebrew poetry is parallelism.[4] Within the use of parallelism, the Prophets are known to use other literary devices such as metaphor, hyperbole, and repetition.

Prophecies Are Predictive

Many of the prophecies predict future events. The question is, "Are these predictions limited to the immediate situation or do they have any future fulfillment?" First, we must establish that there is not a "secret" to understanding the prophecies. When we believe there is such a secret, we tend toward a curiosity that ends in unhelpful speculation, such as the temptation to try to understand prophecy in light of contemporary events. But this can only privilege those who understand the secret message. However, again, there is no secret. The ultimate message is faithfulness to the covenant, a covenant that will ultimately be fulfilled in Christ. That's it. If we must drill down further, we could say that they do so by way of being a corrective warning to Israel and by applying the Torah to particular situations.

Most prophetic literature is not predictive. It is forth-telling, not foretelling. However, when prophecy predicts, what do we do? We should first remember that the prophecies served to build faith so that Israel would trust God. Therefore, when preaching, show how the prophecy came true. Seeing God's hand at work built Israel's faith, and it will build ours as well. So when we show them how the prophecies were fulfilled, we are building faith within our people. When we come to difficult passages we must let 1 Peter 1:12 encourage our hearts because, "It was revealed to [the prophets] that they were serving not themselves but you, in the things that have now been announced to you through those who preached the good news to you by the Holy Spirit." Thus, reading the Prophets provides encouragement—these words our designed to build our faith.

The Prophecies Are Messianic

Second Corinthians 1:20 assures us that all the promises of God find their fulfillment in Christ Jesus. Therefore, "interpreters will miss the heart of the prophecy when they fail to link it to Jesus Christ."[5] What is significant is that, even without explicit Messianic allusions in the text, the Prophets show hints of a new covenant that is coming. "From this perspective there is considerable agreement between what it means to preach from the prophets and what it means to preach from the New Testament."[6] This is because we are preaching the fulfillment of what they prophesied.

Prophecies May Be Contextually Conditional

So you find yourself preaching a prophecy that is strong and direct. Thus, borrowing from the spirit of the genre, you want to be the same. You can; it's there.

---

4. This section is dependent on the section on Hebrew poetry in chapter 8.
5. Sidney Greidanus, *The Modern Preacher and the Ancient Text: Interpreting and Preaching Biblical Literature* (Grand Rapids: Eerdmans, 1988), 258.
6. Sailhamer, "Preaching from the Prophets," 116.

However, remember that often there is an "if" in the passage. Jeremiah's words are encouraging, "If at any time I declare concerning a nation or a kingdom, that I will pluck up and break down and destroy it, and if that nation, concerning which I have spoken, turns from its evil, I will relent of the disaster that I intended to do to it" (Jer 18:7–8). God is giving them an opportunity to obey and to live. This is central to understanding the work of the Prophets.

This is both good and bad news. The good news is that the prophecies of judgment are conditioned on repentance. Thus, if people repent, the prophecies will not come true. The bad news is that so are the promises of blessing. The most popular one that comes to mind is 2 Chronicles 7:14. "If my people who are called by my name humble themselves, and pray and seek my face and turn from their wicked ways, then I will hear from heaven and will forgive their sin and heal their land." The promise comes on the condition of the humility of the people. In reality, this is good news as well. Humility is where we want to be. The blessing that attends the humility is God's affirmation of a life well lived.

That prophecies are conditional is clear enough. However, understanding those conditions comes on the other side of understanding the context of the situation in which they were written. Thus they are "contextually conditional."

Prophecies Are Hopeful

A parent warns a child to protect him, not to curse him. "Don't drive the car like that or you will kill yourself," is not intended to indicate inevitability, but provide protection. The loving parent is trying to protect the child. Prophecies are porous directives that allow the loving-kindness of God to seep through. Remember Jeremiah 18:7–8 quoted above. If nations repent God will in fact relent of the disaster that he intends.

Thus, the promises are a way of extending hope, a hope that is conditioned with obedience. "God's word of judgment does not cast the future in iron, predetermining its very outcome, for God remains in control of his words and is free to respond to human repentance and prayer."[7] In this way we are distinguishing from the words and their objective. The words sound like condemnation, but their purpose is restoration. Again, we are reading the text in light of the book and in light of the author's purpose.

This is how the Prophets are gospel oriented. Oh, to have been with Jesus when he spelled out the rich meaning of the Old Testament for his disciples, and explained how each page was rushing up to meet the Messiah. It's all there. And for all the things we may not know about the Prophets, we do know this: they offer hope on the other side of repentance. Christ offers hope on the other side of repentance (Matt 4:17). Thus, the message the prophets speak is the same as we modern preachers speak. We tell people of the hope that is in Christ. After all, the first Christian sermon was based on the prophet Joel (Acts 2:16–21). There is hope there. When we preach the Prophets, we are preaching in the flow of hope.

The Prophecies Have Unique Literary Structure

The structure of each book is not so much chronological as it is topical. Some books are more chronological such as Ezekiel, Haggai, and Zechariah. However,

---

7. Greidanus, *The Modern Preacher and the Ancient Text*, 234.

most of the books are composed with a loose chronological or topical arrangement. In either case, there is unity in the thematic development.

The Prophets primarily use the means of poetry to communicate their message. There are narration and prayers, but the actual prophecies usually take the form of sermon-speeches that are poetry. This means that what we said about poetry applies here. Again, the staple of prophecy is the use of Hebrew parallelism. If you understand the function of parallelism, then you have unlocked the way much of the prophecies function and can structure sermons accordingly.[8]

COMMUNICATION: RECAPTURING THE VOICE OF GOD IN THE PROPHETS

Preach the Text, Not the Event Behind the Text

How much historical context should you actually include when preaching? The answer to this question ties into the nature of the Bible itself. Remember, our philosophy of preaching flows from our theology of preaching. We believe that Scripture is one literary unit. This is a shocking revelation, but it is nonetheless true. As one literary unit, it has one driving idea that it is supporting. The Testaments, the books, and the chapters all have smaller ideas that support the larger driving idea. To return to our question, "How much background material do I include?" The answer is enough to get the main idea of the text across without distracting the listener. In other words, my responsibility is not to give them a lesson in biblical backgrounds, but I cannot ignore it altogether either. Some listeners may be interested in backgrounds. However, I intentionally distill what I say about backgrounds based on this question: How critical is this information to communicate the main idea of the text? With background information there is always the temptation to be interesting without being helpful.

There is a secondary concern. Namely, how much information do I need to set up for my people to understand subsequent texts? Thus, if preaching through a book, I might include more background material than was necessary in one sermon because it will be essential in helping people follow future sermons.

Remember, the meaning of the text is not derived solely from the historical backgrounds. We are preaching texts, not events. So it is not a question of, "What cultural events give this text meaning?" Rather, the question is, "What does the Bible say in this text?" Of course there are interpretive helps in the biblical backgrounds and historical information. They are valuable. However, if we knew exactly what kind of fish swallowed Jonah, the fashion sensibilities of the Ninevites, or the type of worm that ate the branch, those details would not yield the meaning of the text. Why? Because the meaning of the book of Jonah is given to us by Christ in Matthew 12:38–41. The point is that the meaning of Jonah is not derived from digging deeper behind the text, but by allowing the rest of Scripture to inform the text. This is what it is to be wholly biblical. So the primary question we should ask is, "What about this text points me to look further within the text of the Bible to find the answer?" In the end, you can die without knowing biblical backgrounds, but I would rather die not knowing backgrounds than not knowing the Bible. I understand the former serves the latter. However, this is a reminder that the Bible is our first look. So

---

8. Ibid., 245–49.

when we have the text before us, we are asking how this text fits into the flow of the book, and then how the flow of the book fits into redemptive history. First we take a micro-look, then a macro-look. This is especially necessary because the New Testament interprets the prophecies for us.

Exploit the Metaphors

The metaphor gives us a window into the mind of the biblical author, telling us what is important to him. For example, listen to Jeremiah's use of metaphor in Jeremiah 15:16 (NRSV),

> Your words were found, and I ate them,
> and your words became to me a joy
> and the delight of my heart;
> for I am called by your name,
> O LORD, God of hosts.

Why does he describe the word of God like food that he ingests? Well, it's simply more powerful that way. He could have said, "The way you speak is so important to me that I love it and willingly obey it." And he did say all that. It's wrapped up in the metaphor. The metaphor just says it better. With a metaphor you say more with fewer words.

Notice the incredible metaphor of Micah 6:1–2 (NRSV).

> Hear what the LORD says:
> Rise, plead your case before the mountains,
> and let the hills hear your voice.
> Hear, you mountains, the controversy of the LORD,
> and you enduring foundations of the earth,
> for the LORD has a controversy against his people,
> and he will contend with Israel.

God is putting his people on trial. The indictment will be so real, that it is as if the mountains will hear it. The whole world will know it. This speaks to the severity of the offense. God is so angered by this that he is calling on the mountains themselves to give witness. The watching/listening mountains, who don't "know" anything are personified and serve to demonstrate how deeply God hates sin and how widely he will make the judgment known. Locate all the meanings embedded in the literary devices and unpack them.

Look to the Immediate Fulfillment

When prophecies point to specific events that are to occur, look for the historical events that actually occurred and point to them. Think for a moment. If there are events that are going to occur, what is God's purpose in sharing them? If these are tragic events, a predictive prophecy serves to warn. In other words, they may have the chance to repent. If they do not repent, when the calamity comes, then they will make the connection with what the prophet says. In repentance, one believes God because of pending judgment. In rejection, one believes God after the judgment. Either way, God builds their faith!

Look to Further Fulfillment

In some cases prophecies have dual fulfillment. They point to the now and to the later. This is especially true of messianic prophecies. When this is the case, show this to the people. The classic example is Isaiah 7:10–17. The wicked King Ahaz would not ask a sign from God even though God told him to do so. God responded, "Therefore the Lord himself will give you a sign. Behold, the virgin shall conceive and bear a son, and shall call his name Immanuel" (7:14). This messianic prophecy is used by Matthew to signify that Jesus was the Christ child (Matt 1:23). However, it also had meaning in the immediate context as well. Show your people the first context, so you can get to the later.

Preach the Prophecy in Light of the Whole

When you get to a messianic prophecy, show your people its New Testament parallel. People are generally unaware of the unified nature of Scripture, how it is one organic whole. Showing the relationship between the texts will encourage them to see it this way. One of our goals in preaching is to teach people how to read their Bibles. If they are going to understand the New Testament, especially the Gospels, they need to understand how the Old Testament is the backdrop for the New Testament.

One caution here: don't forget your text! If you do go to a parallel text in the New Testament, don't stay there. Simply show them the connection and how it is fulfilled in Jesus Christ. Then, come back to your text and finish preaching and applying its message to your people.

Panning Out

How do we understand the context? We ask how the author of the book is using this prophecy. In other words, "What theme does this pitch to within the book?" Think for a minute of the classic example of Jeremiah 29:11: "For I know the plans I have for you, declares the LORD, plans for welfare and not for evil, to give you a future and a hope." This is a wonderful prophecy of hope. It is tempting is to read this verse and apply it to the individual who is currently struggling with no hope. However, in the context the hope is only partially immediate. God is warning of his judgment upon the exiles. They could have hope that God would help them, but verse 10 says ultimate hope will come later—after 70 years of judgment.

If we pan out a little further to Jeremiah 31:31–34, we see one of the greatest promises of all, namely that God will do a new thing.

> "And no longer shall each one teach his neighbor and each his brother saying, 'Know the LORD,' for they shall all know me, from the least of them to the greatest, declares the LORD. "For I will forgive their iniquity, and I will remember their sin no more." (31:34)

So ultimately there is great hope. The preacher, then, is taking the listener on a journey. He is showing the immediate hope that is in the text, if repentance were to take place. We also have hope in Christ if we repent, and even after we repent we can have restored fellowship with God when we daily repent of sin. So Israel and the modern Christian are responding to this text under two different theological schemes—one relating to the old covenant, and one relating to the new covenant. The text is still applicable—however, the preacher should be careful to teach his people how to apply the prophecy of the old covenant in the shadow the new.

Preach with Hope

The prophets were tough. The reason is that they were calling Israel back to the covenant. Sometimes this was done with dramatic words. For those who were practicing injustice toward their countrymen God was "devising disaster from which you cannot remove your necks" (Mic 2:3). So, is there a way to preach these texts with any sense of hope? The answer is implied in the fact of the prophecy. The prophetic call for repentance implies that there was hope for those who would turn. Without dulling the edge of the prophecy, we are to preach in a way that shows the joy of repentance and surrender in obedience. They were to be obedient to the conditions of the old covenant, while we are throwing ourselves at the mercy of the new covenant.[9]

Preach Under the Shadow

When we read a prophet, we understand that ultimately that prophecy is about Christ (Luke 24:44). How is the so? Scripture does not suggest that the person of Christ is mentioned in every verse. However, it does suggest that the shadow of redemption is cast over all of Scripture. Think of Christ stepping out of heaven in eternity past. The light emanating from the throne of God causes a shadow to fall over all that will take place from creation, flood, fall, old covenant, new covenant, and consummation.

So, when preaching Christ from a prophet, it is wise not to tack on the story of Christ as an unrelated afterthought. It is equally unwise to try to find a messianic literary allusion to Christ where one does not exist. What is more appropriate is to make clear verbal connections in the pulpit:

> "This prophet is calling Israel to respond to God's old covenant this way . . . "
> "Yet we have a new covenant in Christ . . . "
> "So in a parallel sense the New Testament affirms this truth in this way . . . "
> "Christ gives us the power to keep the New Testament affirmation . . . "

This approach connects the application of the Old Testament prophetic exhortation to its New Testament parallel while teaching that the ability to keep the New Testament exhortation is through Christ. So in a concise way the truth of the Old Testament prophecy is affirmed and applied, while ultimately what is affirmed is the glory of Christ who gives us grace to honor the exhortation.

---

9. Walter Kaiser observes that the prophets have one central message, repentance. The response will determine whether blessing or judgment is to follow. See Walter C. Kaiser Jr., *Toward an Exegetical Theology: Biblical Exegesis for Preaching and Teaching* (Grand Rapids: Baker, 1981), 193.

Know the Landscape

It is wise when preaching through a Major or Minor Prophet, to know the landscape of the entire book before you begin. The thematic order may be difficult to follow, but people will follow you if you will show them the structure of the book as you preach. Of course, being able to do so requires that you read through the book multiple times until you gain a good handle on its structure.[10]

STRUCTURING A SERMON FROM A PROPHETIC TEXT

1. Use the Poetic Structure

In addressing prophecy, the most common genre that we engage is prophetic poetry. Some books are entirely prophecy. This means that we are following the strophe structure as was discussed in our previous chapter on Psalms. The divisions of the strophe can serve like "points" supporting a theme.[11]

One cautionary note: while it is true that the strophe structure is like using points, it is not identical to the points of a New Testament epistle. Often the prophets are like prosecuting attorneys, arguing a case insomuch as they layer on several indictments before getting to their closing arguments. The classic example is Isaiah 1 where Isaiah rails against Israel before the encouraging words of verses 18–20 (NKJV):

> "Come now let us reason together,"
> Says the LORD:
> "Though your sins are like scarlet,
> They shall be as white as snow;
> Though they are red like crimson,
> They will be as wool.
> If you are willing and obedient,
> You shall eat the good of the land;
> But if you refuse and rebel,
> You shall be devoured by the sword";
> For the mouth of the LORD has spoken.

The sermon should reanimate this movement by turning around the movements of the text leading up to the main idea. Then, after the main idea is stated, application can be culled out of the main idea. In the example below, four movements lead up to the main idea, which comes very near the end, then application comes from the main idea.

2. Watch for Hybrids

When preaching Prophets, there will be times when the Hebrew poetry is mixed with other genres. The most obvious one is narrative. So, there may be the chance

---

10. For a helpful guide to reading the Prophets, see "Guidelines for Interpreting Prophecy" in Köstenberger and Patterson, 346–358.

11. There are different subgenres within the genre of prophecy. Kaiser notes there are also "woe oracles," "the prophetic lawsuit," and "oracles against foreign nations" in Walter C. Kaiser Jr., *Preaching and Teaching from the Old Testament* (Grand Rapids: Baker, 2003), 110–13. So, while there are sub-genres within the genre of Prophecy, this should not affect the structure when crafting a sermon.

to preach using a narrative or a "scene" structure. Even if narrative structure is not the formal structure for the sermon, it will need to be managed well because the Prophets are responding to specific, local situations. Hosea 1 and 3 are almost all narrative; the rest of the book is prophecy in poetic form. Jonah is almost all narrative with the exception of chapter 2, which is Jonah's poetic prayer. In the examples the preacher will have the opportunity to alter sermon structure in the same series, based on the genre of the text. Even when preaching the poetic prophetic discourses, the preacher can point out in each of the respective sermons that they are framed in a narrative context.

At other times the poetry will be mixed with, or be composed of, clear imperatives. In the example below there are multiple reasons given (Mic 6:1–7) for the clear commands in 6:8. So the genre is a progressive narrative that leads the original audience (Israel) to remember what they already know. The choice was made to treat the first three sections at a fast pace in the effort to move the listener to what God wants them to do—namely to remember what they already know he wants—doing justice, loving kindness, and walking humbly with God.

3. Consider One Sermon on an Entire Minor Prophet

The terse approach and quick pace of the Minor Prophets lend themselves to preaching them in one sermon apiece. In this approach, you would outline the entire book noting the main divisions and moving the divisions toward the main theme of the book.[12] A great example of this is the book of Jonah. The narrative moves quickly, reaches a dramatic climax, and has a provocative ending.

Sample Sermon

A Heart of Responsive Obedience, Micah 6:8

> PREACHING STRATEGY
>
> It seems the text is raising this question: What does God want from us? However, the answer to this question, given in v. 8, is more significant in light of the first several verses. So the approach is to walk through the movements of the prophetic poetry reaching the climax of v. 8. After v. 8, the main idea is clear. Then application can be made.

Introduction

When I was in junior high, I tried windsurfing one vacation. It was not the picturesque stuff of extreme athletes but a gangly adolescent trying to stay afloat. However, when I came home from vacation I quickly bragged that I was a windsurfer, which I was (kind of). You know, it was my thing. My newfound status as a windsurfer was in jeopardy when a friend asked me to go to a lake to windsurf. Now I was in trouble. As I climbed on

---

12. See treatment of Zephaniah in Alison Lo, "Preaching the Minor Prophets," in *Reclaiming the Old Testament for Christian Preaching*, ed. Grenville J. R. Kent, Paul Kissling, and Laurence A. Turner (Downers Grove: InterVarsity, 2010), 212–14.

the board, I was shocked that I actually stayed on. And, what's more, I actually stayed on the board and glided effortlessly into the middle of the lake. It was there that I realized that I had no idea how to get back. I was fine when the wind was at my back, but I had nothing to offer when the wind was against me. So now I had two options: I could sit down on the board, or I could keep going, fooling no one, and pretend that I was in complete control.

Occasionally I find myself drifting from God. Things get hard and the wind is no longer at my back. And here is this dual temptation: we can just keep going pretending nothing is wrong, or we can sit down, immobilized by our fear of repentance. This is my temptation more often than I would like to admit. And this was Israel's problem. The wind was no longer at her back. The people had to repent, but they did not want to.

CONTEXT: Micah is addressing Israel in a time of national disobedience, especially in areas of social injustice.

TRANSITION: So, because of their disobedience, God calls them into the courtroom . . .

The courtroom imagery is implicit in the text, so it is employed here.

MOVE ONE (vv. 1–2)

They had drifted so far from God that he puts them on trial with all the mountains as the jury.

MOVE TWO (vv. 3–5)

Using some sarcasm, God reminds Israel of all he has done to help her, then asks if his graciousness is why the people are rejecting him.

MOVE THREE (vv. 6–7)

The defendant tries to offer subpar sacrifices to appease God. This is not unlike the story of the wealthy young man in Luke 18 who was willing to give God everything, but that which was most precious to him. The fact that God will not accept these sacrifices shows what he really wants—he wants our hearts.

This first three moves can be accomplished at a pretty fast clip. After all, I really want to get to the main idea so the application can take place. So the idea is to go fast enough to sustain attention, but slow enough to build interest while being faithful to the text.

MOVE FOUR (v. 8)

This is not everything God wants, but it is a summary statement like James 1:27 or Matthew 22:34. What we learn is that God wants a heart, but more specifically he wants a heart of obedience. What is a heart of obedience?

1. A heart of obedience does justice.
2. A heart of obedience is faithful to those in need.
3. A heart of obedience walks carefully with God.

Notice he begins with, "you know what God requires." In other words, they already knew this. So now we are getting the full picture. God wants obedience, but the kind of obedience defined as responsiveness.

Main Idea: God wants a heart of responsive obedience.

Yet, if they were to have known this already (v. 8), where would they have learned it? From the covenant language that is in the text: "LORD," "Israel," "My people." All of this is covenant language. They should know by the covenant, sealed by the representative sacrifice, that God wants their hearts not just outward demonstrations of obedience. In the same way, we should know from the new covenant, sealed by the atoning sacrifice of Christ, that God wants our hearts. We should know this.

Conclusion

We are to respond to God by turning to his discipline, not from it (Prov 1:23). He wants us to receive his reproof and respond with a heart of responsive obedience.

REFLECTION

1. Why was Christ considered a prophet?
2. How do you preach with hope from a prophet?
3. How does a literary device have meaning?
4. Is it possible to preach an entire Minor Prophet in one sermon?
5. What genres might you find in one pericope while preaching a prophet?

RECOMMENDED SOURCES

Alexander, Desmond. *From Eden to the New Jerusalem*. Grand Rapids: Kregel, 2008.
Chisolm, Robert B. *Handbook on the Prophets*. Grand Rapids: Baker, 2002.
Köstenberger, Andreas J, and Richard D. Patterson. "Guidelines for Interpreting Prophecy." Pages 346–58 in *Invitation to Biblical Interpretation: Exploring the Hermeneutical Triad of History, Literature, and Theology*. Grand Rapids: Kregel, 2011.
Lo, Allison. "Preaching the Minor Prophets." Pages 212–14 in *Reclaiming the Old Testament for Christian Preaching*. Edited by Grenville J. R. Kent, Paul Kissling, and Laurence A. Turner. Downers Grove: InterVarsity, 2010.
Sailhamer, John. "Preaching from the Prophets." Pages 115–36 in *Preaching the Old Testament*. Edited by Scott Gibson. Grand Rapids: Baker, 2006.

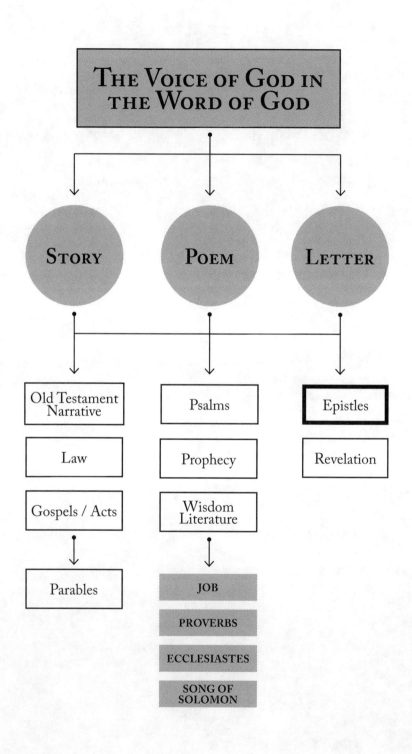

THE VOICE OF GOD IN THE WORD OF GOD

STORY

POEM

LETTER

Old Testament Narrative

Law

Gospels / Acts

Parables

Psalms

Prophecy

Wisdom Literature

JOB

PROVERBS

ECCLESIASTES

SONG OF SOLOMON

Epistles

Revelation

Chapter 11

RECAPTURING THE VOICE OF
GOD IN THE EPISTLES

THERE ARE AT LEAST FIVE MAJOR PERIODS OF COMMUNICATION:
(1) ORAL, (2) WRITTEN, (3) LITERATE, (4) PRINT, AND (5) ELECTRON-
IC.[1] Looking at those five periods on a page, it may seem that the most dramatic shift
was the last one: from print to electronic. I am typing this on an electronic screen.
In fact, I really do not know where this document is. It exists, but I'm not exactly
sure where or in what form it exists. This is the world of electronic communication,
and it is currently impossible to conceive of a world without it. You might be reading this through an electronic medium. If so, then you are not holding a book but a
medium that is transporting this book to you. And you might be like me; you don't
really know where the book is. Generally people do not think of where books or
documents are located; mediums are purely utilitarian. They serve a purpose. Books
are increasingly more about what they do than what they are.

However radical the shift from print to electronic mediums may have been, that is not
the biggest shift in the communication periods above. Far and away, the biggest shift
is between the first two, from oral to written. The oral culture does something no other
culture does. When someone is communicating with words to ears in real time, there is
the unavoidable presence that always accompanies the words. So when something was
first written down and given to another person, it was the first time that the sender of the
message was removed from the message itself. All content. No presence. For the first
time, communication consisted solely of what it was, and not who was attached to it.

This shift did something that all the others would follow. It created distance.
From the first time that communication could take place without the communicator
being present, the message was distanced from the messenger. All that could be
communicated nonverbally was lost in the written form. So, anything other than oral
communication is a distant presence.[2] Text-driven preaching is an attempt to close
this distance by re-presenting the text, and not forcing our own ideas on the text.[3]

---

1. This suggested pentad is sliced many different ways by different communication theorists. For a look
at the history of communication, I suggest the classic David Crowley and Paul Heyer, *Communication in
History: Technology, Culture, Society* (New York: Longman, 1999).

2. See Thomas Long, *Preaching and the Literary Forms of the Bible* (Philadelphia: Fortress, 1989),
108–9.

3. "It is the interpreter's job to represent the text, not the prejudices, feelings, judgments, or concerns of

This distant presence is exactly what is expressed in the Epistles. We see Paul longing to be with the people to whom he wrote.[4] However, he is providentially hindered. So, he tries to recreate his presence through the medium of a letter. However, the letters are not like any other medium. Yes, they are letters, but not the free flowing rambling according to the whims of the writer that we are accustomed to in letters. Rather, these letters are highly structured expressions of theology and practice.[5]

BREAD AND BUTTER

The Epistles are the bread and butter of most evangelical, pastoral preaching. After all, we are in fact a New Testament church, naturally leaning toward texts that express life on this side of the new covenant. However, there is another reason that drives us to the Epistles; they are intensely practical. When Paul lays out explicit commands on sexuality (1 Corinthians 7), or abuses in worship (1 Corinthians 14), or even dealing with a contentious church member (Titus 3:9–11), the Epistles scream for us to practice them. These two reasons alone make the Epistles the main stay of most of our contemporary preaching.

Since the Epistles are commonly preached in our pulpits, we are left with two temptations. First, there is a tendency to move beyond preaching the Epistles primarily to preaching them exclusively. This is extremely dangerous because the Epistles were not to be read in a vacuum of Old Testament theology, or the old covenant narrative. Think of Paul's encouragement to the Galatians that the blessing of Abraham came to the Gentiles through Christ.

Think also of the argument of the book of Hebrews. Hebrews is, in many ways, an exposition of Psalm 110.[6] That psalm is mentioned in Hebrews 1:3, 7; 8:1; and 10:12. Without an understanding of this psalm, one would not know how to understand the whole of the book of Hebrews. This is not to mention the exodus metaphor woven though the book, the priestly allusions, or the entire roll call of faith in chapter 11. All this is to say that staying in the Epistles to the exclusion of the Old Testament will actually keep people from understanding the Epistles. The Epistles not only quote the Old Testament, but are built on the exegetical and theological framework of the Old Testament.

The example above is especially relevant because Psalm 110 is the most quoted Psalm in the New Testament. The in King Jesus' triumph richness of the Messiah was a wonderful encouragement to the New Testament Christians. Even though they were persecuted by the Roman government, Jesus was the Messiah. All his enemies will be under him at some point. What a Savior. This is a richness that could only be brought to them against the backdrop of the Old Testament.

Perhaps the most explicit preaching verses in the New Testament are 2 Timothy 4:1–2, "I charge you in the presence of God and of Christ Jesus, who is to judge the

the exegete." Walter C. Kaiser Jr., *Toward an Exegetical Theology: Biblical Exegesis for Preaching and Teaching* (Grand Rapids: Baker, 1981), 45.

4. For example, note the familial language of 1 Thessalonians alone: Paul refers to the Thessalonians as "brothers" (2:1, 9), he loves them like a mother (2:7), and challenges them like a father (2:11–12).

5. The letters themselves follow many of the conventions of the period. See Leland Ryken, *Words of Delight: A Literary Introduction to the Bible* (Grand Rapids: Baker, 1987), 432–33.

6. See the author's preface in David Allen, *Hebrews*, New American Commentary (Nashville: B&H, 2010).

living and the dead, and by his appearing and his kingdom: preach the word." Now, here is the question: What was "the word" that Timothy was to preach? Clearly it was not the New Testament since he did not live with a complete canon as we understand it. The answer is found 3:15: "You have been acquainted with the sacred writings, which are able to make you wise for salvation through faith in Christ Jesus."

So, what exactly were these sacred writings? They were not the New Testament Scriptures but the Old Testament Scriptures. What a provocative revelation. Paul told Timothy that he knew the Old Testament Scriptures that would lead to faith in Christ. Therefore when he says "Preach the Word," he was speaking of the Old Testament. More expressly, he is saying, "Preach the way to Christ from the Old Testament."

We have something that Timothy did not: the complete canon of Scripture. Therefore we preach the New Testament and how it completes the Old Testament. However, my fear is that while we have something Timothy did not have, Timothy had something we do not have: a thoroughgoing understanding of the Old Testament. So, while we wave the banner for the value of the Epistles, we must remember that they are built on the foundation of the Old Testament. The Epistles may be the bread and butter of our preaching, but exclusively preaching the Epistles will not give the whole story. Man shall not live on bread and butter alone.

Also, the Epistles, by their nature, are anticipatory. They called for believers to look for an existence beyond the one they were currently experiencing. Jesus came preaching that the kingdom was near (Matt 4:17). The disciples were likewise convinced that the time was upon them (Acts 1:1–8). Thus, Peter encourages us to live "preparing your minds for action, and being sober-minded, set your hope fully on the grace that will be brought to you at the revelation of Jesus Christ" (1 Pet 1:13).

Ever since Pentecost, Christians have been called to anticipate the second coming of Christ. The first Christians believed his return was the next event on the calendar, and they lived with both expectation and hope. In trials they were to "Be patient, therefore, brothers, until the coming of the Lord. See how the farmer waits for the precious fruit of the earth, being patient about it, until it receives the early and the late rains. You also, be patient. Establish your hearts, for the coming of the Lord is at hand" (Jas 5:7–8).

When they were downhearted, they were to remember that

> . . . we do not want you to be uninformed, brothers, about those who are asleep, that you may not grieve as others do who have no hope . . . Therefore encourage one another with these words . . . For God has not destined us for wrath, but to obtain salvation through our Lord Jesus Christ, who died for us so that whether we are awake or asleep we might live with him. Therefore encourage one another and build one another up, just as you are doing. (1 Thess 4:13, 18; 5:9–11)

The New Testament believers were living under heavy-handed persecution. They longed for their Messiah who would ride in on a white horse and destroy the enemies with one word (Rev 19:11–21). If our preaching of the Epistles does not build anticipation and hope of Christ's return, then we have missed something. Or, more pointedly, we have transplanted something. By our silence we appear to agree with confused Christians who think living for this life is all there is, that there is nothing more to life than this present age. Such believers need to be rocked back into reality, the reality that the real world is the world they cannot see. The real hope is the hope they can't find in anything else.

INTERPRETATION: HEARING THE VOICE IN THE EPISTLES

The Epistles Have a Macro-Structure

Most of the Epistles have a clear structure to them.[7] There is often a doctrinal section and a practical section. Perhaps the most obvious example of a structured epistle is the epistle to the Ephesians. The first three chapters of doctrine work out what it is to be in Christ. The hinge of the book leading to the practical section is 4:1, "I therefore, a prisoner for the Lord, urge you to walk in a manner worthy of the calling to which you have been called" (Eph 4:1). This structure is even true of the smaller books such as Philemon, 1 John, 2 John, and Jude, though on a much smaller scale. However, there are notable exceptions to this.

The book of Hebrews lacks the structure that the others have and instead reads more like a sermon. As noted earlier, some argue that the book of Hebrews is one long sermon, an exposition of Psalm 110.

The other notable exception to the structure in the Epistles is the book of James. The book of James reads like Proverbs. There are generally five themes that are woven throughout the book, and the structure seems inconsequential to its argument. In fact, one could isolate the individual sections and preach them by themselves, with minimal discussion of the context, and not lose much of the meaning. I don't think this is true of any other epistle, but it is true of James.

The Epistles Have a Micro-Structure

One of the joys of preaching Epistles is that so much hangs on so little. Huge doors of theology hang on small hinges of exegetical nuance. Getting the text correct is critically important. However, perhaps more than other genres, the Epistles demonstrate that meaning may be communicated on the structural level. Therefore, the structure of the text is very important and at times may be the clue to the meaning of a text. Let's look at one example.

Preaching though Titus, I struggled with the qualification that an elder must have children ". . . who are believers and not open to the charge of debauchery or insubordination" (Titus 1:6). We have some help from the 1 Timothy 3:4 text that states that an elder must keep his child submissive in order to test his mettle for leadership within the church. This makes perfect sense. However, the Titus qualification is stronger and seems to imply that a potential pastor with a child that does not have saving faith is disqualified.[8] What exactly does this mean? The answer, I believe, is in the micro-structure of the text.

---

7. For an extremely helpful macro-view of the Pauline Epistles, see John Polhill, *Paul and His Letters* (Nashville: B&H Academic, 1999).

8. The following discussion was influenced by John Banker, *Semantic Structural Analysis of Titus* (Dallas: Summer Institute of Linguistics, 1994). While most commentaries argue from historical, theological, or biblical grounds, linguists may build a case from the semantic structure of the text. I find these linguistic tools helpful in dealing with difficult texts, especially when there is not an obvious theological

Notice the affirmative/opposite construction of the text: believers/not accused of debauchery or insubordination. They are to be this (believers); they are not to be that (charged with wild living or rebellion). This structure is used at least two other times in the immediate context:

1:7	God's Steward	Not arrogant, etc.
2:2	Reverent	Not slanderers, etc.

In these cases what follows the "not" is the exact opposite of the affirmation. Therefore, we could ask if there is a linguistic clue to the meaning of verse 6 and its reference to children who must be "believers." What is the opposite of insubordination? It is Christian faith, yes, but a specific application of it, namely, that the child buys into the leadership of the father who, in this case, is a pastor. Therefore while the text implies Christian faith, it is stronger than that. It seems to be saying that the children of an elder must buy in; they must believe in what their father is doing. This is an argument from the semantic structure of the text. It is an argument from the micro-level of the text.

The Epistles Have an Objective or Theme

While the structure of the epistle may have to do with the theological or practical aim of the book, the objective of the book has to do with the personalities of the writer and the recipient. The objective of the Gospels is expressed clearly enough by the individual writers. And this is no less true in the Epistles. They were written to correct a certain practice, or encourage another practice, or lead someone to a fuller faith.

Perhaps this is clearest in the book of Galatians when, in 1:6, Paul gets right to it: "I am so astonished that you are so quickly deserting him who called you in the grace of Christ and are turning to a different gospel." Everything else that is said in Galatians flows out of this astonishment that they have left what ought to have been their principle love to follow after something else.

Sometimes the themes are not stated up front, but they emerge throughout the letter. For example, the Pastoral Epistles begin with affirmations of the calling of Timothy and Titus (1 Tim 1:1–3; 2 Tim 1:1–6; Titus 1:1–4). It is the personal appeal of a father to a son. This tenor is evoked throughout the entire book. And, like a true loving father, Paul is not afraid to bring the hammer down on the theological or practical problems that are in the church. So, interestingly, these warm introductions lead to some of the sternest warnings so that Titus may in every respect show himself a model of good works and that Timothy may persist in his calling so that he might "save himself and others" (1 Tim 4:16).

Many times the theme will emerge through word pictures. Think about how metaphoric the Epistles are: Paul describes the church anthropomorphically as both the body and the bride. We are called not to let the world pour us into its mold, but to be living sacrifices, and we are encouraged to be vessels fit for use. All of these

---

or biblical resolution to a problem. The one cited above is produced by the linguists of the Summer Institute of Linguistics who use the resources as guides for translators working in oral cultures. The Semantic Structural Analysis and Exegetical Guides for various books can be ordered at *www.sil.org/ resources*.

wonderful word pictures should be exploited for their meaning.[9] However, the temptation in preaching is to "run away with the metaphor." For example, a sermon on being vessels fit for use that traces every possible use of a first-century vessel and gets much more out of the metaphor than could have possibly been intended by the author. The meaning of the metaphor is governed by the context, and the context is governed by the theme of the book. That is what drives the letter.

In each of the cases above there is a pastoral bent. The letter was written to right a wrong (1 Cor 1:11), to encourage (Ephesians 1:3–14), or to teach a doctrine (Phil 2:5–11). This reality affects the spirit of how we preach. The idea is that the metaphor exists to serve the truth. The metaphor is not itself to be served. Information about the metaphor, outside of what is demanded by the context, is unhelpful and can be distracting.

The Epistles Are Generally Didactic

The Epistles are often working out one theological idea or the application of a theological idea. Therefore, the sermons themselves tend to be didactic. The question is, how do you preach didactic sermons, with such a strong teaching bent, while keeping them lively and invigorating?

One of the reasons the biblical Epistles are didactic is because the writers, in some sense, are trying to recreate their presence. Paul comments about his weak presence and strong letters in 2 Corinthians 10:8–11. This is a clue, not to Paul's weakness, but to the idea that communication really is re-presentation. Paul wants the reading of the letter to be the type of experience that recreates his presence in the room. Thus, many of the letters have an oral dimension to them. In other words, they are didactic and they are written for the ear as much as they eye. After all, it only took one person to read the letters to the whole church, who would then hear the letter.[10]

The Epistles Have Loaded Introductions and Conclusions

The opening of a letter often provides clues to its interpretation. From the introduction one can observe the intended audience, the purpose of the book, and any theological themes that may be developed. "New Testament writers often send strong signals about their purposes in the opening section of the letter, and you should pay extra attention to that section."[11] In the conclusion, the content is usually personal, creating unique challenges for the preacher.

The preacher has been walking through an epistle, tending to the semantic structure, and then stumbles upon the end of a book with its warm and personal

---

9. For a helpful discussion of metaphor and literary technique in the Epistles, see Ryken, *Words*, 435–39.

10. This is true especially of the books of Hebrews and James. See discussion of the oral nature of the book of Hebrews in Andreas J. Köstenberger and Richard Patterson, *Invitation to Biblical Interpretation: Exploring the Hermeneutical Triad of History, Literature, and Theology* (Grand Rapids: Kregel, 2011), 476–79. See the insightful discussion on the oral nature of the book of James and how to capitalize on the oral effects in preaching in David Lim, "Text-Driven Preaching and the Aurality of the Text: Reanimating Aural Effects in Preaching James" (Ph.D. diss., Southwestern Baptist Theological Seminary, 2011).

11. Terry G. Carter, J. Scott Duvall, and J. Daniel Hays, *Preaching God's Word: A Hands-on Approach to Preparing, Developing, and Delivering the Sermon* (Grand Rapids: Zondervan, 2005), 174.

benediction, perhaps even peppered with personal names. Then he wonders, *What in the world do I do with this?* However, we are wrong to think there is nothing there exegetically since the conclusion is part of the letter and is consistent with the overall theme and purpose of the book.

The Commands Are Built on Foundations

The Epistles often use the imperative mood. They give commands: "Walk in the spirit"; "Do not get drunk with wine." It is tempting when preaching these commands to preach them as isolated edicts for right behavior. However, every imperative is built on an indicative. The imperative is the command; the indicative is the reason for the command. Therefore, preaching must be balanced around these two realities. The old axiom of parenting, "rules without relationship leads to rebellion," is very real in the preaching moment. If we give people rules without the reason behind them, there is little motivation to obey. And more importantly, Scripture is not written that way. The God who seeks a relationship with us builds his rules on the foundation of his love relationship with us. This is just how good he is.[12]

The Epistles Are Occasional Letters

All of the rich doctrine, all of the robust commands, and all of the exaltation of Christ in the Epistles are situational. The Epistles are what we call "occasional letters." That is, there was something specific going on in the life of the author and in the congregation that motivated the writing of the letter. For example, 1 Corinthians was written to correct some significant abuses in the church, 1 Peter to encourage in the midst of suffering, and Galatians to correct the abuse of legalism. All of the Epistles are written to real people in the middle of real first-century situations. This makes translating them to a modern audience difficult. What exactly does a preacher do with head coverings and meat sacrificed to idols? Since the Epistles were written for a specific context, how are they to be applied in the twenty-first century? This is a fair question. Let's deal with a few strategies.

COMMUNICATION: RECAPTURING THE VOICE IN THE EPISTLES

Preach the Book Systematically

There is a tremendous advantage to serial exposition—that is, preaching through books of the Bible. In this way one does not need to set up the context with each sermon, but can briefly refer the listener back to previous themes. For a one-time sermon, listeners are advantaged if they understand that the author is working through a particular doctrinal section or practical section. So, the message in an individual sermon must be tied back to the theme.[13]

To use our example above, if you are preaching anywhere in Ephesians 4, 5, or 6, you will want to mention from time to time that this is an outworking of the theme of being "in Christ" that is a significant theme in chapters 1–3. Paul helps us here by

---

12. Bryan Chapell effectively makes the point that the imperatives are always built on indicatives. See his talk in the Expository Preaching Workshop, March 6, 2012. Accessed March, 10, 2014, http://swbts.edu/media/item/412/plenary-session-6.

13. To understand a book's theme, I recommend reading some introductory surveys. There are several helpful ones such as Donald Guthrie, *New Testament Introduction* (Grand Rapids: InterVarsity, 1990).

pointing back to this theme throughout the book. Remember, the first three chapters are doctrinal and the last three practical. However, throughout the practical section he repeats the phrase "walking worthy" to remind us that all of this practical application is an outworking of the doctrinal portions of the text. Consider this simple outline for Ephesians.

Chapters 1–3 Doctrine
    Hinge: "Walk in a manner worthy of the calling to which you have been called" (4:1).

Chapters 4–6 Practice
    Don't walk like the Gentiles (4:17).
    Walk in love (5:1).
    Walk as children of light (5:8).
    Look carefully how you walk (5:16).

The repetition of the walking metaphor helps us understand that this is theology being lived out in practice. Paul wanted the Ephesians to understand this and therefore he used the metaphor repeatedly. We can do the same with great effect. While often the theme is not as obvious, it is best to point the listener back to the macro structure of the book.[14]

Listen to the Tone of the Text

When preaching an epistle, it is important to take on the tone of the text we are preaching. The listener should feel the stern rebuke of the apostle, the gentle encouragement, or the rhetorical verve of the brilliant apostle as he unravels a theological knot with simplicity and grace. All of this should be felt by the listener. While such feelings seem subjective, I am not sure I know how to say it more clearly. Those who teach oral interpretation teach that when we are trying to interpret a poem orally, or read the Scripture, the words should be pronounced with a pitch, rate, and volume that accentuate their meaning in the context. This is exactly what we are trying to do in the preaching of the text. Since these are not removed pieces of art, but personal letters, the listener should feel this in the communication of the truth.

How do we do this? The answer is quite simple. If we study and meditate on the text long enough we will be able to feel what the writer is feeling and to know what he wants to say, the way he wants to say it. The biblical writers were adept at not just communicating propositional truth but also tremendous emotion through their words. When we come to a passage that is unusually forthright and strong, we allow it to land with all of the force of the text. We are not just getting into the mind of the apostle; we are getting into his heart. And, the genre demands this. These are letters, and they are personal.

As a part of this strategy, it is helpful to back up occasionally and tie the theme of the book to the theme of Scripture. Perhaps as we preach the narratives of Scripture we become intuitive about saying, "Here is the story, but watch how this plays into the drama of Scripture." That type of narrative pointing allows the listener not to

14. See outline of Ephesians and his discussion of the relationship between Colossians and Ephesians in Peter O'Brien, *The Letter to the Ephesians*, The Pillar New Testament Commentary (Grand Rapids: Eerdmans, 1999), v–vii, 9–10.

lose sight of the fact that every story fits into *the* story. However, that is also true of Epistles. When teasing out the theme, often it's helpful to show how this theme not only fits into the letter as a whole, but also how it fits into the grand narrative of Scripture. The Epistles are written from the perspective of a dispersed church waiting for redemption. That is a great story to which every theme is tied.[15]

Effectively Place the Main Idea in the Structure of the Sermon

It is possible to state the main idea right up front. In a deductive sermon we are working from the main idea. It is stated at the beginning. However, it seems that if we structure our sermons the same way each time, the sermons could get predictable. It takes a masterful communicator to use the same style over and over again and not be boring. Yet the opposite is true for the rest of us who are average communicators; we are greatly advantaged by using a variety of structures. So, how do we sustain that variety when preaching through an epistle? Our ultimate goal is not variety nor creativity, but clarity. We first want to get the text right, but then we want to communicate its message in the most compelling way possible. Once the idea is clear, there are two ways we can make the structure more compelling and interesting: using variety with the main idea, and following the flow of the text. Let's discuss both of these in the examples below.

Since my examples are both from deductive type sermons, the most obvious approach is to give the main idea up front. The most common approach to this is what Hadden Robinson calls the "Subject-Completed" outline.[16] Robinson's approach will also be used to establish the structure for the sample given at the end of this chapter. In this approach, the subject is given up front and it is completed with each one of the points being a complement. The biggest advantage of this approach is its clarity. The biggest disadvantage is its predictability. A subject-completed outline may look like this:

Text: Colossians 1:15–18
Subject: Jesus is everything.

1. Jesus is everything because of his reflection of the Father (v. 15a).
2. Jesus is everything because of his creation of all things (vv. 15b–17).
3. Jesus is everything because of his resurrection from the dead (v. 18).

Notice that each of the points completes the subject. The subject stated up front gives the sermon interest because of its laser focus on one topic. More importantly, the subject-completed approach mirrors the way that Paul develops his argument. Duplicating the structure of the text in your sermon may seem "uncreative" or "boring," but doing what the text does is our goal in preaching.

Now think of a totally different type of text. Look at this passage from Titus 3:9–11.

But avoid foolish controversies, genealogies, dissensions, and quarrels about the law, for they are unprofitable and worthless.

---

15. Among the many resources that illustrate the narrative of Scripture, see Craig Bartholomew and Michael Goheen, *The Drama of Scripture: Finding Our Place in the Biblical Story* (Grand Rapids: Baker, 2004).

16. See Haddon Robinson, *Biblical Preaching: The Development and Delivery of Expository Messages* (Grand Rapids: Baker, 1980), 117, Figure 1.

> As for a person who stirs up division, after warning him once and then twice, have nothing more to do with him, knowing that such a person is warped and sinful; he is self-condemned.

The temptation in this text might be to have an outline with three clear points: avoid, warn, and know. However, in the last point the "know" is actually "knowing," a participle, that modifies the warning. In other words, Paul is not prescribing a three step process: avoid, warn, and know. Rather he is saying (1) there are some things that need to be avoided, and (2) there are some people who need to be confronted because they are self-condemned. In other words, the knowledge here is the motivation for the confrontation. Think about this possible outline:

Text: Titus 3:9–11
Subject: How do you handle divisive people?

1. You handle division by avoiding certain things (v. 9).
2. You handle division with proper confrontation (vv. 10–11).

Sometimes we like the beginning, middle, and ending feel of a three-point outline, but in this case it does not represent the text. So, we want to avoid the temptation of a neat and clean three point outline when it just is not there.

Now, as a further example of variety, let's look at the variety of sermons that are possible when preaching through the short epistle of Titus:

1:1–4. Paul's calling and motivation for writing the book. Sermon Shape: This will be a simple one or two point sermon.

1:5–9. Qualifications for Elders. Sermon Shape: This, on the other hand, is a lengthy and rather unwieldy list of qualifications. For the sake of clarity, it would be advisable to group these around the macro categories of qualification.

2:1–10. Paul writes a long list of admonitions that are gender and age specific, describing how one is to live out their theology. Sermon Structure: The most natural divisions are the ages: older men, older women, etc.

2:11–14. One of the most amazing Christological passages in the NT, this explains the effect of God bringing Christ into the world. Sermon Structure: This passage has three participles that naturally divide the text.

We could go on, but the point is that while each of these is a deductive epistolary text, they all have unique structures. And so should our sermons. In this way we are not being creative on our own, but we are borrowing the creativity of the text, and we are accomplishing our goal of teaching people the Scripture. So, allow the text to speak for itself and use variety when doing so. Again, in most cases the variety will not need to be forced, rather it is oozing up from the text itself.

Tend to the Introductions and Conclusions

The introductions to a letter are the natural time to introduce the entire book when preaching through a series. The challenge will be developing a main idea that is honest with the text and compelling at the same time. For some books this will not be difficult. The introduction to Romans is a theological treatise in and of itself as are the introductions to the books of Hebrews, 1 John, Galatians, and Titus. It would not be difficult for an idea and a structure to emerge that renders a full sermon. However, we have more difficulty with the shorter introductions. In such cases, we can introduce themes for the entire book and then explore those themes. This way we cover the introduction, while introducing the entire letter.

When preaching the introductions and conclusions, there is nothing wrong with allowing the humanity of the text to come to the surface. We do not know why Tychicus, Zenus, and Artimus are mentioned at the end of Titus. We are not even sure who they are. However, their presence reminds us that there was an immediate audience that received these letters and that all of the magnificent doctrine espoused in them was always cradled in the day-to-day life of the human condition. The book of Romans is perhaps the theological stalwart of the Epistles, yet in chapter 16 Paul mentions over 30 people by name. This is a pressing reminder to the preacher that theology is not removed from life; that which is teased out in the seminary classroom or the study must be lived out in the world. Doctrine without a view toward people is fire without heat or light. The introductions and conclusions are a great time to remind people, and preachers, of this essential truth.

In that same way, the introductions and conclusions speak to the nature and strategy of the church. Early Christians needed hope in the "only wise God" (Rom 16:27). Encouragement was in the nature of the church. However, one cannot read the benedictions of Paul without being struck by his engagement in the lives of people. Paul was remarkably engaged in people's lives. For Paul, being ready in season and out of season included pastoral instruction, preaching before world leaders, and managing with care and grace the relationships that God put in his life. Paul was not afraid to engage people on an individual level, as well as the large crowds. We know this from his introductions and conclusions.

So when we preach the introductions and conclusions, we must first mine the theology in them and its application to people's lives; then we must note the humanity that gives hands and feet to the theology.

Distinguish Between the Indicative and the Imperative

Clearly differentiating between the indicative and imperative in an epistolary argument is a simple sermon strategy. Be balanced and do not avoid the indicative. Preaching that ignores the biblical basis for a command and the divine enablement for obedience to that command will weary and dishearten the congregation. But do not make the mistake of avoiding the imperative either. Preaching that is constantly piling on indicatives, relishing in the truths of the text without the implications of the text assumes one can engage the mind without engaging the will. The truth is, Scripture itself does not function that way. It challenges, rebukes, and exhorts, and we preachers are commanded to do the same (2 Tim 4:2).

Take for example Galatians 5:16, "But I say, walk by the Spirit and you will not gratify the desires of the flesh." The command is a strong one. It is repeated a few verses later in a more passive form, "If we live by the Spirit, let us also walk by the Spirit" (5:25). However, this is not an isolated command. It is preceded by these words in verse 24, "And those who belong to Christ Jesus have crucified the flesh with its passions and desires." Now we begin to see that the reason we walk in the Spirit and not the flesh is because it is evidence of true conversion, i.e., those who are in Christ have crucified the flesh. We pan out and notice that the first verse of chapter 5 reads, "For freedom Christ has set us free; stand firm therefore, and do not submit again to a yoke of slavery." This indicative/imperative combination helps us understand verses 16 and 25. The motivation to walk by the Spirit and to crucify the flesh is that Christ has delivered us from bondage. Why would we want to return to that bondage? It makes no sense whatsoever.

As mentioned earlier we must never preach the imperatives without the indicatives. We never preach the commands without the promises.[17] Without the foundation of the promises/indicatives, the tilt toward legalism is certain.

Distinguish between Understanding and Doing

There are passages that are hard to understand and others that are hard to do. Some passages are difficult because they are hard to understand. Other passages are difficult because they are easy to understand, but they are hard to do. For example, Paul's exhortation in 1 Corinthians 6:12 that we are to flee sexual immorality is a difficult text to follow in our culture. The honest contemporary preacher has to embrace the reality that pornography is readily available and fornication is not only accepted, it's expected. What is worse is that sexual immorality is no longer seen as a sin, but as a full expression of one's self. The logic, therefore, is that when one frustrates one's sexual expression, he is limiting his soul and therefore the human self, one of the worst crimes one could commit in our culture today. This is a hard text, not because it is hard to understand, but because it is hard to do.

We deal with the texts that are difficult to apply by finding a cultural equivalent. Paul taught that people should not eat meat sacrificed to idols in 1 Corinthians 8. And brilliantly he makes a theological argument. His argument is that there really is no such thing as meat sacrificed to idols because idols do not exist (8:4). The implication is that the meat cannot have anything inherently wrong with it because there is nothing that can taint the meat. The problem is that not everyone understands this (8:7). The reader follows Paul's logic and thinks that the answer is to get all these un-knowledgeable people knowledgeable. Paul says it is the opposite. If we have the knowledge, but do not respect their lack of it, then "by your knowledge this weak person is destroyed, the brother for whom Christ died" (8:11). When preaching, one must unpack the historical context. However, if we stop there we have only provided an illustration for our theology but have not really helped our people. The preacher must ask the question, "Are there modern equivalents to this?" Are there "grey" areas that are not inherently right or wrong, but become right or wrong based on the context? Am I tempted to destroy a brother based on the presumption of my reach for freedom? There are a number of sensitive cultural issues such as appropriate/inappropriate entertainment, alcohol consumption, and stewardship of money where believers are tempted to waive the banner of freedom higher than the banner of love for others. The goal is to connect the ancient problem to the current one and make appropriate application.

On the other hand, there are many other texts such as the household codes and personal admonitions (Titus 2:1–10) and the qualifications for a minister (1 Tim 3:1–7) that are not hard-to-do as much as they are hard-to-understand. In these cases the strategy is simple: be clear. Where there is no clarity, the church will suffer. So when

---

17. See David Jackman, *Preaching and Teaching the New Testament*, Proclamation Trust DVD.

Scripture teaches on divorce, moral purity, gender roles, or any other number of difficult subjects, please do the congregation the service of being clear. Once you have been clear, there are two friends that must accompany your clarity, namely love and understanding. By this I mean that a preacher whose message is clear must make sure that his tone is one of love and affirmation. His tone should also include the fact that he understands how contemporary people might think these things are strange. There is nothing wrong with being honest about that. There is a line of thinking that has clarity without charity; this does not serve the church, but tilts the scales toward legalism. There is another type of preaching that has charity without clarity; this leaves people in the bondage of disobedience. Neither extreme serves the church.

STRUCTURING A SERMON FROM THE EPISTLES

1. Move from the Macro to the Micro

When preparing any text it is best to begin with the macrostructure and move to the micro-structure. In this way we are safeguarding ourselves from reading meaning into words and sentences and disregarding the context of the book. Carter, Duvall, and Hays suggest that when preaching Epistles, the "major pitfall is ignoring or disregarding the historical or literary context."[18] This pitfall is avoided when moving from the macro view to the micro view. If you are preaching through a book, then you have already done the heavy lifting of book level context, by reading through it several times. When you come to the individual text, it will be more natural.[19] So we begin with looking at the major themes of the book, then the structural divisions within the book, then the context of the individual unit of text to be preached, then to the sentence and clause level, and finally to the word study level. This approach also protects us from building a sermon around a word study that ignores the word in context.

2. Choose Where to Place the Main Idea

Since the Epistles are generally deductive it makes sense to give the full main idea at the beginning of the sermon, and this is usually done at the end of the introduction. The introduction is inductive leading to the main idea of the sermon; then the sermon works from the idea presented in the introduction. However, Epistles are very effective in the subject-compliment format that was observed in chapter 2. In this way the subject of the sermon is raised in the introduction and each point represents a compliment to that subject. This, I think, works best for Colossians 1:15–19. The subject is "Why is Christ supreme?" Paul answers that question with four reasons. Thus the sermon should raise that question in the introduction and allow the text to answer the question.[20]

---

18. See Carter, Duvall, and Hays, *Preaching God's Word*, 179–82.

19. The best work I have seen on preparing a text-driven sermon is found in the unpublished preaching notes of Dr. David Allen. I have learned much from them, especially when dealing with Epistles. Allen is a linguist, and his perspective is based on principles of Semantic Structural Analysis. The synopsis of his approach has been published in David L. Allen, "Preparing a Text-Driven Sermon," in *Text-Driven Preaching: God's Word at the Heart of Every Sermon*, ed. Daniel L. Akin, David L. Allen, and Ned L. Mathews (Nashville: B&H Academic, 2010).

20. The structure of this example is interesting because of its repetition. Some see that Paul is defending his proposition of the supremacy of Christ with four propositions, and others with five. It depends if the

Watch for Genre in a Genre

Many of the genres we have mentioned are hybrids. One would think that this is not the case in the Epistles, but it is. In the Epistles, there will always be a narrative backdrop that will influence interpretation (see, for example, the letter to Philemon) and often times there are hymns. Epistles will contain their own sub-genres such as domestic codes, slogans, and lists of vices and virtues.[21] Most commentators believe Colossians 1:15–20 is an early Christian hymn. It has a strophe structure and is supported by key rhetorical markers of repetition: firstborn (vv. 15, 18) and "things in heaven and on earth" (vv. 16, 20). This is wonderful because once noted, it is a clue to help us find the meaning.[22]

Sermon Sample

Jesus is Everything, Colossians 1:15–18

> PREACHING STRATEGY
>
> *The text is raising the question, "Why is Christ supreme over all things?" The answer is in four or five simple propositions in vv. 15–20. This sermon only addresses the first three.*

Introduction

When Copernicus discovered that the earth was not the center of the universe, but the sun was the center, he set in motion what is called "The Copernican Revolution." There were some that disagreed and could not believe that the earth was not the center. However, concerning those who disagreed with Copernicus, how much did they actually change the place of the sun? Not one degree.

We often make odd statements such as, "I made Christ the Lord of my life." I know what is meant, and I'm not trying to play semantic games, but the truth is that we cannot make Christ anything, much less what God has already declared that he is. Christ is Lord. God has declared it to be so. He is the center. The question is not what I will make Christ, the question is will I rearrange my life around that reality of his supremacy? Because my life isn't everything, ministry isn't everything, making money, or status, or work, or recognition are not everything; Jesus is everything.

> The introduction sets up the theology of this text. This leads nicely into the context where the Colossians are faced with a question: Will they believe that Jesus is something or that he is everything?

---

exegete will take the idea of Christ being the *pleroma*, fullness (v. 19), of God as a stand alone reason for the supremacy of Christ or fold it into the idea of *eikon*, image (v. 15). It seems that both are defensible.

21. Köstenberger and Patterson, *Invitation*, 473–76.

22. See Douglas Moo, *The Letters to the Colossians and to Philemon*, Pillar New Testament Commentary (Grand Rapids: Eerdmans, 2008), 107–37.

CONTEXT

TRANSITION: So why is Christ everything?

Text: Colossians 1:15–18

> The sermon structure is simple because the text is laid out in a simple way. Note however that the first point is only half a verse. I believe v. 15b is better grouped with vv. 16 and 17.

1. **Jesus is everything because of his reflection of the Father (v. 15).**

   Paul uses an interesting word, *eikon*—image, this is the perfect mirror reflection of God; Image/invisible—this is the juxtaposition of what we can and cannot see, thus Jesus is the tangible of that which is intangible. Firstborn—This speaks to the supremacy of Christ above anyone else. It is a reference to the Hebrew cultural idea of the firstborn having all the rights. He is both preexistent and preeminent. John 1:1–5. Jesus proves his supremacy because he is the exact tangible expression of the God who is invisible.

2. **Jesus is everything because of his creation of the world (vv. 16–17).**

   All (*panta*) things—is used four times. Thus everything is under the dominion of Christ. He is pitting contrasting ideas—heaven/earth; visible/invisible. Jesus is supreme because everything that exists was created by Jesus, through Jesus, and for Jesus.

3. **Jesus is everything because of his resurrection from the dead (v. 18).**

   Jesus is supreme in the church. Because of his resurrection from the dead he earned the right to be first in all things.

Conclusion

   Before I was married, God used singleness to help me understand that marriage is not everything. Jesus is everything. In that moment he taught me that I did not have to be married, but I did have to recognize the supremacy of Christ in my life. Marriage wasn't everything; Jesus was everything. Having children isn't everything; Jesus is everything.

REFLECTION

1. What are the advantages to serial exposition?
2. What does it mean to tend to the macro-structure of an epistle?
3. What does it mean to tend to the micro-structure of an epistle?
4. How do you preach an introduction or conclusion?
5. Why is placement of the main idea important?

Recommended Reading

Abernathy, David. *An Exegetical Summary of 1 Peter*. Dallas: Summer Institute of Linguistics, 2008. (Any book in this series is recommended.)

Banker, John. *Semantic Structural Analysis of Titus*. Dallas: Summer Institute of Linguistics, 1994. (Any book in this series is recommended.)

Blailock, Edward M. "The Epistolary Literature." Pages 545–56 in *Expositor's Bible Commentary*, vol. 1. Grand Rapids: Zondervan, 1979.

Harris, Murray. *Colossians and Philemon*. Exegetical Guide to the Greek New Testament. Grand Rapids: Eerdmans, 1991.

Polhill, John B. *Paul and His Letters*. Nashville: B&H Academic, 1999.

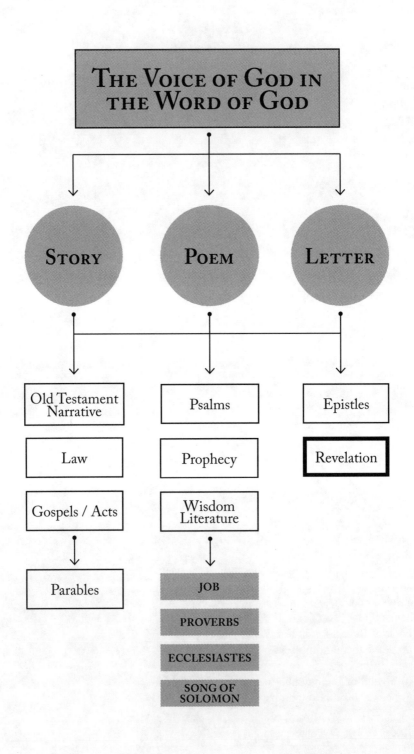

THE VOICE OF GOD IN THE WORD OF GOD

STORY

POEM

LETTER

Old Testament Narrative

Law

Gospels / Acts

Parables

Psalms

Prophecy

Wisdom Literature

JOB

PROVERBS

ECCLESIASTES

SONG OF SOLOMON

Epistles

Revelation

Chapter 12

RECAPTURING THE VOICE OF
GOD IN REVELATION

THE BOOK TO END THE BOOK IS AN INCREDIBLE BOOK. Some look at it as a road map through which they can navigate modern events; therefore, they go slow. They stop to gaze at the magnificent visions in the book, and as they gaze they wonder exactly why it is written this way. They poke and prod; they squeeze and mix, until what is extracted from this vision becomes a blend of modern events glazed over with speculation and hope. And then there are the rest of us, the minimalists. On the whole Christians look at the back of the book, Revelation, and they understand that they win. That is quite enough. If you know the end, then why read it? After all, the bizarre images are beyond interpretation anyway. Perhaps it's for this reason that the book of Revelation is largely ignored today. It's neglected from a mix of apathy and a fear of the unknown. Why take the time to understand and unpack the contents of John's book when listeners do not care for the bizarre? How does understanding the book of Revelation actually help people? Why bother? The answer to these questions is found in the first verse.

The book of Revelation, from beginning to end, is a book about Jesus. The book never gets past the first verse, "The revelation of Jesus Christ." This is Jesus Christ revealed. You do not have to love end times prophecy to love Revelation; you simply have to love Jesus. To love Jesus is to love him revealed.

The preposition "of" implies that this is the Revelation from Jesus Christ.[1] Meaning, this is what Christ said to John. However, what Christ said is all about Christ. So Revelation is about Jesus, but more specifically it is about how Christ wants us to understand Christ. It is a self-portrait of Jesus. How could it be anything but fascinating? What is there not to love, given the Author and the content? The challenge for the preacher is to know how to extract that content. How do you preach the book of Revelation in a way that will give people a full glimpse of its content, yet not leave them intimidated by the details? The answer to those questions lies in the sermon structure.

At the end of the day, the modern preacher has to help people overcome how they imagine Jesus. How do people imagine Christ? Since the church calendar is

---

1. This could be considered a plenary genitive. Osborne understands the preposition as a subjective genitive, not an objective genitive; thus, it is revelation "from" Jesus not necessarily about Jesus. Yet, it is no matter since the content of so much of the book is the identity of Christ. See Grant R. Osborne, *Revelation*, Baker Exegetical Commentary on the New Testament (Grand Rapids: Baker, 2002), 52.

built around Easter and Christmas, it is no wonder that people see Christ first as a baby. The soft newborn nestled in the hay, lying there helpless. Bethlehem, baby Jesus. The second way they think of Jesus is crucified—the victim of Roman torture. Calvary, whipped Jesus. If they picture him any other way, it is often as a peace loving hippie. Jesus is sitting on a Galilean hillside with his disciples, just outside of his VW van. Peter is playing the acoustic guitar while Jesus lectures on the value of recycling. Galilee, hippie Jesus. Yet, Jesus is none of that. Jesus is not a baby. Jesus is not dying. Jesus is not a Jewish peasant strolling the hillside as an intellectual guide. Those are the images that are burned on our minds, and they are tied to events that actually happened. The problem is not that the images aren't real; it's just that they are so outdated. Consequently, our people are fixated on who Jesus was, not who he is. It is true that Jesus Christ is the same yesterday, today, and forever. His character does not change, but in the sovereign rule and plan of God, he did subject himself to time. He was a baby, but he grew. He grew to be a man, but he died. He died, but he rose. And now he wants us to understand him as he is—the ruling monarch of all eternity. That is who he is. That is what Christ wants us to know about Christ. That is what people miss when we neglect to preach Revelation. We fail to fixate on the hope that awaits us (1 Pet 1:13). Jesus' words are critical because the self-revelation of his future coming tells us how we are to live now.

INTRODUCING JESUS

The introduction to the book of Revelation is perhaps the most descriptive of any of the New Testament books.

> The revelation of Jesus Christ, which God gave him to show to his servants the things that must soon take place. He made it known by sending his angel to his servant John, who bore witness to the word of God and to the testimony of Jesus Christ, even to all that he saw. Blessed is the one who reads aloud the words of this prophecy, and blessed are those who hear, and who keep what is written in it, for the time is near. (Rev 1:1–3)

As noted in the first verse, this book is described as a "revelation." This is a revelation from Jesus, about Jesus. And yet, there is more. It is also described as a testimony (v. 2). So again, this is not just any revelation; it is a self-revelation. Notice the progress of communication in this testimony:

From God to Jesus
From Jesus to the angel
From the angel to John
From John to us.

This testimony is certain because it is coming from God himself.

Finally, the book is prophecy (v. 3). There is prediction of end times events, but much more. If the Old Testament is any guide, prophecy typically contains more proclaiming than predicting. The book of Revelation has its share of proclaiming, so the book has a function that is corrective. In the end this is a letter to the churches, so it functions like epistolary genre as well.[2] In other words, the purpose of the prophecy is to prepare us for Christ's return, not to scratch an itch of curiosity. So the book is a self-revelation of Jesus that tells us how to live in light of the reality that he is coming soon. That is something to preach. So now, let's look at issues of interpretation and communication.

INTERPRETATION: HEARING THE VOICE IN REVELATION

Revelation Is Jesus Revealed

As noted, the first challenge is to make Revelation about Jesus. Revelation contains prophecy, but it's not about prophecy. Revelation contains a description of heaven, but it's not about heaven. Revelation has strong prophetic words to the church, but it is not about encouragement to the church. The book from beginning to end is about Jesus. So, the way to make the book compelling and provocative is to show its true character as a revelation of Christ.

Revelation Has a Unique Genre and Structure

This unique structure is identified in 1:19. John is told to "Write therefore things that you have seen, those that are and those that are to take place after this." This has commonly been seen as an outline of the entire book. The things that he has seen appear in chapter 1. The things that are, are in chapters 2–3. And the things that will take place are in chapters 5–22. This has to do with the content of the book, since the first chapter deals with introductory matters, 2 and 3 are the letters to the seven churches, and the rest is the revelation of the future.

The structure of the book can also be seen through a narrative framework in the four visions marked by the phrase "in the spirit" (1:9; 4:2; 17:3; 21:10), and there is also a unique structuring device with the use of the series of sevens.[3]

It is easy to miss the unique genre of the book. In fact, it might be second nature to refer to the book as apocalyptic, but that might be too simplistic and it hardly helps us preach it.[4] What is the genre of the book? Ian Paul notes, "Revelation changes its microgenre from one place to another, and this is particularly marked in chapter 1, where we have apocalyptic (vv. 1 and 7), blessing (v. 3), doxology (v. 5), prophecy (v. 8) as well as clear markers of the epistolary genre (vv. 4 and 9)."[5] Chapters 2 and 3 are epistolary. Narrative and prophecy are woven throughout the book so what we have said about shaping the sermon by these other genres applies here. The reality is that the book of Revelation, as do so many of the biblical books, contains multiple genres. "The book falls into the overall genre of prophecy but corresponds to apocalyptic writings in many respects."[6] And yet, as noted above, the whole book has a narrative framework to it; thus, when preaching through the book, the preacher must

2. Andreas J. Köstenberger and Richard D. Patterson, *Invitation to Biblical Interpretation: Exploring the Hermeneutical Triad of History, Literature, and Theology* (Grand Rapids: Kregel, 2011), 531.

3. Ibid., 533–36.

4. See Paige Patterson's helpful discussion of the unique genre in Revelation. Paige Patterson, *Revelation,* New American Commentary (Nashville: B&H, 2012), 24–25.

5. Ian Paul, "Preaching from the Book of Revelation," in *Preaching the New Testament*, ed. Ian Paul and David Wenham (Downers Grove, IL: InterVarsity, 2013), 162.

6. Köstenberger and Patterson, *Invitation to Biblical Interpretation*, 531.

communicate the setting, plot, scene structure, rising tension, and releasing tension in the macro narrative. Along the way, preaching through Revelation will necessitate switching sermon structures during the series.

Of course, in a sense the narrative of Revelation mirrors the narrative of the whole of Scripture. Revelation is, after all, the consummation of the whole Bible. In this way, the intertextuality of the book is not just a unique feature, but rather the threads that hold the narrative of the Bible together to form one complete vision.[7]

Remember also that the structure of Revelation has a visionary feel to it. John is telling us the things that he has "seen." The preacher's challenge is to tell the vision. John wrote what he saw, and we speak what he wrote about that vision. In the translation process, make sure that people see what you are saying.[8]

Revelation Is Intertextual

Revelation is the most intertextual of all the books. Meaning, the book is dependent on the Old Testament. Ian Paul notes that in 404 verses there are 676 allusions to the Old Testament:

Isaiah	128
Psalms	99
Ezekiel	92
Daniel	82
Exodus	53[9]

While some allusions are easier to grasp than others, it is difficult to overstate the importance of highlighting these intertextual links.[10] First, like all the books of the Bible, intertextuality demonstrates the remarkable unity of the Scripture. Generally the allusions describe the epic coming of the Messiah to redeem his people.[11] The Hebrew people had often been under persecution. They were persecuted by the Egyptians, the Assyrians, and then the Romans. They were told that one day their Messiah would come. So many of the prophets spoke about the rider who would come (Isa 63:1–6) while they prayed that God would rend the heavens and come down (Isa 64:1).

And he came. However, while they got the Messiah they wanted, they did not get the Messiah they were expecting. He came, but he also left without dealing justice on their enemies. Where is the justice? Well, he brings it here in the book of Revelation. And so much of the justice they hoped for is tied up in the reality that the long promised Messiah of Psalm 2 has finally come and will most certainly return.

---

7. For the relationship of Revelation to biblical theology, see T. Desmond Alexander, *From Eden to the New Jerusalem: An Introduction to Biblical Theology* (Grand Rapids: Kregel, 2008).

8. Köstenberger and Patterson provide an outline of the book based on the visions of the book. See Köstenberger and Patterson, *Invitation to Biblical Interpretation*, 558–59.

9. Paul, "Preaching from the Book of Revelation," 165.

10. Köstenberger sees three types of allusions: embedded, implied, and incidental. Köstenberger and Patterson, *Invitation to Biblical Interpretation*, 542–43.

11. See Leland Ryken's discussion on "The Book of Revelation as Epic" in Leland Ryken, *Words of Delight: A Literary Introduction to the Bible* (Grand Rapids: Baker, 1987), 481–82.

Revelation Has a Unique Imagery

No other book in the Bible uses as much imagery as the book of Revelation. Approaches to the imagery of Revelation swing wildly from the hyper-allegorical to those that ignore the imagery all together. There is a reason the imagery is there. We must locate the reason and show how it relates to the interpretation and application of the text. The objective is to "read the symbols in the vocabulary of the first century and then to interpret them for the [twenty-first]-century church in terms of their final and complete fulfillment."[12] For example, when we see Jesus on a white horse (Rev 19:11) the imagery conveys Christ as ruling all things. Thus what needs to be communicated is Christ's complete and total domination that is loaded in that image. In this way we are considering the cultural context, the imagery, and applying it to the contemporary situation.[13]

Revelation Is Prophetic More Than Predictive

The book claims to be prophetic (1:3; 22:6–7, 10, 18–19). However, is this prophecy predicting the future, or does it serve as a warning to the church? The answer is, of course, "both." The book warns about future events. However, because this is true, one homiletic approach has dominated its preaching over the years—namely preaching it only as a template for understanding current and future events. Those events may in fact be there. However, if no event unfolds in contemporary times that we can explicitly tie to a prophecy in the book of Revelation, the book still has an incredible impact. The reason for this is that a prophetic book functions to teach more than to predict. Think prophetic, not speculative.

Revelation Is Personal

Under the rule of the Roman Emperor Domitian, the people to whom John is writing were severely persecuted. They knew nothing of the Christian liberty we enjoy in the contemporary West. This gives us a good sense of the "underground" nature of the book.[14] Imagine these cultural subversives, holed up in house churches. John writes, using all of the Old Testament imagery they would understand to speak of the Messiah and tells them that he has seen him. Yet, he is not the Jewish peasant they remember. He is actually the reigning Messiah. He is coming back in defense of his bride, and he will take out all of his enemies. This is the Jesus whom John saw, and the One whom they will see. Revelation is personal because Christ will personally come back for his persecuted bride.

COMMUNICATION: RECAPTURING THE VOICE IN REVELATION

The Structure of the Sermon

Sermon structures from Revelation may have more variety than any other book. This is because there are multiple subgenres in the book. There will be times in the

---

12. Robert H. Mounce, *The Book of Revelation*, rev ed., New International Commentary on the New Testament (Grand Rapids: Eerdmans, 1998), 30.
13. See the seven steps to interpreting symbolic language in Köstenberger and Patterson, *Invitation to Biblical Interpretation*, 551–57.
14. See David Jackman, *Preaching and Teaching New Testament: Gospels, Letters, Acts and Revelation* (London: The Proclamation Trust), DVD.

book where one can use a deductive approach, as if preaching an epistle. This is clear from chapters 2 and 3 especially. However, there are some times when the best approach is a simple list—a descriptive approach; times when a narrative structure is best; and other times when there is prophecy that functions like poetry. So, let's look at those structural options.

Descriptive. In descriptive literature, there may not be any divisions as we normally understand them. In the example below from Revelation 19:11–16, there simply is no outline in the text, so I chose to have no "points" in the sermon. The sermon has an outline; it just does not have major headings like a traditional sermon.

The text describes the Warrior Messiah. The ordering of the words, in this instance, is of less importance. One could fairly divide the text into two aspects of the Warrior Messiah: his identity and his activity. This would work. Still, my fear is that while I try to maintain the form of "points," I lose something in the text. The priority is the structure of the text, not maintaining a pre-determined homiletic form.

Narrative. Much of the book is narrative and can be developed by scenes. We have noted that the structure of individual stories fits into the larger framework of the story of the book. This is especially true in Revelation. In fact, the tension built in the original stories is never quite released until the Lamb is worshiped fully and the last battle is fought. Therefore, when preaching Revelation, be sure to remind them of the big picture. Such reminders are especially helpful when dealing with the tougher texts.

Chapters 4 and 5 are examples of passages that read like descriptions, but they have a narrative feel to them—especially chapter 5 when John, while looking for a lion, sees a lamb. And a slain Lamb at that. This chapter has the traditional narrative structure of setting, rising tension, and release of tension.

Prophecy. The letters to the seven churches are epistolary prophecy. They are not predictive as much as they are corrective. They are filled with indictments and commands. Therefore, like an epistle, this can be more easily arranged in a traditional point-by-point outline.

Remember this book is intertextual (more on this below). This is critical. Most of what you are reading is, by design, dependent on the Old Testament sources. So when trying to interpret what a word or phrase says, remember it is possible to understand what it "says" without understanding what it "means." The meaning is often embedded in the language of the Old Testament, either by quotation, allusion, or both. In the example below, the entire passage is a fulfillment of Psalm 2. In Psalm 2, the nations take up counsel together against "the Anointed One," and in Revelation 19 the prophecy was fulfilled. This is a clear allusion. In case the allusion is not clear enough, John uses an almost exact quote from Psalm 2:9 in verse 15, "he will rule them with a rod of iron." Why John used this, and how John used this, is loaded with meaning. So be sure and drill down there. The preacher will have the opportunity here to show the intertextual nature of Revelation and its dependence on the Old Testament.

Showing the OT allusions and references should be fluid in the sermon. Meaning, you can use them or not, and when you do, it will be to varying degrees. The question the interpreter is always asking is, "What does this text mean in light of the whole of Scripture?" Intertextuality is important because it helps people see the

Bible wholly. To recognize these connections. You may have them turn to the passage, or you may just mention it.

Preach Jesus

The most obvious way to demonstrate the interconnectedness of Revelation to the rest of the Bible is to preach the Christological passages of the book. The passages about Christ proper are nothing short of amazing. Think about these images of Christ. He is the magnificent source of light in 1:9–20, the strong Lamb, who is also the Lion and the Shepherd, in chapter 5 and 7:17, the groom and Warrior Messiah in chapter 19, and the source of all light in heaven in 21:23. So a great way to introduce this would be to preach a short series, five–eight sermons, on the major Christological passages of the book. This should have the effect of changing people's opinion about the book while whetting their appetite for more.[15]

Assuming you preach straight through the book, you will want to stop and point to Jesus throughout. This should not be difficult, and it has a great practical benefit. While you might be tempted to bog down in the details of the book, stopping to point to Jesus will remind your people of the end game. They will be reminded where all of this is going.

Additionally, we must be careful about preaching our own end times views instead of preaching Jesus. We should be careful not to preach sermons that are merely platforms for ideas that were decided long before the series was complete.

Mix It Up

Since there are shifts in the genre, there can be shifts in the sermon structure. A sermon from chapter 1 might feel like it has too much biblical background information for our liking, but it is a necessary framework for the message that is coming. The letters to the churches are favorite preaching material. They are clear and explicit. Major portions of what follows are descriptions of events that will come. A sermon from this last section may feel like a list of descriptions for the reason that is exactly what it is. The variety this provides in preaching is very compelling. Variety in genre means there will be great variety in the length of text chosen.

Chapter 1 is a good example. There is wisdom in taking the first three verses alone. There is a lot there and it serves as a good introduction to the book. Additionally, there is also wisdom in taking verses 4–20 as a sermon text. You could break the passage up from verses 4–8 and verses 9–20. However, if you do, be sure and recast the vision in the second sermon. It is one literary unit. Much of the book is narrative, so for a narrative text you will want to take a bigger text to give the full narrative. For example, chapters 4 and 5 could be preached together.

Point to the Book Structure from Time to Time

Revelation can seem like a labyrinth. The listener may wonder how he will wade through all of the information that is coming his way. It is always wise to point

---

15. Craig Blaising argues that the theme of the book is "Jesus is coming" and it is initially addressed in 1:7 and throughout the book thereafter in his insightful and helpful address, "Jesus Is Coming," which was delivered at the Advanced Expository Preaching-Workshop, Southwestern Baptist Theological Seminary, Oct. 7, 2013.

to the macro-structure of a book, but maybe more so in Revelation than in other books. Help your listeners see the momentum of the book, leading up to the climactic ending.

A good way to do this would be to present the book visually as you preach through it, assuming the technology is available. There is much that video technology cannot do, but one thing that it can do well is to provide a view of the macro-structure of a book. People will enjoy seeing where you are, and this will create much needed sign posts for navigating such a dense book. Start by choosing a simple outline for the book. Then graphically recreate it in a normal list, or a time-line format, to point your people in the right direction. Then, from time to time, show it to them. Be careful not to overdo it. But done well, a visual timeline or outline could help them keep their bearings as you walk through a dense book.

Show and Tell

When preaching Revelation it is important to constantly show the correlation with other books of Scripture. Pointing out intertextuality is always important in preaching, but in Revelation it is critically important. The faith of your people will grow as they see the organic unity of the Bible: hope fulfilled in the person of Jesus.

The key is to find the connections. The primary way we achieve this is through simply reading and rereading Scripture. However, the work of scholars can also help us. So, when we see a quotation of or an allusion to another passage, we will need to do some exegetical work on the Old Testament text from which John is drawing. There may be a reason John is using that particular text. A reason that will come to light when we study the passage he is referencing.

Think of it this way. John is writing to people who know their Bibles. Because of this, John's words were a means of tying together so much of what they already knew. They knew it, but did not know how it all fit together. John is showing how all they had learned about and thought of is coming to fruition. Revelation indeed.

Preach with Eyes on Those in Front of You

Revelation was written for an immediate audience, and we preach to one as well. They were privileged to see the future, and so are we. However, the function of eschatology is to prepare us, not to inform us. The book is for the obedient, not the curious. So, when approaching the book, show the immediate implications of the text to the listener.

The task may seem daunting given the strange nature of the book, but it can be done. And the starting place is hope. The book gives us incredible hope. After all, there are seven blessings mentioned in the book—future reward for immediate obedience.[16] There is hope in a coming Messiah, a new world, and a new heaven.

Preach the Victory

When preaching the book of Revelation, preach it in light of Christ's coming victory. Christ will come back. He will bring the royal beat down on his enemies. Christ will conquer. It is encouraging to see Christ, our Warrior Messiah, coming to defend his bride and take out the enemy. The consummation that he brings can

---

16. Simon Kistemaker, *Revelation*, New Testament Commentary (Grand Rapids: Baker, 2001), 5.

be imagined now.[17] Preaching this image of Christ as victor, Christ defending the helpless, helps us crush the emasculated picture of Christ seared into our minds by the popular culture. He is not that. He is who Revelation reveals him to be in all of his majesty and glory. So preach to people who need hope and tell them that help is on the way. Preach to a potentially persecuted people to teach them that help will be on the way. Jesus is coming back. Jesus will defend. Jesus will protect.

Sample Sermon

The Warrior Messiah (Rev 19:11–16)

> PREACHING STRATEGY
>
> The text answers the question of the identity and the activity of the rider on the white horse. The sermon simply allows the text to answer that question.

Main Idea: Jesus Christ is the Warrior Messiah who wars with his Word.

Introduction

> I decided not to do a fully orbed introduction. The reason is that the text is so magnificent with imagery that a "normal" introduction might distract from its majesty. Sometimes it is more effective to jump right in. So the introduction of the sermon was simply an exposition of v. 11 with some important background information added. One option would be to begin with Psalm 2 since Revelation 19 is its fulfillment.

"And I saw heaven opened . . . " (v.11).

All through the book of Revelation, God is giving John little pictures into heaven. A window here or a door there. However, now it is as if God has thrown the entire cargo doors of heaven open. No holding back. John can see everything inside. Here is what John sees. Look at verse 11. He sees a horse. This is not a show horse or a parade horse; what he sees is a war horse. The imagery of a white horse is that of a Roman general returning from battle. This is a picture of a warrior.

However, the first-century Palestinian Jewish audience would have seen something more clearly. They would have heard in this passage a ring of Isaiah 63—their Warrior Messiah was to return on a white horse. The Messiah who is coming back to war on their behalf. So who is this Warrior Messiah?

---

17. Stephen S. Smalley, *The Revelation to John: A Commentary on the Greek Text of the Apocalypse* (Downers Grove: InterVarsity, 2005), 17.

The one sitting on it is "Faithful and True . . . " This is a reference to Christ. He is anticipated in Matthew 24:29–30; he is anticipated in Isaiah 63:1–3. They were expecting a Warrior Messiah, and here he is.

So here is the idea of the passage: Jesus is the Warrior Messiah. The rest of the passage is simply the identity and the activity of the Warrior Messiah.

PREACHING STRATEGY

As stated above this text is a simple list. Two divisions are present, but they are not very helpful. They are referenced in the beginning and not repeated. This text describes, so the sermon must simply work through this description.

The Identity of the Warrior Messiah

He judges and makes war (v. 11). He is coming back to bring right judgement. These statements are symbolic of his entire activity. **His eyes are a flame of fire (v. 12).** Jesus can see everything. His eyes are penetrating like two lasers. His eyes are like a raging fire. This speaks of his omniscience (sees all) and judgment (repays all).

And on his head are many diadems (v. 12). Jesus has many crowns, indicating an unlimited sovereignty. Perhaps this contrast is intentional. After all, Satan came on a white horse. This description of the presence of the One who is faithful and true exposes the false and the fake. His Sovereignty is also seen in verse 12: "On his robe and on his thigh he has a name written, King of kings and Lord of lords . . ." This is a banner that is going across his chest and his thigh. This is the divinity of Christ stressed.

So, now we have someone who has all authority, he can see all, and has all power—he is the only One in a position to make right judgment.

And he has a name written on him that no one knows but himself (v. 12). There is a parallel here to Philippians 2:9. This is a secret name. The name will never be known.

A robe dipped in blood (v. 13). This is an allusion to Isaiah 63:1–6 and the "treading in the wine press." This is the blood of his enemies, not his own as in 1:5; 5:9; 7:14. This is not the blood of Jesus; it is the blood of the ones he has conquered. The idea is tied to the winepress. What help it gives the martyrs to know that the enemy's blood is on his robe. This is a text that is intended to show a vision of Christ as the conquering and ruling Warrior Messiah.

Illustration: This is not normally how we think of Christ, is it? We normally think of him as a baby, a hippie, or a victim of crucifixion. Baby Jesus. Hippie Jesus. Whipped Jesus. The problem with these images is not that they do not have historical value; it's just that they are so outdated. That is who Jesus was; this is who Jesus is.

The armies which are in heaven. They did not come to fight; they came to watch.

PREACHING STRATEGY

The list-like nature of this text demands that the sermon be interrupted for illustration along the way. This pauses the heaviness since it gets heavier still in the following verses.

TRANSITION: The first four verses describe what he is, the last two describe what he will do, so now notice . . .

The Activity of the Messiah Warrior

From his mouth comes a sharp sword (v. 14). Isa. 11:4—Messianic King will strike with one word. When it ends, Jesus will destroy them with one word. This is the power of the word of judgment.

Rod of Iron (v. 15). This is an allusion from Psalm 2:9—he will rule them with a rod of iron. He will dominate them, and his judgment and wrath will be as unyielding as iron.

Treading the Wine Press (v. 15). This is first mentioned in Joel 3:13. The fierce anger of God. The idea is that Jesus tramples his enemies as one would tread on grapes.

Conclusion

Well, are you ready for the battle? Actually, there is no battle. Notice the army's robes were white and clean—they did not come to fight; they came to watch. Jesus will end it all with one word. In fact the whole chapter ends with the unceremonious words, "the rest were slain" (v. 21). It is Christ who ends the battle, not us.

The application to this passage is actually found in Psalm 2:10–12. The purpose is not to prepare us for battle, but to get us to ask, "Do we fear him alone?" and "Do we trust him alone"?

PREACHING STRATEGY

Revelation 19:11–16 is the fulfillment of Psalm 2. John uses the language of Psalm 2 to help us see this. The intertextual nature of this text is critical for two practical preaching reasons: (1) There is no application to this idea of Jesus as warrior in Revelation 19, but there is in Psalm 2. Thus we can borrow the application from Psalm 2. (2) Seeing Psalm 2 and Revelation 19 together, it is abundantly clear that it is Christ who fights the battle. We are present as spectators to his victory. Only One has a sword.

QUESTIONS

1. What is the genre of Revelation, and why is this a trick question?
2. How many sermon structures are possible when preaching Revelation?
3. What does it mean to preach Revelation from the macro view or the micro view?

4. How do you make application when preaching Revelation?
5. What does it mean that Revelation is intertextual, and what difference does it make when preaching?

RECOMMENDED RESOURCES

Alexander, T. Desmond. *From Eden to the New Jerusalem: An Introduction to Biblical Theology*. Grand Rapids: Kregel, 2008.

Jackman, David. *Preaching and Teaching New Testament: Gospels, Letters, Acts and Revelation*. London: The Proclamation Trust, 2008.

Mounce, Robert H. *The Book of Revelation*. Rev ed. New International Commentary on the New Testament. Grand Rapids: Eerdmans, 1998.

Osborne, Grant R. *Revelation*. Baker Exegetical Commentary on the New Testament. Grand Rapids: Baker, 2002.

Patterson, Paige. *Revelation*. New American Commentary. Nashville: B&H, 2012.

Selected Bibliography

The following select bibliography includes works cited and resources for the preacher wanting to dig further. Not all the works are equally helpful since some are listed for their contribution to the field.

General

Adam, Peter. *Speaking God's Word: A Practical Theology of Preaching*. Downers Grove: InterVarsity, 1996.

Allen, David L. "A Tale of Two Roads: Homiletics and Biblical Authority." *Journal of the Evangelical Theological Society*. 43 (2000): 489–515.

Ash, Christopher. *The Priority of Preaching*. Ross-shire, Scotland: Christian Focus, 2009.

Autrey, Denny. *Factors Influencing the Sermonic Structure of Jean Claude and His Influence on Homiletics*. Southwestern Baptist Theological Seminary. Fort Worth, TX. 2013.

Beale, G. K. *The Right Doctrine from the Wrong Texts? Essays on the Use of the Old Testament in the New*. Grand Rapids: Baker, 1994.

Blomberg, Craig L., Robert L. Hubbard, and William W. Klein. *Introduction to Biblical Interpretation*. Waco, TX: Word, 1993.

Broadus, John A. *On the Preparation and Delivery of Sermons*. 4th ed. Revised by Vernon L. Stanfield. San Francisco: Harper & Row, 1986.

Brown, H. C., Jr., H. Gordon Clinard, Jesse J. Northcutt, and Al Fasol. *Steps to the Sermon*. Nashville: B&H, 1996.

Bunyan, John. *The Pilgrim's Progress*. Springdale, PA: Whitaker House, 1981.

Carson, D. A. *Biblical Interpretation and the Church*. Nashville: Nelson, 1984.

———. *Hermeneutics, Authority, and Canon*. Grand Rapids: Zondervan, 1986.

Claude, Jean. *Essay on the Composition of a Sermon: With Notes and Illustrations and One Hundred Skeletons of Sermons by Charles Simeon*. Reprint ed. Grand Rapids: Baker, 1979.

Cox, James W. *A Guide to Biblical Preaching*. Nashville: Abingdon, 1976.

Dever, Mark. *The Message of the New Testament: Promises Kept*. Wheaton: Crossway, 2005.

———. *The Message of the Old Testament: Promises Made*. Wheaton: Crossway, 2006.

Dodd, C. H. *According to the Scriptures: The Sub-Structure of New Testament Theology*. Stone Lectures. New York: Scribner's, 1953.

Duvall, J. Scott, and J. Daniel Hays. *Grasping God's Word: A Hands-on Approach to Reading, Interpreting, and Applying the Bible*. Grand Rapids: Zondervan, 2001.

Ellis, E. Earle. *The Old Testament in Early Christianity: Canon and Interpretation in the Light of Modern Research*. Wissenschaftliche Untersuchungen Zum Neuen Testament. 2. Reihe. Grand Rapids; Tübingen: Baker; Mohr Siebeck, 1991.

Eswine, Zack. *Preaching to a Post-Everything World: Crafting Biblical Sermons to Connect with Our Culture.* Grand Rapids: Baker, 2008.

Feinberg, John S. *Continuity and Discontinuity: Perspectives on the Relationship between the Old and New Testaments: Essays in Honor of S Lewis Johnson, Jr.* Westchester, IL: Crossway, 1988.

Goldingay, John. *Models for Interpretation of Scripture.* Grand Rapids: Eerdmans, 1995.

Gorman, Michael J. *Elements of Biblical Exegesis: A Basic Guide for Students and Ministers.* Rev. ed. Peabody, MA: Hendrickson, 2009.

Hall, E. Eugene, and James L. Heflin. *Proclaim the Word: The Basis of Preaching.* Nashville: Broadman, 1985.

Hopkins, Charles. *Charles Simeon of Cambridge,* Eugene, OR: Wipf and Stock, 2012.

Jackman, David. *I Believe in the Bible.* London: Hodder & Stoughton, 2000.

Kaiser, Walter C., Jr. *Toward an Exegetical Theology: Biblical Exegesis for Preaching and Teaching.* Grand Rapids, Baker, 1981.

Killinger, John. *Fundamentals of Preaching.* Philadelphia: Fortress, 1985.

Ladd, George Eldon, and Donald A. Hagner. *A Theology of the New Testament.* Rev ed. Grand Rapids: Eerdmans, 1993.

Lischer, Richard. *A Theology of Preaching: The Dynamcis of the Gospel.* Eugene, OR: Wipf & Stock, 2001.

Lloyd-Jones, D. Martyn. *Preaching and Preachers.* Grand Rapids: Zondervan, 2012.

Long, Thomas G. *The Senses of Preaching.* Louisville: John Knox, 1988.

MacArthur, John, Jr., and the Master's Seminary Faculty. *Preaching: How to Preach Biblically.* Nashville: Thomas Nelson, 2005.

———. *Rediscovering Expository Preaching.* Dallas: Word, 1992.

Marshall, Howard I. *New Testament Theology: Many Witnesses, One Gospel.* Downers Grove: InterVarsity, 2004.

Richard, Ramesh. *Preparing Evangelistic Sermons: A Seven-Step Method for Preaching Salvation.* Grand Rapids: Baker, 2005.

———. *Preparing Expository Sermons: A Seven-Step Method for Biblical Preaching.* Grand Rapids: Baker, 2001.

Roberts, Vaughan. *God's Big Picture: Tracing the Storyline of the Bible.* Downers Grove: InterVarsity, 2002.

Steward, James S. *Preaching.* London: Hodder & Stoughton, 1955.

Smith, Steven. *Dying to Preach: Embracing the Cross in the Pulpit.* Grand Rapids: Kregel, 2008.

Willhite, Keith, and Scott Gibson. *The Big Idea of Biblical Preaching.* Grand Rapids: Baker, 1998.

Wilson, Paul Scott. *The Four Pages of the Sermon.* Nashville: Abingdon, 1999.

———. *The Practice of Preaching.* Nashville: Abingdon, 1995.

WORKS RELATED TO EXPOSITION, INTERPRETATION, AND GENRE

Achtemeiter, Elizabeth. *Preaching from the Old Testament.* Philadelphia: Westminster, 1984.

Akin, Daniel L., Bill Curtis, and Stephen Rummage, eds. *Engaging Exposition.* Nashville: B&H Academic, 2011.

Akin, Daniel L., David Lewis Allen, and Ned Lee Mathews. *Text-Driven Preaching: God's Word at the Heart of Every Sermon.* Nashville: B&H Academic, 2010.

Alexander, T. Desmond. *From Paradise to Promised Land: An Introduction to the Pentateuch.* 2nd ed. Grand Rapids: Paternoster, 2002.

———. *From Eden to the New Jerusalem: An Introduction to Biblical Theology.* Grand Rapids: Kregel, 2008.

Allen, Ronald. "A Response to Genre Criticism—Sensus Literalis." Pages 193–203 in *Hermeneutics, Inerrancy, and the Bible*. Edited by Earl D. Radmacher and Robert D. Preus. Grand Rapids: Zondervan, 1984.

Allen, Ronald J. "Feeling and Form in Biblical Interpretation." *Encounter* 43 (1982): 99–107.

Alter, Robert, and Frank Kermode, eds. *The Literary Guide to the Bible* Cambridge, MA: Harvard University Press, 1987.

Arthurs, Jeffrey D. *Biblical Interpretation Through Rhetorical Criticism: Augmenting the Grammatical/Historical Approach*. Diss. Purdue University, 1992. Ann Arbor: UMI, 1993.

———. *Preaching with Variety: How to Re-create the Dynamics of Biblical Genres*. Grand Rapids: Kregel, 2007.

Aune, David E. *The New Testament in Its Literary Environment*. Library of Early Christianity. Philadelphia: Westminster, 1987.

Awbrey, Ben E. *"A Critical Examination of the Theory and Practice of John F. MacArthur's Expository Preaching."* Th.D. dissertation. New Orleans Baptist Theological Seminary, 1990.

Bailey, James L., and Lyle D. Vander Broek. *Literary Forms in the New Testament: A Handbook*. Louisville: Westminster/John Knox, 1992.

Baird, J. Arthur. "Genre Analysis as a Method of Historical Criticism." *Book of Seminar Papers* (1972): 385–411.

Bar-Efrat, S. "Some Observations on the Analysis of Structure in Biblical Narrative." *Vetus Testamentum* 30 (1980): 154–73.

Berkhof, Louis. *Principles of Biblical Interpretation*. Grand Rapids: Baker, 1950.

Best, Ernest. *From Text to Sermon: Responsible Use of the New Testament in Preaching*. Atlanta: John Knox, 1978.

Blomberg, Craig L., Robert L. Hubbard, and William W. Klein. *Introduction to Biblical Interpretation*. Waco, TX: Word, 1993.

Blomberg, Craig L., and Jennifer Foutz Markley. *A Handbook of New Testament Exegesis*. Grand Rapids: Baker, 2010.

Carter, Terry G., J. Scott Duvall, J. Daniel Hays. *Preaching God's Word: A Hands-on Approach to Preparing, Developing, and Delivering the Sermon*. Grand Rapids: Zondervan, 2005.

Carson, D. A. "Accept No Substitutes: 6 Reasons Not to Abandon Expository Preaching." *Leadership* 18 (1996).

Chapell, Bryan. *Christ-Centered Preaching: Redeeming the Expository Sermon*. 2nd ed. Grand Rapids: Baker Academic, 2005.

———. "The Future of Expository Preaching." *Preaching* 20 (September–October 2004).

———. "The Future of Expository Preaching." *Preaching* 20 (November–December 2004).

Clements, Roy. "Expository Preaching in a Postmodern World." *Evangelical Review of Theology* 23 (1999): 174–82.

Chisholm, Robert B., Jr. *From Exegesis to Exposition: A Practical Guide to Using Biblical Hebrew*. Grand Rapids: Baker, 1998.

Clowney, Edmund P. *Preaching and Biblical Theology*. Grand Rapids: Eerdmans, 1961.

———. *Preaching Christ in All of Scripture*. Wheaton: Crossway, 2003.

Collins, John Joseph. "Towards the Morphology of a Genre: Introduction." *Semeia* 14 (1979): 1–20.

Cooper, Lamar E. "Interpreting the Poetical Books for Preaching." *Faith and Mission* 13 (1995): 85–97.

Cox, James W. *Biblical Preaching: An Expositor's Treasury*. Philadelphia: Westminster, 1983.

————. "How Good Is Your Expository Preaching?" *Pulpit Digest* edition (November–December 1979).

Craddock, Fred B. *Preaching*. Nashville: Abingdon, 1985.

Dever, Mark, and Greg Gilbert. *Preach: Theology Meets Practice*. Nashville: B&H, 2012.

Dockery, David S. *Biblical Interpretation Then and Now: Contemporary Hermeneutics in the Light of the Early Church*. Grand Rapids: Baker, 1992.

————. *Foundations for Biblical Interpretation*. Nashville: B&H, 1994.

Doriani, Daniel M. *Getting the Message: A Plan for Interpreting and Applying the Bible*. Phillipsburg: P&R, 1996.

Duduit, Michael. *Communicate with Power*. Grand Rapids: Baker, 1996.

Fee, Gordon D., and Douglas K. Stuart. *How to Read the Bible for All Its Worth*. 2nd ed. Grand Rapids: Zondervan, 1993.

Fokkelman, J. P. *Reading Biblical Narrative*. Louisville: Westminster/John Knox, 1999.

Goldingay, John. "Preaching on the Stories in Scripture." *Anvil* 2 (1990): 105–14.

Goldsworthy, Graeme. *According to Plan: The Unfolding Revelation of God in the Bible*. Downers Grove: InterVarsity, 2002.

————. *Gospel-Centred Hermeneutics: Foundations and Principles of Evangelical Biblical Interpretation*. Downers Grove: InterVarsity Academic, 2006.

————. *Preaching the Whole Bible as Christian Scripture: The Application of Biblical Theology to Expository Preaching*. Grand Rapids: Eerdmans, 2000.

Greidanus, Sidney. *The Modern Preacher and the Ancient Text: Interpreting and Preaching Biblical Literature*. Grand Rapids: Eerdmans, 1988.

Hall, E. Eugene, and James L. Heflin. *Proclaim the Word: The Basics of Preaching*. Nashville: Broadman, 1985.

Hamilton, James M., Jr. "Biblical Theology and Preaching," http://www.jamesmhamilton. org/renown/wp-content/uploads/2010/07/tdp-pp-193-218.pdf

————. *God's Glory in Salvation through Judgment: A Biblical Theology*. Crossway, 2010.

————. *What Is Biblical Theology? A Guide to the Bible's Story, Symbolism, and Patterns*. Wheaton: Crossway, 2013.

House, H. Wayne, and Daniel G. Garland. *God's Message, Your Sermon: Discover, Develop, and Deliver What God Meant by What He Said*. Nashville: Thomas Nelson, 2007.

Howell, Mark A. *"Hermeneutical Bridges and Homiletical Methods: A Comparative Analysis of the New Homiletic and Expository Preaching Theory."* Ph.D. Dissertation. Southeastern Baptist Theological Seminary, 1999.

Howell, W. S. *Fenelon's Dialogues on Eloquence*. Princeton, NJ: Princeton University Press, 1951.

Hughes, R. Kent, Leland Ryken, and Todd A. Wilson. *Preach the Word: Essays on Expository Preaching in Honor of R. Kent Hughes*. Wheaton: Crossway, 2007.

Johnson, Dennis. *Him We Proclaim: Preaching Christ from All the Scriptures*. Phillipsburg, NJ: P&R, 2007.

Kaiser, Walter C., Jr. *Preaching and Teaching from the Old Testament*. Grand Rapids: Baker, 2003.

Klein, George L. *Reclaiming the Prophetic Mantle: Preaching the Old Testament Faithfully*. Baptist Sunday School Board, 1992.

Köstenberger, Andreas J., and Richard Patterson. *Invitation to Biblical Interpretation: Exploring the Hermeneutical Triad of History, Literature, and Theology*. Grand Rapids: Kregel, 2011.

Kuruvilla, Abraham. *Privilege the Text!: A Theological Hermeneutic for Preaching*. Chicago: Moody, 2013.

————. *Text to Praxis: Hermeneutics and Homiletics in Dialogue*. T&T Clark, 2009.

Liefield, Walter L. *New Testament Exposition: From Text to Sermon.* Grand Rapids: Zondervan, 1984.

Long, Thomas G. *Preaching and the Literary Forms of the Bible.* Philadelphia: Fortress, 1989.

Longman, Tremper, III. *Literary Approaches to Biblical Interpretation.* Grand Rapids: Zondervan, 1987.

Mathewson, Steven. *The Art of Preaching the Old Testament.* Grand Rapids: Baker, 2002.

McDill, Wayne. *The Twelve Essential Skills for Great Preaching.* Nashville: B&H, 1994.

Mohler, Albert R. *Preaching the Centrality of Scripture.* Edinburgh: Banner of Truth, 2003.

Montgomery, R. Ames. *Expository Preaching.* New York: Revell, 1939.

Mulder, David. *Narrative Preaching.* Saint Louis: CPH, 1996.

Osborne, Grant R. "Genre Criticism." Pages 163–90 in *Hermeneutics, Inerrancy, and the Bible.* Edited by Earl D. Radmacher and Robert D. Preus. Grand Rapids: Zondervan, 1984.

—————. *The Hermeneutical Spiral: A Comprehensive Introduction to Biblical Interpretation.* Downers Grove: InterVarsity, 1991.

Paul, Ian, and David Wenham, eds. *Preaching the New Testament.* Downers Grove: InterVarsity, 2013.

Piper, John. "Preaching as Expository Exultation for the Glory of God." in *Preaching the Cross.* Mark Dever, J. Ligon Duncan III, R. Albert Mohler Jr., and C. J. Mahaney. Wheaton: Crossway, 2007.

Quicke, Michael J. *360-Degree Preaching: Hearing, Speaking, and Living the Word.* Grand Rapids: Baker, 2003.

Robinson, Haddon W. "What Is Expository Preaching?" *Bibliotheca Sacra* 131.

Richard, Ramesh. *Scripture Sculpture.* Grand Rapids: Baker, 1995.

Robinson, Haddon W. *Biblical Preaching: The Development and Delivery of Expository Messages.* Grand Rapids: Baker, 1980.

—————. *Biblical Sermons: How Twelve Preachers Apply the Principles of Biblical Preaching.* Grand Rapids: Baker, 1989.

Robinson, Haddon W., and Craig Brian Larson. *The Art and Craft of Biblical Preaching: A Comprehensive Resource for Today's Communicators.* Grand Rapids: Zondervan, 2005.

Ryken, Leland. *How to Read the Bible as Literature.* Zondervan, 1984.

—————. *Words of Delight: A Literary Introduction to the Bible.* Grand Rapids: Baker, 1987.

Ryken, Leland, and Tremper Longman III, eds. *A Complete Literary Guide to the Bible.* Grand Rapids: Zondervan, 1993.

Ryle, John Charles. *Expository Thoughts on the Gospels: St. Matthew.* New York: Robert Carter, 1857.

Sandy, D. Brent, and Ronald L. Giese Jr. *Cracking Old Testament Codes: A Guide to Interpreting the Literary Genres of the Old Testament.* Nashville: B&H, 1995.

Silva, Moisés. *God, Language and Scripture.* Grand Rapids: Zondervan, 1990.

—————. *Has the Church Misread the Bible?* Grand Rapids: Zondervan, 1987.

Steimle, Edmund A. *Preaching the Story.* Philadelphia: Fortress, 1980.

Stott, John R. W. *Between Two Worlds: The Art of Preaching in the Twentieth Century.* Grand Rapids: Eerdmans, 1982.

—————. "Biblical Preaching Is Expository Preaching." in *Evangelical Roots: A Tribute to Wilbur Smith.* Edited by Kenneth S. Kantzer. New York: Thomas Nelson, 1978.

—————. *Understanding the Bible.* Grand Rapids: Lamplighter, 1972.

Stout, Harry S. *The New England Soul: Preaching and Religious Culture in Colonial New England.* Oxford: Oxford University Press, 1986.

Sunukjian, Donald R. *Invitation to Biblical Preaching: Proclaiming Truth with Clarity and Relevance*. Grand Rapids: Kregel, 2007.

Vanhoozer, Kevin. *Is There a Meaning in This Text?: The Bible, the Reader, and the Morality of Literary Knowledge*. Grand Rapids: Zondervan, 1998.

Unger, Merrill F. *Principles of Expository Preaching*. Grand Rapids: Zondervan, 1955.

Vines, Jerry, and Jim Shaddix. *Power in the Pulpit: How to Prepare and Deliver Expository Sermons*. Chicago: Moody, 1999.

Von Rad, Gerhard. *Biblical Interpretations in Preaching*. Nashville: Abingdon, 1973.

Voobus, Arthur, and Henry Grady Davis. *The Gospel in Study and Preaching*. Philadelphia: Fortress, 1966.

Wilson, Paul Scott. *The New Interpreter's Handbook of Preaching*. Nashville: Abingdon, 2008.

_____. *The Practice of Preaching*. Rev ed. Nashville: Abingdon, 2007.

OLD TESTAMENT NARRATIVE

Alexander, T. Desmond. *From Paradise to the Promised Land: An Introduction to the Main Themes of the Pentateuch*. Grand Rapids: Baker, 1995.

Alter, Robert. *The Art of Biblical Narrative*. New York: Basic, 1981.

Arthurs, Jeffrey D. "The Implications of the Plot Structure of Biblical Narrative for Homiletics." M.A. thesis. Western Conservative Baptist Seminary, 1987.

Ellingsen, Mark. *The Integrity of Biblical Narrative: Story in Theology and Proclamation*. Minneapolis: Augsburg Fortress, 1990.

Fokkelman, J. P. *Narrative Art and Poetry in the Books of Samuel*. A Full Interpretation Based on Stylistic and Structural Analysis. 4 volumes. Asssen: Van Gorcum, 1981.

_____. *Narrative Art in Genesis*: Specimens of Stylistic and Structural Analysis. Assen Van Gorcum, 1975.

Gibson, Scott M. *Preaching the Old Testament*. Grand Rapids: Baker, 2006.

Goldsworthy, Graeme. *Gospel and Kingdom*. Paternoster, 1981.

Gow, Murray D. *The Book of Ruth: Its Structure, Theme, and Purpose*. Leicester, England: Apollos, 1990.

Green, Joel B., and Michael Pasquarello. *Narrative Reading, Narrative Preaching: Reuniting New Testament Interpretation and Proclamation*. Grand Rapids: Baker Academic, 2003.

Greidanus, Sidney. *Preaching Christ from Genesis: Foundations for Expository Sermons*. Grand Rapids: Eerdmans, 2007.

_____. *Preaching Christ from the Old Testament: A Contemporary Hermeneutical Method*. Grand Rapids: Eerdmans, 1999.

_____. *Sola Scriptura: Problems and Principles in Preaching Historical Texts*. Toronto: Wedge Publishing Foundation.

Gunn, David M. *The Story of King David: Genre and Interpretation*. Sheffield University of Sheffield Press, 1978.

Hicks, R. Lansing. "Form and Content: A Hermeneutical Application." in *Translating and Understanding the Old Testament: Essays in Honor of Herbert Gordon May*. Edited by Harry T. Frank and William L. Reed. Nashville: Abingdon, 1970.

Holbert, John C. *Preaching Old Testament: Proclamation and Narrative in the Hebrew Bible*. Nashville: Abingdon, 1991.

Howard, David M., Jr., and Michael A. Grisanti. *Giving the Sense: Understanding and Using Old Testament Historical Texts*. Grand Rapids: Kregel, 2003.

Kaiser, Walter C., Jr. *The Old Testament in Contemporary Preaching*. Grand Rapids: Baker, 1973.

_____. *Preaching and Teaching from the Old Testament: A Guide for the Church.* Grand Rapids: Baker, 2003.

Kline, Meredith G. *Treaty of the Great King: The Covenant Structure of Deuteronomy: Studies and Commentary.* Grand Rapids: Eerdmans, 1963.

Mathews, Kenneth A., and R. Kent Hughes. *Leviticus: Holy God, Holy People.* Wheaton: Crossway, 2009.

Mathewson, Steven D. *The Art of Preaching Old Testament Narrative.* Grand Rapids: Baker, 2002.

Pratt, Richard L., Jr. *He Gave Us Stories: The Bible Student's Guide to Interpreting Old Testament Narratives.* Phillipsburg, NJ: P&R, 1990.

Robinson, Haddon W. "Preaching Narrative." Unpublished class notes from Pr6324, Gordon-Conwell Theological Seminary, 1998.

Sailhamer, John. *The Meaning of the Pentateuch: Revelation, Composition and Interpretation.* Downers Grove: InterVarsity, 2009.

_____. *The Pentateuch as Narrative.* Grand Rapids: Zondervan, 1992.

Sternberg, Meir. *The Poetics of Biblical Narrative: Ideological Literature and the Drama of Reading.* Bloomington, IN: Indiana University Press, 1985.

Stevenson, Dwight Eshelman. *Preaching on the Books of the Old Testament.* New York: Harper, 1961.

Stuart, Douglas K. *Old Testament Exegesis: A Handbook for Students and Pastors.* 4th ed. Louisville: Westminster John Knox, 2009.

Wegner, Paul D. *Using Old Testament Hebrew in Preaching: A Guide for Students and Pastors.* Grand Rapids: Kregel, 2009.

PSALMS

Alter, Robert. *The Art of Biblical Poetry.* New York: Basic, 1985.

Bateman, Herbert W. I. V., and D. Brent Sandy. *Interpreting the Psalms for Teaching and Preaching.* St. Louis: Chalice, 2010.

Belcher, Richard P., Jr. *The Messiah and the Psalms: Preaching Christ from All the Psalms.* Fearn, UK: Christian Focus, 2006.

Bellinger, W. H. *Psalms: Reading and Studying the Book of Praise.* Peabody, MA: Hendrickson, 1990.

Brueggemann, Walter. *The Message of the Psalms: A Theological Commentary.* Augsburg Old Testament Studies. Minneapolis: Fortress, 1984.

Firth, David G. "Preaching Praise Poetry." *Reclaiming the Old Testament for Christian Preaching.* Downers Grove: InterVarsity Academic, 2010.

Fokkelman, J. P. *Major Poems of the Hebrew Bible at the Interface of Hermeneutics and Structure Analysis.* Edited by Greenville J. R. Kent, Paul J. Kissling, and Laurence A. Turner. Van Gorcum, 1998.

_____. *Reading Biblical Poetry: An Introductory Guide.* Translated by Ineke Smit. Louisville: Westminster John Knox, 2001.

Freedman, David Noel. "Pottery, Poetry, and Prophecy: An Essay on Biblical Poetry." *Journal of Biblical Literature* 96, no. 1 (1977): 5–26.

Fugato, Mark D., and David M. Howard Jr. *Interpreting the Psalms: An Exegetical Handbook.* Handbooks for Old Testament Exegesis. Grand Rapids: Kregel, 2007.

Geller, Stephen A. *Parallelism in Early Biblical Poetry.* Missoula: Scholars, 1979.

Kugel, James L. *The Idea of Biblical Poetry: Parallelism and Its History.* New Haven, CT: Yale University Press, 1981.

Lewis, C. S. *Reflections on the Psalms.* New York: Harcourt, Brace, and Jovanovich, 1958.

Longman, Tremper, III. *How to Read the Psalms.* Downers Grove: InterVarsity, 1988.

Mays, James Luther, Patrick D. Miller, and Gene M. Tucker. *Preaching and Teaching the Psalms*. Louisville: Westminster John Knox, 2006.

McCann, J. Clinton, Jr., and James C. Howell. *Preaching the Psalms*. Nashville: Abingdon, 2001.

Miller, Patrick D., Jr. *Interpreting the Psalms*. Philadelphia: Fortress, 1986.

O'Donnell, Douglas Sean. *God's Lyrics: Rediscovering Worship Through Old Testament Songs*. Phillipsburg, NJ: P&R, 2010.

Parsons, Greg W. "Guidelines for Understanding and Proclaiming the Psalms." *Bibliotheca Sacra* 147 (1990): 169–87.

Ryken, Leland. *Words of Delight: A Literary Introduction to the Bible*. Grand Rapids: Baker, 1987.

Sedgwick, Colin J. "Preaching from the Psalms." *Expository Times* 103 (1992): 361–64.

Sharpe, Lamoyne. *Preaching Thru the Psalms*. Dacula, GA: L. Sharpe, 1978.

Smith, Kenneth W. "Preaching the Psalms with Respect for Their Inspired Design." *Journal of the Evangelical Homiletics Society* 3 (2003): 4–31.

Tornfelt, John V. "Preaching the Psalms: Understanding the Chiastic Structures for Greater Clarity." *The Journal of the Evangelical Homiletics Society* 2, no. 2 (December 2002): 4–31.

Velema, W. H., and Susan van der Ree. "Preaching on the Psalms." *Evangelical Review of Theology* 21 (July 1997): 258–67.

Wallace, Howard Neil. *Words to God, Word from God: The Psalms in the Prayer and Preaching of the Church*. Burlington, VT: Ashgate, 2005.

Waltke, Bruce K. "A Canonical Process Approach to the Psalms." Pages 3–18 in *Tradition and Testament: Essays in Honor of C. L. Feinberg*. Edited by J. S. Feinberg and P. D. Feinberg. Chicago: Moody, 1981.

_____. "Psalms: Theology of." Pages 1100–115 in *New International Dictionary of Old Testament Theology and Exegesis*, vol. 4. Edited by Willem VanGemeren. Grand Rapids: Zondervan, 1997.

Westermann, Claus. *Praise and Lament in the Psalms*. John Knox, 1981.

_____. *The Psalms: Structure, Content and Message*. Minneapolis: Augsburg, 1980.

Wilson, Gerald H. "The Shape of the Book of Psalms." *Interpretation* 46, no. 2 (1992): 129–42.

Yates, Kyle M. *Preaching from the Psalms*. New York: Harper, 1948.

Zenger, Erich, and Linda M. Maloney. *A God of Vengeance? Understanding the Psalms of Divine Wrath*. Louisville: Westminster John Knox, 1996.

WISDOM LITERATURE

Alleman, Herbert C. "Personal Religion: How to Preach from the Wisdom Books and the Psalms." *Interpretation* 2, no. 3 (July 1948): 299–312.

Arthurs, Jeffrey D. "Short Sentences Long Remembered: Preaching Genre-Sensitive Sermons from Proverbs." *Journal of the Evangelical Homiletics Society* 5 (2005).

Bullock, C. Hassell. *An Introduction to the Old Testament Poetic Books*. Chicago: Moody, 1988.

Crenshaw, James. *Old Testament Wisdom: An Introduction*. Atlanta: John Knox, 1981.

Davis, Ellen F. "Demanding Deliverance." in *Preaching from Psalms, Oracles, and Parables*. Edited by Roger Alling and David J. Schlafer. Harrisburg, PA: Morehouse, 2006.

Decker, Barbara. *Proverbs for Parenting: A Topical Guide for Child Raising from the Book of Proverbs*. Boise, ID: Lynn's Bookshelf, 1989.

Dorsey, David A. *The Literary Structure of the Old Testament: A Commentary on Genesis–Malachi*. Grand Rapids: Baker, 1999.

Estes, Daniel J. *Handbook on the Wisdom Books and Psalms*. Grand Rapids: Baker Academic, 2005.

_____. *Job*. Teach the Text Commentary Series. Grand Rapids, Baker, 2013.

Goldsworthy, Graeme. *Gospel and Wisdom*. Milton Keynes, UK: Paternoster, 1987.

Greidanus, Sidney. *Preaching Christ from Ecclesiastes: Foundations for Expository Sermons*. Grand Rapids: Eerdmans, 2010.

Holbert, John C. *Preaching Job*. St. Louis: Chalice, 1999.

Jackman, David. *Preaching and Teaching Old Testament: Narrative, Prophecy, Poetry, Wisdom*. 4 DVDs. London: The Proclamation Trust, 2008.

Kidner, Derek. *The Wisdom of Proverbs, Job, and Ecclesiastes*. Downers Grove: InterVarsity, 1985.

Kitchen, John A. *Proverbs*. Mentor Commentary. Inverness, Scotland: Mentor, 2006.

O'Donnell, Douglas Sean. *The Beginning and End of Wisdom: Preaching Christ from the First and Last Chapters of Proverbs, Ecclesiastes, and Job*. Wheaton: Crossway, 2011.

Ortlund, Raymond C. *Proverbs:Wisdom That Works*. Wheaton: Crossway, 2012.

Perry, T. Anthony. *Wisdom Literature and the Structure of Proverbs*. University Park, PA: Pennsylvania State University Press, 1993.

Ryken, Philip Graham. *Ecclesiastes: Why Everything Matters*. Wheaton: Crossway, 2010.

Thompson, J. M. *The Form and Function of Proverbs in Ancient Israel*. The Hague: Mouton, 1974.

Trible, Phyllis. "Wisdom Builds a Poem: The Architecture of Proverbs 1:20–33." *Journal of Biblical Literature* 94 (1975): 509–18.

Waltke, Bruce K. *The Book of Proverbs: Chapters 1–15*. New International Commentary on the Old Testament. Grand Rapids: Eerdmans, 2004.

_____. *The Book of Proverbs: Chapters 15–31*. New International Commentary on the Old Testament. Grand Rapids: Eerdmans, 2005.

PROPHECY

Alexander, T. Desmond. "Jonah and Genre." *Tyndale Bulletin* 36 (1985): 35–59.

Blackwood, Andrew Watterson. *Preaching from Prophetic Books*. New York: Abingdon-Cokesbury, 1951.

Childs, Brevard Springs. "Canonical Shape of the Prophetic Literature." *Interpretation* 32, no. 1 (1978): 46–55.

Chisholm, Robert B., Jr. *Handbook on the Prophets*. Grand Rapids: Baker Academic, 2002.

_____. *Interpreting the Minor Prophets*. Grand Rapids, Zondervan, 1990.

Garrett, Duane A. "The Structure of Amos as a Testimony to Its Integrity." *Journal of the Evangelical Theological Society* 27, no. 3 (1984): 275–76.

_____. "The Structure of Joel." *Journal of the Evangelical Theological Society* 28, no. 3 (1985): 289–97.

Gooding, David W. "The Literary Structure of the Book of Daniel and Its Implications." *Tyndale Bulletin* 32 (1981): 43–79.

Greidanus, Sidney. *Preaching Christ from Daniel: Foundations for Expository Sermons*. Grand Rapids: Eerdmans, 2012.

Kaiser, Walter C. *Preaching and Teaching the Last Things: Old Testament Eschatology for the Life of the Church*. Grand Rapids: Baker Academic, 2011.

VanGemeren, Willem. *Interpreting the Prophetic Word: An Introduction to the Prophetic Literature of the Old Testament*. Grand Rapids: Zondervan, 1996.

Yates, Kyle. *Preaching from the Prophets*. Nashville: Broadman, 1942.

GOSPELS/ACTS

Aune, David E. "The Problem of the Genre of the Gospels: A Critique of C. H. Talbert's What Is a Gospel?" in *Gospel Perspectives*. Studies of History and Tradition in the Four Gospels. Volume Two. Edited by R. T. France and David Wenham. 9–60. Sheffield: JSOT, 1981.

Barnes, Stanley. *Sermons on Acts 16*. Greenville, SC: Ambassador, 2001.

Bauckham, Richard. *The Gospels for All Christians: Rethinking the Gospel Audiences*. Grand Rapids: Eerdmans, 1998.

Beasley-Murray, George Raymond. *Preaching the Gospel from the Gospels*. Peabody, MA: Hendrickson, 1996.

Blomberg, Craig. *Jesus and the Gospels: An Introduction and Survey*. Nashville: B&H Academic, 2009.

Boice, James Montgomery. *Acts: An Expositional Commentary*. Grand Rapids: Baker, 1997.

Borgman, Paul. *The Way According to Luke: Hearing the Whole Story of Luke-Acts*. Grand Rapids: Eerdmans, 2006.

Burridge, Richard A. *Four Gospels, One Jesus*. 2nd ed. London: SPCK, 2005.

_____. *What Are the Gospels?: A Comparison with Graeco-Roman Biography*. 2nd ed. Grand Rapids, Eerdmans, 2004.

Clark, David J., and Jan de Waard. "Discourse Structure in Matthew's Gospel." *Scriptura*, no. 1 (1982): 1–97.

Combrink, H. J. B. "The Structure of the Gospel of Matthew as Narrative." *Tyndale Bulletin* 34 (1983): 61–90.

Craddock, Fred B. *The Gospels*. Interpreting Biblical Texts Series. Abingdon, 1981.

Edwards, Glen. "Preaching from Mark's Gospel." *Southwestern Journal of Theology* 21, no. 1 (1978): 55–69.

Fokkelman, J. P., and Ineke Smit. *Reading Biblical Narrative: A Practical Guide*. Tools for Biblical Study. Leiden: Deo, 1999.

Gathercole, Simon J. *The Preexistent Son: Recovering the Christologies of Matthew, Mark, and Luke*. Grand Rapids: Eerdmans, 2006.

Hendriksen, William. *Exposition of the Gospel According to John*. Baker New Testament Commentary. Grand Rapids: Baker, 1953.

Jackman, David. *Preaching and Teaching: New Testament: Gospels, Letters, Acts and Revelation*. 3 DVDs. London: The Proclamation Trust, 2008.

Kuruvilla, Abraham. *Mark: A Theological Commentary for Preachers*. Eugene, OR: Wipf & Stock, 2012.

Michie, Donald, and David M. Rhoads. *Mark as Story: An Introduction to the Narrative of a Gospel*. Philadelphia: Fortress, 1982.

Pennington, Jonathan T. *Reading the Gospels Wisely: A Narrative and Theological Introduction*. Grand Rapids: Baker Academic, 2012.

Phillips, John. *Exploring Acts. Volume 1: Acts. 1–12*. Chicago: Moody, 1989.

Polhill, John B. *Acts*. Nashville: B&H, 1992.

Ressequie, James L. *Narrative Criticism of the New Testament: An Introduction*. Grand Rapids: Baker Academic, 2005.

Rhoads, David, and Donald Michie. *Mark as Story: An Introduction to the Narrative of a Gospel*. Philadelphia: Fortress, 1983.

Ryle, John Charles. *Expository Thoughts on the Gospels: St. Mark*. Reprint ed. Carlisle, PA: The Banner of Truth Trust, 1994.

Scott, Bernard Brandon. *The Word of God in Words: Reading and Preaching*. Philadelphia: Fortress, 1985.

Smith, D. Moody. *Interpreting the Gospels for Preaching*. Philadelphia: Fortress, 1980.

_____. *John*. Proclamation Commentaries. Philadelphia: Fortress, 1986.

Strauss, Mark L. *Four Portraits, One Jesus: An Introduction to Jesus and the Gospels.* Grand Rapids: Zondervan, 2007.

Talbert, Charles H. *What Is a Gospel? The Genre of the Canonical Gospels.* Philadelphia: Fortress, 1977.

Tannehill, Robert C. "The Disciples in Mark: The Function of a Narrative Role," *Journal of Religion* 57 (1977): 386–405.

Wallis, Ethel E. "Four Gospels, Four Discourse Genre." *Evangelical Journal* 1, no. 2 (1983): 78–91.

Wilder, Amos. *Early Christian Rhetoric: The Language of the Gospel.* Peabody, MA: Hendricksen, 1964.

Wirada, Timothy. *Interpreting Gospel Narratives: Scenes, People, and Theology.* Nashville: B&H, 2010.

Yates, Kyle Monroe. *Preaching from John's Gospel.* Nashville: Broadman, 1964.

PARABLES

Bailey, Kenneth E. *Poet and Peasant and Through Peasant Eyes: A Literary-Cultural Approach to the Parables in Luke.* Grand Rapids: Eerdmans, 1983.

Blomberg, Craig L. *Interpreting the Parables.* Downers Grove: InterVarsity, 1990.

_____. *Preaching the Parables: From Responsible Interpretation to Powerful Proclamation.* Grand Rapids: Baker Academic, 2004.

_____. "Preaching the Parables: Preserving Three Main Points." *Perspectives in Religious Studies* 11 (1984): 31–41.

Brauninger, Dallas A. *Preaching the Parables.* Series 3, Cycle A. Lima, Ohio: CSS, 2003.

Chenoweth, Ben. "Identifying the Talents: Contextual Clues for the Interpretation of the Parable of the Talents (Matthew 25:14–30)." *Tyndale Bulletin* 56 (2005): 61–72.

Keach, Benjamin. *Exposition of the Parables in the Bible.* Grand Rapids: Kregel, 1974.

Sider, John W. *Interpreting the Parables: A Hermeneutical Guide to Their Meaning.* Studies in Contemporary Interpretation. Grand Rapids: Zondervan, 1995.

Snodgrass, Klyne. *Stories with Intent: A Comprehensive Guide to the Parables of Jesus.* Grand Rapids, MI: Eerdmans, 2008.

Stein, Robert H. *An Introduction to the Parables of Jesus.* Philadelphia: Westminster, 1981.

Wenham, David. *The Parables of Jesus.* Jesus Library. Downers Grove: InterVarsity, 1989.

NEW TESTAMENT EPISTLES

Aune, David E. *The New Testament and Its Literary Environment.* Philadelphia: Westminster, 1987.

Betz, Hans Dieter. "The Literary Composition and Function of Paul's Letter to the Galatians," *New Testament Studies* 21 (1975): 353–379.

Blaiklock, Edward M. "The Epistolary Literature." In *The Expositor's Bible Commentary.* Vol. 1. Edited by Frank E. Gaebelein. Grand Rapids, MI: Zondervan, 1979.

Collins, Raymond. *Preaching the Epistles.* New York: Paulist, 1996.

DeJong, James A. "Principled Paraenesis: Reading and Preaching the Ethical Material of the New Testament Letters." *Pro Rege* 10 (1982): 26–34.

Greidanus, Sidney. "Preaching from Paul Today." in *Dictionary of Paul and His Letters: A Compendium of Contemporary Biblical Scholarship.* Edited by Gerald F. Hawthorne et al. Downers Grove: InterVarsity, 1993.

Hendriksen, William, and Simon Kristemaker. *Exposition of Thessalonians, the Pastorals, and Hebrews.* Grand Rapids: Baker, 1995.

Mumaw, John R. *Preach the Word: Expository Preaching from the Book of Ephesians.* Scottsdale: Herald, 1987.

Porter, Stanley, and Thomas H. Olbricht, eds. *Rhetoric and the New Testament*. Sheffield: Journal for the Study of the New Testament Supplement Series 90. Sheffield, 1990.

Russell, Walter B., III. "Rhetorical Analysis of the Book of Galatians, Part 1." *Bib Sac* 150 (1993): 341–58. See also "Part 2," 416–39.

Schreiner, Thomas R. *Interpreting the Pauline Epistles*. Grand Rapids: Baker, 1990.

Smith, D. Moody. *First, Second, and Third John*. Interpretation: A Bible Commentary for Teaching and Preaching. Louisville: John Knox, 1991.

APOCALYPTIC LITERATURE/REVELATION

Bultmann, Rudolf Karl. *This World and the Beyond: Marburg Sermons*. New York: Scribner's, 1960.

Craddock, Fred B. "Preaching the Book of Revelation." *Interpretation* 40 (1986): 270–82.

Goldsworthy, Graeme. *The Lamb and the Lion: The Gospel in Revelation*. Nashville: Thomas Nelson, 1984.

Gooding, David W. "The Literary Structure of the Book of Daniel and Its Implications." *Tyndale Bulletin* 32 (1981): 43–79.

Hamilton, James M., Jr. *Revelation: The Spirit Speaks to the Churches*. Preaching the Word. Wheaton: Crossway, 2012.

Paul, Ian. "Preaching from the Book of Revelation." Pages 158–172 in *Preaching the New Testament*. Edited by Ian Paul and David Wenham. Downers Grove: InterVarsity Academic, 2013.

Jacobsen, David Schnasa. *Preaching in the New Creation: The Promise of New Testament Apocalyptic Texts*. Louisville: Westminster John Knox, 1999.

Jeter, Joseph R., and Cornish R. Rogers. *Preaching through the Apocalypse: Sermons from Revelation*. St. Louis: Chalice, 1992.

Jones, Larry Paul, and Jerry L. Sumney. *Preaching Apocalyptic Texts*. St. Louis: Chalice, 1999.

Kistemaker, Simon. *Revelation*. New Testament Commentary. Grand Rapids: Baker, 2001.

Mounce, Robert H. *The Book of Revelation*. Rev. ed. New International Commentary on the New Testament. Grand Rapids: Eerdmans, 1998.

Osborne, Grant R. *Revelation*. Baker Exegetical Commentary on the New Testament. Grand Rapids: Baker, 2002.

Patterson, Paige. *Revelation*. New American Commentary. Nashville: B&H, 2012.

Smalley, Stephen S. *The Revelation to John: A Commentary on the Greek Text of the Apocalypse*. Downers Grove: InterVarsity, 2005.

Wilcox, Michael. *The Message of Revelation*. The Bible Speaks Today Series. Downers Grove: InterVarsity Academic, 2006.

WEBSITES[1]

Christ in Genesis: http://headhearthand.org/blog/2010/10/14/christ-in-genesis

Guide to Interpreting Song of Solomon: http://headhearthand.org/blog/2010/10/21/guide-to-interpreting-the-song-of-solomon

Guide to Interpreting the Prophets: http://headhearthand.org/blog/2010/10/25/guide-to-interpreting-the-prophets

How Do You Do Expositional Preaching Poorly? http://www.9marks.org/answers/how-do-you-do-expositional-preaching-poorly

Lectures on the Pentateuch and Genesis: http://headhearthand.org/blog/2011/09/01/lectures-on-pentateuch-and-genesis

---

1. These sites were accessible at the time of writing.

Lectures on Exodus–Leviticus: http://headhearthand.org/blog/2011/09/10/
   lectures-on-exodus-leviticus
The Old Testament on One Page: http://headhearthand.org/blog/2011/09/02/
   the-old-testament-on-one-page
Preaching Christ in the Old Testament: http://thegospelcoalition.org/preaching-christ/
Proclamation Trust: http://www.proctrust.org.uk
Preaching through Joshua: http://www.preaching.com/resources/articles/11661049
Old Testament Introduction Lectures (audio & PDF available): http://headhearthand.org/
   blog/2011/09/29/old-testament-introduction-lectures
Should Preachers Show Their Work? Or, Should Our Preaching Train People to Read the
   Bible? http://jimhamilton.info/2011/10/18/should-preachers-show-their-work-or-
   should-our-preaching-train-people-to-read-the-bible/?utm_source=feedburner&utm_
   medium=feed&utm_campaign=Feed%3A+
   ForHisRenown+%28For+His+Renown%29
Simeon Trust: http://simeontrust.net/
Preaching Christ from Exodus: http://simeontrust.net/index.
   php?option=com_content&view=article&id=281&Itemid=571
Preaching Christ from Joshua: http://simeontrust.net/index.
   php?option=com_content&view=article&id=282&Itemid=572
Preaching Christ from the Prophets: http://simeontrust.net/index.
   php?option=com_content&view=article&id=283&Itemid=573
Three Thoughts on Preaching: http://biblicalpreaching.net/category/specific-text
25 Pointers for Preaching Epistles Effectively: http://networkedblogs.com/zPJQ3
Two Vital Old Testament Questions: http://headhearthand.org/blog/2013/03/05/
   two-vital-old-testament-questions/

NAME INDEX

222

SUBJECT INDEX

A
Acts, structure of   *86–87*
affect   *131*
affective   *137*
allegorizing   *53–54, 112*
allegory   *109, 152, 201*
allusion   *172, 202, 204*
analytical   *137, 139*
apocalyptic   *199*
appeal   *98*
application   *49, 52, 56, 58, 60, 70*
audience   *108*
authorial intent   *49–50, 53, 57, 96–97*

C
canonical context   *74, 124*
characters   *42–43, 88, 110*
characters, main   *95–96*
Christ in the OT   *45–47, 49, 55–56, 125–26, 136, 153, 157, 167*
compliment   *51*
conclusion   *184, 189*
contextually conditional   *167–68*

D
deductive   *51, 116, 187*
descriptive approach   *202*
dialogue, purpose of   *88*
discourse   *89–90, 99*
divine revelation   *6, 11–15, 25, 39, 47, 134*
double parables   *106–7, 113, 115*

E
Ecclesiastes, structure of   *150*
exegetical idea   *19*
expository preaching   *1, 24, 47*

F
fulfillment, future   *171*
fulfillment, immediate   *170*

G
genealogies   *91*
genre   *5, 7, 15, 17, 20–21, 27–28, 30–34, 87, 93, 98, 126, 192, 199, 203*

God, voice of   *6–8, 14–15*
Gospels   *12*
Gospels, genre of   *80, 81–82, 87–88*
Gospels, structure of   *83–86*

H
Hebrew poetry   *126–27*
historical context   *190*
historical reconstruction   *94*
historical setting   *166*

I
illustrations   *130–31*
image of God   *11, 13*
imagery   *130–31, 201, 203*
indicative-imperative   *185, 189–90*
inductive   *45, 51, 105, 107, 116, 153*
inductive/deductive   *51, 58*
inspiration, doctrine of   *40*
interpretation   *17, 22, 30, 41, 80, 118, 137, 184*
intertextuality   *91, 200, 202, 204*
introduction   *184, 188–89*

J
Job, structure of   *147*

L
law, categories of   *69*
law, purpose of   *66–68, 70, 73*
letter   *28*
lines   *132*
literal method   *152, 156*
literary devices   *166*

M
macro-level meaning   *18, 39, 57, 68, 74, 83, 93–94, 109, 114, 153–54, 156–57, 171, 182, 191*
main idea   *10, 51–52, 52, 58–60, 118, 187, 191*
metaphor   *170, 184*
micro-level meaning   *18, 74, 132, 182–83, 191*
moralism   *49–50, 72*
moralizing   *54*
movement   *129*
multiple genres   *99*
mythological method   *152*

SCRIPTURE INDEX

Daniel
7:13–14   *96*

Hosea
1   *174*
3   *174*

Joel
2   *91*
3:13   *207*
9   *48*

Jonah
1:17   *55*
4:11   *44*

Micah
2:3   *172*
5:2   *98*
6:1–2   *170*
6:1–7   *174*
6:8   *6, 174*

Matthew
1   *56*
1:1–17   *55, 91*
1:22–23   *84*
1:23   *171*
2:5–6   *84*
2:6   *98*
2:15   *84*
2:17–18   *84*
2:23   *84*
3:1–3   *84*
3:17   *157*
4:1–11   *84*
4:14–16   *84*
4:17   *79, 166, 168, 181*
5:1   *140*
5:1–7:29   *83*
5:1–11   *157*
5:3   *97*
5:5   *135*
5–7   *87, 89*
5:16   *73*
5:17   *69–71, 75*
5:17–19   *46, 66*
5:18   *71*
5:21–22   *71*
5:27–28   *71*
5:31–34   *71*
5:38–39   *71*
5:43–44   *71*
6:19–24   *150*
7:24   *157*
7:24–27   *106*
8:17   *84*
9:36   *98*
10:1–11:1   *83*
11:10   *84*

11:16–19   *106*
11:20   *166*
11:25–30   *72*
12:1–8   *72*
12:15–21   *166*
12:17–21   *84*
12:24–30   *106*
12:38–41   *169*
12:39–40   *55*
12:39–41   *41*
12:42   *153*
13   *89–91, 99, 118, 125, 166*
13:1–3   *125*
13:1–23   *22, 113, 116*
13:1–53   *83*
13:9   *6*
13:10–16   *109*
13:14–15   *84*
13:18–30   *109*
13:24–30, 36–43   *117*
13:31–35   *107*
13:34–35   *135*
13:44–45   *117*
13:44–46   *107*
13:47–50   *22, 106*
16:1–4   *87*
16:14   *165*
17:1–13   *38*
17:10–13   *84*
18   *89*
18:1–19:1   *83*
18:12–14   *98, 107, 114*
18:23–35   *106*
20:1–16   *106, 113*
21:4–5   *84*
21:28–32   *106*
21:33–41   *106*
22:1–14   *106*
22:34   *175*
22:37–40   *72–73*
22:44   *135*
23–25   *89*
24   *38*
24:1–26:1   *83*
24:29–30   *206*
24:37–38   *41*
24:43–44   *106*
24:45–51   *106*
25:1–13   *106*
25:14–30   *106, 219*
26:27–28   *56*
26:31   *98*
26:64   *135*
27:9–10   *84*

Mark
1:17–20   *84*
1:24   *84*
1:25–28   *84*
1:27   *84*
1:29–34   *84*
2   *95*

2:1–12   *84*
2:7   *84*
2:10   *96*
2:23–28   *84*
2:27–28   *72*
3:22   *84*
4:1–20   *109*
4:1–34   *89*
4:3–9   *106*
4:10–12   *109*
4:13–20   *106*
4:26–29   *106*
4:35–41   *84*
4:41   *84*
5   *94*
5:7   *84*
5:35–43   *84*
5:42   *84*
6:3   *84*
6:14–15   *84*
8:11–13   *87*
8:31   *84*
9:31   *84*
10:33–34   *85*
11:32   *165*
12:1–12   *106*
12:41–44   *94*
14:62   *135*
15:39   *85*

Luke
1:31   *85*
1:47   *85*
1:69   *85*
1:71   *85*
1:77   *85*
2:1   *81*
2:1–21   *94*
2:11   *85*
2:30   *85*
3:23–37   *91*
3:26   *41*
4   *38, 85*
6:20   *97*
6:20–49   *89*
6:47–49   *106*
7:31–35   *106*
7:41–43   *106*
7:50   *85*
8:9–15   *109*
8:12   *85*
8:48   *85*
9:51–24:53   *111*
10:25–37   *106*
10:29, 36   *113*
11:5–8   *106*
11:29–32   *41*
12   *89*
12:16–21   *106*
12:39–40   *107*
12:42–48   *106*
13:1–20   *100*